DIGITAL LIBRARIES

Digital Libraries

Policy, Planning and Practice

Edited by

JUDITH ANDREWS
University of Central England

DEREK LAW
University of Strathclyde

ASHGATE

Chapter 7 of this book is based on *Digital Preservation and Metadata: History, Theory, Practice* by Susan Lazinger © 2001 Libraries Unlimited, Englewood, Colorado, USA; +1 (800) 225 5800; www.lu.com. Adapted by permission of the publisher.

Published by
Ashgate Publishing Limited
Gower House
Croft Road
Aldershot
Hants GU11 3HR
England

Ashgate Publishing Company
Suite 420
101 Cherry Street
Burlington, VT 05401–4405
USA

Ashgate website: http://www.ashgate.com

British Library Cataloguing in Publication Data
Digital libraries : policy, planning and practice
  1.Digital libraries
  I.Andrews, Judith II.Law, D.G. (Derek G.)
  025'.00285

Library of Congress Cataloging-in-Publication Data
Digital libraries : policy, planning, and practice / edited by Judith Andrews and Derek Law.
    p. cm.
  Includes bibliographical references and index.
  ISBN 0–7546–3448–5
    1. Digital libraries. 2. Digital libraries--Great Britain--Case studies. 3. Digital libraries--United States--Case studies. I. Andrews, Judith. II. Law, Derek G.

  ZA4080.D543 2004
  025'.00285--dc22

2003063850

ISBN 0 7546 3448 5

Printed and bound in Great Britain by MPG Books Ltd, Bodmin, Cornwall

Contents

Part 3:   The Way Ahead

List of Figures

List of Tables

List of Contributors

Judith Andrews is Director of Library Services at the University of Central England and has worked at UCE since 1989. Prior to that she worked in three other UK academic libraries. She has served on the Steering Groups of a number of funded projects including one of the eLib Training projects.

Until his death in November 2003, *Gerald Bernbom* served as Director of Research and Academic Computing and Special Assistant to the Vice President for Information Technology at Indiana University, with responsibility for digital libraries, massive data storage, and the IU Advanced Visualization Lab. He had been a member of the IT organization at Indiana since 1990, with assignments in data administration, video networking, and IT architecture. In 1997 he served as Visiting Program Officer to the Coalition for Networked Information in Washington, DC. He wrote, presented and conducted workshops in areas including electronic records management, digital libraries, library/IT partnerships, and institution-wide information strategies.

Mel Collier is Director of Library and Information Services at Tilburg University, the Netherlands. He is also Research Professor at the University of Northumbria, UK, and an independent consultant. Formerly, he was a Director of Dawson Holdings PLC. Prior to that he was Head of Division of Learning Development at De Montfort University. His previous career was in academic libraries in universities and polytechnics. Since the early 1970s he has been active in research into the library applications of information technology. He has directed several major national and European research projects. He has written, and collaborated on, numerous research reports, edited works and journal articles. He has served on a number of professional, national and international bodies including membership of the Library and Information Commission, chairing its research committee. He chaired the Library and Information Advisory Committee of the British Council.

Pete Dalton is Director of the evidence base research centre within Library Services at the University of Central England in Birmingham (UCE) and Director of the eVALUEd project. He has particular research interests in the areas of: evaluation methodologies and techniques; evaluation in the library and information sector and education and training of library and information workers. Pete is also an elected Council member of the UK Evaluation Society.

Mary Wallace Davidson currently heads the William and Gayle Cook Music Library at Indiana University, USA, where she also coordinates the program in music librarianship at the School of Library and Information Science, teaching music bibliography and librarianship. The author of many articles on American music libraries and librarianship, she has also published on 18th-century manuscripts, 19th-century American music periodicals, and musical copyright, and engages in research on both copyright and metadata for the Variations2 project. Long active in the Music Library Association (president from 1983 to 1985), she has served on its legislation.

Alan Dawson is senior researcher/programmer in the Centre for Digital Library Research at the University of Strathclyde, Scotland. He has over 20 years experience of delivering user services and finding practical solutions to information handling problems in the higher education sector, having previously worked as a research assistant, information officer, programmer, educational content specialist and technical consultant, with spells as webmaster at the University of Glasgow and manager of the BUBL Information Service. His current interests cover many areas of digital library development, aiming to combine theory with practice and help turn research projects into user services.

Chris Dodd is the University of Central England Digital Library manager and has been in post since August 2000. Chris has worked in various roles over the last few years in the civil service, local government and research. This has included working in the Department for Work and Pensions, Wolverhampton Public Libraries, Camden Public Libraries and the Libraries Partnership–West Midlands, the latter as Research Officer on a British Library funded project entitled 'Futures Together'. Chris has been an external assessor for the National Lottery New Opportunities Fund and undertaken research on behalf of Re:Source (UK Council for Museums, Libraries and Archives).

Jon W. Dunn is Assistant Director for Technology in the Digital Library Program at Indiana University, USA, overseeing the development and management of software systems to support Indiana University's (IU's) digital library collections. Prior to that, he worked in the Cook Music Library at IU from 1994–1998 as Technical Director for the Variations Project. He is currently serving as an investigator on the Variations2 project, is responsible for overseeing design and development of the Variations2 testbed system, and has written and presented on digital libraries and music information technology.

Edward A. Fox is Director of the Networked Digital Library of Theses and Dissertations. He began work in this area in 1987 in connection with a workshop on SGML and electronic dissertations. Dr Fox holds a PhD and MS in Computer Science from Cornell University, and a BS from MIT. Since 1983 he has been at Virginia Polytechnic Institute and State University (VPI & SU or Virginia Tech), where he serves as Professor of Computer Science. He directs the Internet Technology Innovation Center at Virginia Tech, Digital Library Research Laboratory, and Computing and Information Technology Interactive Digital Educational Library (CITIDEL).

Marcos A. Gonçalves is a PhD candidate in the Digital Library Research Laboratory at Virginia Tech. Mr Gonçalves holds an MS in Computer Science from UNI-

CAMP, Brazil and a BS from the Federal University of Ceará, also in Brazil. He has worked with the Networked Digital Library of Theses and Dissertations since 1999 and in digital libraries in general since 1996. His research interests include aspects of digital library theory, architecture, and interoperability.

Stevan Harnad was born in Hungary, did his undergraduate work at McGill University and his graduate work at Princeton University, USA, and is currently Canada Research Chair in Cognitive Science at University of Quebec/Montreal. His research is on categorization, communication and cognition. Founder and Editor of *Behavioral and Brain Sciences* (http://www.bbsonline.org/, a paper journal published by Cambridge University Press), *Psycoloquy* (http://psycprints.ecs.soton.ac.uk/, an electronic journal sponsored by the American Psychological Association) and the *CogPrints Electronic Preprint Archive in the Cognitive Sciences* (http://cogprints.ecs.soton.ac.uk/), he is Past President of the Society for Philosophy and Psychology, and author and contributor to over 100 publications, including *Origins and Evolution of Language and Speech* (NY Academy of Science, 1976), *Lateralization in the Nervous System* (Academic Press, 1977), *Peer Commentary on Peer Review: A Case Study in Scientific Quality Control* (Cambridge University Press, 1982), *Categorical Perception: The Groundwork of Cognition* (Cambridge University Press, 1987), *The Selection of Behavior: The Operant Behaviorism of BF Skinner: Comments and Consequences* (Cambridge University Press, 1988) and *Icon, Category, Symbol: Essays on the Foundations and Fringes of Cognition* (in preparation).

Rebecca Hartland-Fox was (until April 2003) a researcher on the eVALUEd project. She has worked in HE and FE libraries and has now moved into the area of library training. Her specialist research areas are Education, HE libraries and Information Design.

Jan R. Holloway is Manager of Publications at University Information Technology Services (UITS) at Indiana University, USA, overseeing publications initiatives for UITS and the Office of the Vice President for Information Technology and CIO. As a long-time contributor to the Association for Computing Machinery (ACM) SIGUCCS special interest group, she has written and presented on issues in IT publishing, and received numerous awards for her publications. She is also a member of the Society for Technical Communication. Before joining Indiana University she was a writer/editor in a research division of the *New York Times*.

Diane Nester Kresh is Director for Public Service Collections at the Library of Congress. She directs a staff responsible for 15 of the Library's reading rooms, including the historic Main Reading Room, and for custody and security of more than 113 million items in the Library's general and special collections. She received her BA degree in Theater and MLS degrees from the Catholic University of America. Diane Kresh was the founder of the Collaborative Digital Reference Service (now QuestionPoint, a service co-developed by LC and OCLC), a project to build a global, web-based, reference service among libraries and research institutions. She is a frequent speaker at professional meetings and conferences and the author of several articles on digital reference services. Ms Kresh is the recipient of the 2001 Federal 100 for her role in launching the Collaborative Digital Reference Service. The award is given by Federal Computer Week to top executives from government, industry and academia who have had the greatest impact on the government systems community and honors those who have 'made a difference in the way organizations develop, acquire and manage information technology.'

Derek Law is Head of the Information Resources Directorate at the University of Strathclyde, UK, and holds a chair in the Department of Computing and Information Sciences there. He has worked in several British universities since 1970 and has published widely since then. Most of his work has been on the development of networked resources in higher education and the creation of national information policy. He is Treasurer of IFLA and immediate past president of CILIPS. He was awarded the Barnard prize for contributions to Medical Informatics in 1993, Fellowship of the Royal Society of Edinburgh in 1999 and was awarded an honorary degree by the Sorbonne in 2000.

Susan S. Lazinger is a faculty member and Head of the Academic Program at the School of Library, Archive and Information Studies of the Hebrew University of Jerusalem. She has published widely on the Israel Inter-University Library Network (ALEPH), on LIS education, on cataloging and classification theory and on digital preservation and metadata. She was the Coordinator of a binational project for developing cooperative distance education courses under the auspices of the North Carolina Israel Project (NCIP) of the Binational Science Foundation in 2000–2001, and is the current Chair of the IFLA Section on Education and Training.

Mike Lesk works for the Internet Archive and started at Rutgers University in fall 2003. He is Visiting Professor in Computer Science at University College London; is on the Visiting Committee for the Harvard University Library; and has worked with the Commission on Preservation and Access. He received the 'Flame' award for lifetime achievement from Usenix in 1994, and is a Fellow of the ACM. In the 1960s, he worked for the SMART project, wrote much of their retrieval code and did many of the retrieval experiments, as well as obtaining a PhD in Chemical Physics. In the 1970s, he worked in the group that built Unix and wrote Unix tools for word processing, compiling, and networking. In the 1980s, he worked on specific information systems applications, mostly with geography and dictionaries, as well as running a research group at Bellcore. And in the 1990s, he worked on a large chemical information system, the CORE project, with Cornell, OCLC, ACS and CAS. From 1998–2002 he was head of the Division of Information and Intelligent Systems at the National Science Foundation.

Ming Luo was born in Jiangsu, China. He received Bachelor's and Master's degrees in Computer Science at Nanjing University of Aeronautics and Astronautics, Nanjing China in 1997 and 2000, respectively. Currently, he is a PhD student in the Department of Computer Science, Virginia Tech, USA. His publications are in the fields of digital image processing, digital libraries and information retrieval. His current research interests also extend into the web services area.

Gail McMillan is a professor at University Libraries and director of the Digital Library and Archives at Virginia Tech, USA. She did her graduate work at the University of Maryland, College Park, spent a year as an archivist for the Smithsonian Institution in Washington, DC, before joined the faculty at Virginia Tech in 1982. The Digital Library and Archives combines the digital initiatives and scholarly communications with the historical resources of Special Collections, the home of original manuscript and archival collections, rare books, and the University Archives. Her department designs and implements systems and procedures that move traditional library services and resources on to the Internet, including faculty-edited journals, EReserve (online course materials), ETDs (electronic theses and dissertations), and the VT ImageBase. See http://scholar.lib.vt.edu.

William H. Mischo is Head, Grainger Engineering Library Information Center and Professor of Library Administration at the University of Illinois at Urbana Champaign (UIUC). Before joining the UIUC Library in 1982, he was at OCLC Inc and Iowa State University. He was a Principal Investigator for the National Science Foundation (NSF) Digital Library Initiatives (DLI–I) grant awarded to UIUC (1994–98) and a follow-on CNRI D-Lib Test Suite project that ended in August 2001. In 1998, he established the Grainger Library Collaborating Partners Program whose members include professional society publishers (AIP, APS, ASCE, IEE, IEEE, ACM, ASM), commercial publishers (Elsevier), and governmental agencies (NRL, NTT Learning Systems-Japan) interested in retrieval and rendering of full-text electronic resources. He is currently the PI on an NSF NSDL (National Science, Engineering, Technology, and Mathematics Digital Library) grant of $760,000 awarded to UIUC in September 2002 and a co-PI on a recently awarded IMLS (Institute of Museum and Library Services) integration grant. Bill Mischo has published nearly 50 articles in library and information science journals and conference proceedings. In 2001, he received the 2001 Homer I. Bernhardt Distinguished Service Award from the American Society for Engineering Education Engineering Libraries Division.

Stephen Pinfield is Assistant Director of Information Services at the University of Nottingham, UK. Amongst his current responsibilities is the directorship of BIOME, a service that began its life as an eLib Phase 1 project. In the late 1990s, he was project manager of the BUILDER hybrid library project, part of eLib Phase 3. During 2000 and 2001, he was a part-time consultant for JISC, tasked with capturing and communicating the lessons of eLib.

Hussein Suleman is a Senior Lecturer in Computer Science at the Univerisity of Cape Town in South Africa. He recently completed his PhD, focusing on simple component models for building digital libraries. His research focus is on topics closely related to matters of interoperability and componentized digital library architecture, with a slant towards resource-poor scenarios. Many of his research efforts are related to innovative and unusual applications and extensions of the OAI Protocol for Metadata Harvesting and its underlying principles.

Stella Thebridge is a Research Fellow in CIRT at UCE and a researcher on the eVALUEd project. She has researched and written about a range of projects involving public and academic libraries, the book trade and archives and museums. Prior to her move to the research sector, Stella worked in a range of public and academic libraries. She is also Associate Editor of *Library and Information Research* (journal of the Library and Information Research Group).

List of Acronyms

5/99	Series of projects funded under the Joint Information Systems Committee Teaching and Learning programme
A & I	Abstracting and Indexing
AACR2	Anglo American Cataloguing Rules. 2nd Edition
ACM	Association for Computing Machinery (USA)
ACRL	Association of College and Research Libraries (USA)
ADAM	Art, Design, Architecture and Media information gateway
ADTP	Australian Digital Theses Project
AHDS	Arts and Humanities Data Service (UK)
AIP	American Institute of Physics
ANGEL	Authenticated Networked Guided Environment for Learning
API	Application Program Interface
APS	American Physical Society
ARL	Association of Research Libraries (USA)
ArtStor	A digital resource devoted to scholarship, teaching and learning in the arts, humanities and related social sciences
ASCE	American Society of Civil Engineers
ASPECT	Access to Scottish Parliamentary Election Candidate Materials 1999
BBC	British Broadcasting Corporation
BDL	Brazilian Digital Library in Science and Technology Project
BIDS	Bath Information and Data Services (UK)
BUBL	BUBL Information Service – an Internet-based information service for the UK higher education community, the Bulletin Board for Libraries
BUFVC	British University Film & Video Council
CAIRNS	Co-operative Academic Information Retrieval Network for Scotland
CDLR	Centre for Digital Library Research
CEDARS	CURL Exemplars in Digital ARchiveS
CLIR	Council on Library and Information Resources
CNI	Coalition for Networked Information
CNRI	Corporation for National Research Initiatives
COM	Component Object Model
COPAC	Joint catalogue of the Consortium of University Research Libraries (UK)
COUNTER	Counting Online Usage of Networked Electronic Resources
CSS	Cascading Style Sheets
DARPA	Defense Advanced Research Projects Agency

DeLIver	Desktop Link to Virtual Engineering Resources
DELOS	Network of Excellence on Digital Libraries
DFG	Deutsch Forschungsgemeinschaft (German Research Foundation)
DLESE	Digital Library for Earth System Education
DLI	Digital Libraries Initiative USA
DNER	Distributed National Electronic Resource
DOIs	Digital Object Identifiers
DOM	XML Document Object Model
DSEP	Deposit System for Electronic Publications
DSpace	Digital repository created to capture, distribute and preserve the intellectual output of MIT
EEVL	Internet guide to engineering, mathematics and computing
EIS	Electronic Information Services
eLib	Electronic Libraries Programme
e-metrics	Measures for Electronic Resources
EQUINOX	Library Performance Measurement and Quality Management System
ETD-MS	Electronic Theses and Dissertations Metadata Standard
ETDs	Electronic Theses and Dissertations
eVALUEd	Project focusing on evaluation of electronic library initiatives based at the University of Central England
FAQ	Frequently Asked Questions
FIGIT	Follett Implementation Group for IT
FRBR	Functional Requirements for Bibliographic Standards
GDL	Glasgow Digital Library
GIS	Geographical Information Systems
GNU	Software system developed by the Free Software Foundation
HE	Higher Education UK
HEADLINE	Hybrid Electronic Access and Delivery in the Library Networked Environment
HEDS	Higher Education Digitisation Service UK
HEFCE	Higher Education Funding Council for England
HERON	Higher Education Resources On Demand (UK)
HPCC	High Performance Computing and Communications Program
HTML	HyperText Markup Language
IBICT	Brazilian Institute for Scientific and Technical Information
ICOLC	International Coalition of Library Consortia
IEE	Institution of Electrical Engineers
IEEE	Institute of Electrical and Electronics Engineers
ILS	Integrated Library System
IMLS	Institute of Museum and Library Services
IMPEL2	Overall name for four related eLib projects which monitored organisational and cultural change
IMS	Instructional Management Systems
IP	Internet Protocol
IU	Indiana University

JANET	Joint Academic Network (UK)
JISC	Joint Information Systems Committee (UK)
JPEG	Joint Pictures Experts Group – compressed graphics format
JSTOR	Journal Storage, the Scholarly Journal Archive
JTAP	Joint Technology Applications Programme (UK)
LAMDA	Electronic document delivery service that draws on the journal collections of ten leading UK academic libraries
LC	Library of Congress
LCSH	Library of Congress Subject Headings
LibQUAL+	Project to define and measure library service quality
LOCKSS	Lots Of Copies Keeps Stuff Safe
MARC	Machine Readable Cataloguing
METS	Metadata Encoding and Transmission Standard
MIA	MODELS Information Architecture
MIEL2 project	Management Information for the Electronic Library
MINERVA	Mapping the INternet Electronic Resources Virtual Archive Web Preservation Project
MODELS	MOving to Distributes Environments for Library Services
MODS	Metadata Object Description Schema
NAL	National Agricultural Library
NARA	National Archives and Records Administration
NCSA	University of Illinois' National Center for Supercomputing Applications
NCSTRL	Networked Computer Science Technical Reference Library, Cornell University
NDIIPP	The National Digital Information Infrastructure and Preservation Program
NDLP	National Digital Library Program
NDLTD	Networked Digital Library of Theses and Dissertations
NEDLIB	Networked European Deposit Library
NEH	National Endowment for the Humanities
NISSAT	National Information System for Science and Technology (India)
NLA	National Library of Australia
NLC	National Library of Canada
NLM	National Library of Medicine
NSDL	National Science, Technology, Engineering, and Mathematics Digital Library
NSF	National Science Foundation
OAI	Open Archives Initiative
OAI-PMH	Open Archives Initiative's Protocol for Metadata Harvesting
OAIS	Open Archival Information System
OCLC	Online Computer Library Center
OCR	Optical Character Recognition
OKI	Open Knowledge Initiative
OMNI	Gateway to Internet resources in Health and Medicine
OPAC	Online Public Access Catalogue

PANDORA	Preserving and Accessing Networked Documentary Resources of Australia
PDF	Portable Document Format
PITAC	President's Information Technology Advisory Committee
PLOS	Public Library of Science – check
PNG	Portable Network Graphics
PRINCE	PRojects In Controlled Environments
QAA	Quality Assurance Agency (UK)
QoS	Quality of Service
RDF	Resource Description Framework
RDN	Resource Discovery Network
RLG	Research Libraries Group
ROADS	Resource Organisation and Discovery in Subject-based services
RSLP	Research Support Libraries Programme (UK)
RTF	Rich Text Format
RUDI	Resource for Urban Design Information
S/L/P	Subscription/License/Pay-per-view
SAN	Storage Area Network
SAPIENS	Scottish Academic Periodicals: Implementing an Effective Networked Service
SCONUL	Society of College, National and University Libraries (UK)
SGML	Standard Generalized Markup Language
SOSIG	Social Science Information Gateway
SPARC	Scholarly Publishing and Academic Resources Coalition
SQL	Standard Query Language
STEM	Science, Technology, Engineering, and Mathematics
STM	Scientific Technical and Medical
SUNY	State University of New York
TeX	Macro processor that provides control over typographical formatting
TIFF	Tagged Image File Format
UCE	University of Central England in Birmingham UK
UCEEL	University of Central England Electronic Library
UI	User Interface
UIUC	University of Illinois at Urbana-Champaign
UKOLN	UK Office of Library and Information Networking
URL	Uniform Resource Locator
VLE	Virtual Learning Environment
W3C	World Wide Web Consortium
XDOD	Xerox Documents On Demand
XHTML	eXtensible HyperText Markup Language
XML	eXtensible Markup Language
XSLT	eXtensible Stylesheet Language Transformations
Z39.50	International Standard, ISO 23950: "Information Retrieval (Z39.50): Application Service Definition and Protocol Specification"

Chapter 1

Introduction

Judith Andrews and Derek Law

This book aims to provide a snapshot of digital library development, highlighting issues of policy and practice in a wide range of related areas, and attempts to show how research has been developed for application in the workplace. The pace of development described in the following chapters clearly illustrates that the issues and challenges facing digital library developers change at a staggering pace. The value of this book is that it provides an overview of how we have arrived at the current position, a consideration of key policy issues that need to be addressed, an insight into the decision-making process of those who are working at 'the coal face' and a vision of future directions.

In his chapter about the development of the Glasgow Digital Library, Alan Dawson states that 'It is not a typical digital library, but there is probably no such thing'. The examples of digital library implementations explored in this book illustrate the truth of this comment. Digital libraries are a common issue throughout the world, yet thrive on a diversity of culture, history and professional practice. With 23 authors from five countries on three continents, this book reflects that fact. As a result, a decision has been taken to allow the authors to speak in their own voice. Therefore, the editors have not harmonized spelling (program and programme), library practice (library patron or library user) or words (fall and autumn).

Chapters 2 and 3 present valuable overviews of the eLib and the digital library research programmes that were established in the UK and US respectively. The projects undertaken under the auspices of these programmes have had a fundamental impact on the development of the digital libraries we see today. In Chapter 2, William H. Mischo provides an overview of federally sponsored digital library research projects and programmes. He also considers the developments achieved by two specific projects at Stanford University and the University of Illinois at Urbana-Champaign. In Chapter 3, Stephen Pinfield draws on the literature about eLib and on his personal experiences of working on the programme to analyse some of its successes and failures. He also highlights some of the key differences between eLib and the US digital library programmes.

Part 1 contains chapters that explore five key digital library policy areas – economics, content, scholarly communication, preservation and evaluation. Mike Lesk, in Chapter 4, considers the economics of digital libraries and discusses the advantages and disadvantages of a range of potential funding mechanisms. These mechanisms include the current model (funding by the community) through to funding by authors, by user subscriptions, via advertising and a number of other potential funding routes. The fifth chapter, by Derek Law, explores the different types of content used to create digital libraries, from born digital material to licensed leased journals. In Chapter 6, Stevan Harnad gives a comprehensive description of how open access works or can be made to work to create a global virtual archive of scholarly research. He began as a somewhat solitary voice in the wilderness but his views have been increasingly adopted by the mainstream of thought on scholarly communication. Notably, he provides a series of FAQs and answers that demolish the arguments against progress. This chapter differs from the rest in that it was not specifically written for the book but has been a living document, developed on-line through collaborative debate and comment, on the web for many months. However, the topic is so relevant to the future of digital libraries that we are delighted that Stevan has agreed to its inclusion here, although the audience he addresses is more that of researchers than librarians. Susan S. Lazinger, in Chapter 7, uses a series of questions to consider issues of policy and practice in digital preservation. The questions include why digital resources should be preserved, what should be preserved, who the stakeholders are and what their responsibilities should be, and how digital resources should be preserved bearing in mind a wide range of technical issues. The final question relates to the complexities of establishing the true costs of digital preservation. In Chapter 8, Pete Dalton, Stella Thebridge and Rebecca Hartland-Fox examine the role of evaluation in relation to electronic information services (EIS). They stress the importance of the role that evaluation should play in the effective management of EIS and provide an overview of the benefits it can bring. The current challenges to effective evaluation are identified and a number of important tools and projects in the field are discussed.

The digital library implementations that are described in Part 2 are very different in nature. They are a metropolitan digital library (Glasgow Digital Library), a single university digital library striving to develop multiple collections with a range of different formats (UCEEL), a single subject digital library that is expanding to include other pilot sites (Variations2), a national/international digital library focusing on one type of publication (National Digital Library of Theses and Dissertations) and a national library of international repute with a wealth of special collections (Library of Congress).

Despite the fundamental differences in mission, many of the chapters in Section 2 highlight a range of common issues, for example metadata, technical standards, authentication, preservation and evaluation. What becomes clear is that there is no single solution to the challenges that digital library developers face in each of these key areas. It is intended that the different approaches described will provide a wide-ranging overview of the issues to be addressed, the solutions that have been adopted and the reasons why these crucial decisions have been made.

Chapters 9 and 10 describe implementations of digital libraries in the UK, the Glasgow Digital Library (GDL) and UCEEL, a digital library being developed at the University of Central England.

Alan Dawson, in Chapter 9, uses the 16 headings identified in Chowdhury & Chowdhury's (1999) classic work on digital library research to describe the development of the GDL. Under each heading is a commentary on issues and problems that were actually encountered in trying to create a digital library, as well as details of any solutions found and lessons learned. There is also a rating of the importance of each heading for the GDL, on a scale from 1 to 5 (1 = not important,

5 = extremely important), and an assessment of the percentage of implementation time spent on matters relating to that heading. A practical overview of the development of UCEEL is provided by Chris Dodd and Judith Andrews in Chapter 10. Like the previous chapter, this description also explores the challenges faced and the reasons for the solutions that were adopted. The final part of the chapter highlights plans for further development of the system.

In Chapter 11, Edward A. Fox, Gail McMillan, Hussein Suleman, Marcos A. Gonçalves and Ming Luo describe the Networked Digital Library of Theses and Dissertations (NDLTD). The NDLTD's goals, objectives, content, management and access are discussed, as well as evaluation, preservation and intellectual property rights. The growing interest in electronic theses and dissertations (EDTs) is discussed and illustrated by an overview of five international projects in the US, Germany, Australia, India and Brazil. The final section of the chapter sets out plans for future developments.

The development of the Variations and Variations2 digital music library projects at Indiana University is reviewed by Jon W. Dunn, Mary Wallace Davidson, Jan R. Holloway and Gerald Bernbom in Chapter 12. In addition, possible future directions are discussed in the context of today's concerns in music research and instruction. Diane Kresh, in Chapter 13, describes the beginnings of the Library of Congress digital program, its integration into core library services, and what the future may hold for the provision of web-based information services.

The final chapter, by Mel Collier, discusses a potential way forward for digital libraries in the context of Tilburg University library. The chapter considers the steps on the way to the development of the first digital libraries, and argues that a fundamental boundary has now been crossed in that it is now possible to create a totally digital library. The second part of the chapter looks to the future and discusses possible enabling factors, future stakeholders and potential barriers.

In conclusion, we wish to thank all the contributors to this book. The opinions are theirs, any errors are ours!

Reference

Chowdhury, G.G. and Chowdhury, S. (1999) 'Digital Library Research: Major Issues and Trends', *Journal of Documentation*, 55 (4), 409–448.

Chapter 2

United States Federal Support for Digital Library Research and its Implications for Digital Library Development

William H. Mischo

Introduction

The United States federal government began formal financial support for digital library research in 1994, with the funding of six projects under the auspices of the federated Digital Library Initiative (now called DLI-1) program. These DLI-1 research and development projects were jointly funded by the National Science Foundation (NSF), the National Aeronautics and Space Administration (NASA), and the Defense Advanced Research Projects Agency (DARPA). The support for the DLI-1 program initially came out of the United States federal government's High Performance Computing and Communications Program (HPCC) and grew out of a community-based series of workshops sponsored by the NSF in 1993–94 (Griffin, 1998).

The six DLI-1 projects were awarded a total of $24 million in federal funding over the four-year lives of the projects. In 1998, at the cessation of the DLI-1 program, federal funding for the DLI-2 program was begun with support from the NSF, NASA, DARPA, the National Library of Medicine (NLM), the Library of Congress (LC), the Federal Bureau of Investigation (FBI), and the National Endowment for the Humanities (NEH). In total, between 1994 and 1999, a total of $68 million in federal research grants was awarded under DLI-1 and DLI-2 (Fox, 1999).

In addition, in 1998, the Corporation for National Research Initiatives (CNRI), under DARPA support, began the three-year *D-Lib Test Suite* program, which provided continuing funding for several of the digital library Testbeds created under DLI-1.

The above programs have also been greatly augmented by projects funded under the NSF-sponsored National Science, Technology, Engineering, and Mathematics Digital Library (NSDL) program and the federal Institute of Museum and Library Services (IMLS) research programs.

When work on the DLI-1 projects began in 1994, the World Wide Web (WWW) was in a nascent stage. At that time, the University of Illinois' National Center for Supercomputing Applications (NCSA) Mosaic 2.0 beta was the web browser of choice, the HTML 2.0 standard was still under development, Netscape had yet to release its first web browser and Microsoft Windows 3.1 was the standard personal computer operating system. Computer and networking technology has changed dramatically over the last ten years and nowhere is this more evident than in the rapidly evolving world of digital library research and implementation. While federally funded digital library research has made some important inroads, it has also occasionally found itself outside the mainstream of a rapidly evolving technology environment.

This review will not attempt to survey and document exhaustively all the federally-sponsored research projects and research programs, but rather will provide an overview of the programs and a more-detailed examination of two DLI-1 projects. This review will also suggest key areas of interest for the development and implementation of digital libraries. Some of these areas have been addressed by federally funded digital library research and some have, at the present, not been addressed.

There is a prolific literature surrounding the definition of a 'digital library' and the distinctions between digital, electronic, and virtual libraries (Chowdhury and Chowdhury, 1999). This paper will utilize the vocabulary suggested by the NSDL program in which digital libraries are described as

> A managed environment of multimedia materials in digital form, designed for the benefit of its user population, structured to facilitate access to its contents, and equipped with aids to navigate the global network . . . with users and holdings totally distributed, but managed as a coherent whole

Alternatively, a 1997 Santa Fe Workshop on digital libraries characterized the digital library as an environment to bring together collections, services, and people in a full life cycle of creation, dissemination, use and preservation activities.

The DLI-1 Projects

Under DLI-1, six university-led consortia were funded to develop and apply robust computing and networking capabilities to make large distributed electronic collections accessible, interoperable, and usable. Each project utilized multi-departmental teams together with commercial vendors or software companies to push the envelope of digital library research. The six funded institutions and their primary focus were:

- The University of Michigan for research on agent technology and mechanisms for improving secondary education.
- Stanford University for the investigation of interoperability among heterogeneous digital libraries and the exploration of distributed object technology.
- The University of California-Berkeley for imaging technologies, government environmental information resources, and database technologies.
- The University of California-Santa Barbara for the Alexandria Project to develop GIS (Geographical Information Systems) and earth modeling distributed libraries.

- Carnegie Mellon University for the study of integrated speech, image, video, and language-understanding software under its Informedia system.
- The University of Illinois at Urbana-Champaign for the development of document representation, processing, indexing, retrieval, and display protocols for full-text physics, computer science, and engineering journals.

All projects included a Testbed and an evaluation component. Most of the projects suffered, certainly in the beginning, from a lack of critical mass of Testbed project digital objects. This caused problems in user testing because of the lack of breadth and depth of the Testbed electronic collections.

It may prove useful to examine the Illinois and Stanford projects in some detail. The Illinois Testbed project, of full-text scientific and engineering journal articles, was carried out by a multi-departmental research team comprising individuals from the university's Graduate School of Library and Information Science (GSLIS), the University Library, the NCSA, and the Department of Computer Science (Mischo and Cole, 1998). The DLI Testbed, housed in the Grainger Engineering Library Information Center, was constructed from source text journal articles supplied in SGML format by a number of professional society publishers.

The Testbed team implemented a web-based retrieval system, called DeLIver (Desktop Link to Virtual Engineering Resources) featuring enhanced access and display capabilities. The DeLIver system was used by over 3000 registered UIUC students and faculty, as well as designated outside researchers. Detailed transaction log data of user search sessions (gathered and merged from both database and web servers) were gathered and an analysis of user search patterns from some 4200 search sessions has been performed.

In addition to enhancing the DeLIver system, in the course of this project Testbed staff developed a metadata-based retrieval and full-text display system based on a relational database model, a cross-repository retrieval system over several of the D-Lib Test Suite collections based on metadata normalizing procedures, a handbook-based full-text system, a Local Resolver server for processing and handling Digital Object Identifiers (DOIs), and a simultaneous search portal that operates over major A&I Services and provides reference linking to publishers' full-texts using OpenURLs and DOIs.

The Illinois Testbed comprised full-text in XML format (converted from the SGML) with RDF (Resource Description Framework) qualified Dublin Core metadata and bit-mapped images of figures for 63 journal titles containing over 100,000 articles from eight scholarly professional societies in physics and engineering. The full-text journal articles for the Testbed were contributed by:

American Institute of Physics (AIP),
American Physical Society (APS),
American Society of Civil Engineers (ASCE),
Association for Computing Machinery (ACM),
Elsevier Science, Ltd,
Institute of Electrical and Electronics Engineers (IEEE), and
Institution of Electrical Engineers (IEE).

In addition, the Testbed contained full-text handbook data from ASM International.

The Stanford Digital Library Project focused on mechanisms for unified access to heterogeneous digital collections and information services. The project attempted to organize search access around a protocol that was tailored for use with distributed objects. The Stanford project was prescient in its focus on metadata schemes and manipulation and in its emphasis on issues connected with search-threading across wide-area networks, search and network reliability factors, and techniques to provide mechanisms to hold communication connections open (to retain state) in a web environment. A refreshingly candid article on the design decisions inherent in the project and their aftermath was published in 1998 (Paepcke *et al.*, 2000).

The Stanford project attempted to develop a working model for distributed searching across heterogeneous collections, services, and objects. These were, and continue to be, important research and implementation issues. Much work has gone into developing standards and best practices for federated and broadcast search systems. This issue will be revisited at the conclusion of this chapter.

The Illinois, Stanford and Michigan projects all addressed issues connected with search interoperability and distributed searching. It is perhaps interesting to contrast these interoperability approaches. The Stanford model employed what they termed a 'shared information bus', which provided the means to perform federated searching across heterogeneous information resources. The Michigan view was built around a collection of collaborating software agents that tied together a set of servers spread throughout the Internet. The Illinois approach utilized broadcast, asynchronous searching of distributed, heterogeneous repositories. All of these approaches helped to define the ongoing conundrum of federated versus broadcast searching and presaged the development of web services technologies.

Overall, the DLI-1 projects served to identify and define important document and data metadata standards, protocols for web-based access, and the issues surrounding federated and broadcast search protocols.

Corporation for National Research Initiatives (CNRI) Support

In 1998, CNRI began the three-year D-Lib Test Suite project to provide continuing support for several of the Testbeds created under DLI-1. These Testbeds, combined into the D-Lib Test Suite, provided a set of digital library collections for research purposes. CNRI provided funding for the continuing development and testing of the DLI-1 Testbeds and also provided a large open resource for research and technology transfer in digital libraries and related fields. The D-Lib Test Suite was coordinated by CNRI with support from DARPA. The five Testbeds supported under this project were:

- The University of Illinois at Urbana-Champaign full-text journal article Testbed.
- The Cornell University NCSTRL (Networked Computer Science Technical Reference Library) running under the Dienst software architecture for distributed collections.

- The Carnegie Mellon Informedia video collection.
- The University of California-Berkeley distributed environmental information system.
- The University of California-Santa Barbara Alexandria Project digital earth prototype.

These Testbeds included large collections of images, video segments, maps, journal articles in eXtensible Markup Language (XML) format, and full-text technical reports.

In the Illinois project, The CNRI D-Lib Test Suite grant provided the Testbed Team with the resources to extend the functionality of the DeLIver system and develop data conversion, dynamic linking, enhanced rendering, extended metadata, and improved retrieval capabilities. In addition, a Collaborating Publishing Partners program was instituted to provide additional support for the Testbed. The Testbed Collaborating Partners supplied both full-text content and monetary support. A total of 11 organizations – professional societies and commercial entities – were members of the Partners program during the three years of the project.

The overarching focus of the Illinois full-text Testbed has been on the design, development, and evaluation of mechanisms that can provide effective access to full-text engineering and physics journal articles within an Internet environment. The primary goals of the Illinois Testbed within the D-Lib Test Suite were:

- The construction and testing of a multi-publisher XML-based full-text Testbed employing emerging document representation techniques and flexible search and rendering capabilities that offer rich links to internal and external resources.
- The development of processing, rendering, metadata, linking, and search technologies and best practices that can be transferred to the Testbed publisher partners within their full-text repository systems.
- The development of integrated retrieval systems employing full-text repositories, A&I services, and metadata resources within the continuum of information resources offered to end-users by Library portals.

One of the cornerstones of the Illinois Testbed, in terms of retrieval capabilities, was the effective integration of the article content and structure revealed by XML with the associated article-level metadata. Across publisher repositories, metadata was normalized into a standard canonical format that allowed the display of consistent short-entry records and provided the capability of cross-article linking. The metadata contained links to internal and external data in the form of forward and backward links to other Testbed articles and links to A&I Service databases (including Ovid INSPEC and Compendex databases) and other full-text repositories, such as the American Institute of Physics, the American Physical Society, and Elsevier.

An important concern of the Testbed Team has been in exploring effective retrieval models for a web-based electronic journal publishing system. The retrieval and display of full-text journal literature in an Internet environment poses a number of issues for both publishers and libraries. It has now become commonplace for both major and small-scale publishers to provide web-based access to full-text journal issues and articles. The work performed under this grant provided important information, in the form of design insights and specific technologies, to the scientific publishing community seeking to establish or improve its full-text repositories.

Probably the most significant contribution of the project was the transfer of technology to our publishing partners and other publishers. This is shown by the rapid evolution of many of the scientific and technical (sci-tech) journal publishers' websites. When this project commenced in 1994, almost none of the scientific or technical publishers provided online access to full-text journal articles. Indeed, even at the outset of the D-Lib Test Suite in 1998, full-text journal article content was provided as static, proprietary Adobe Acrobat files, or even as scanned page images. However, nearly all sci-tech publishers now provide online access to full-text articles, many with features that closely follow those that were originally developed within the Illinois Testbed project. These feature-sets include: full-text display using HTML and Cascading Style Sheets (CSS), internal linking between citations and footnotes, hyperlinks to cited articles using DOIs and OpenURLs, and the display of complex mathematics and special Unicode characters directly in HTML full text.

Much work was also done in dynamically converting well-formed XML into formats that can be displayed in current web browsers (Netscape 6, Mozilla, and Microsoft Internet Explorer). We successfully implemented several different approaches.

Early in the project, prior to the adoption of several key W3C standards, we had implemented our own XML parser (similar to the current SAX parsers), which we used to transform dynamically the XML. However, as the W3C standards evolved we adopted more of the standard technologies and tools for working with XML, namely the XML Document Object Model (DOM) and the eXtensible Stylesheet Language Transformations (XSLT). However, the rendering techniques that we experimented with using both our custom tools and the W3C standard tools are very similar.

The approach that ultimately proved to be the most flexible was dynamically to convert the XML into HTML on the server with references to the appropriate Cascading Style Sheets (CSS) and downloadable fonts. We developed several sophisticated server and client-side scripts that use XSLT and CSS stylesheets for rendering the full-text XML articles as HTML.

We also experimented with rendering the raw, untransformed XML directly in the web browser. However, this approach was hampered by the lack of native XML support in early commercial web browsers, and the fact that the browsers that did support XML did so imperfectly.

One important technique common to all of the above approaches is *metamerge*. Metamerge is the on-the-fly combining of the full-text article with the metadata. This allows the rendered article to contain much value-added information that was not contained in the original article, such as links to cited and citing articles, links to abstracting and indexing services, etc.

The DLI-2 Program

The main DLI-2 program, as funded in 1999, involved 24 awards. Several of the awards continued DLI-1 investigations (Santa Barbara, Carnegie Mellon, Stanford, and Berkeley), albeit in several cases in a modified form. Overall, the DLI-2 projects were perhaps less focused on research and included a number of discipline areas and technologies that were not represented in the DLI-1 foci. For example, DLI-2 grants have addressed digital library issues in anthropology, fine arts, humanities, sheet music, economics, patient care, folk literature, and library and information sciences. DLI-2 awards fall into three major component categories: research, testbed, and applications. There is also an undergraduate education track and an international digital libraries collaborative research component.

The principal investigators for DLI-2 have continued to come from the ranks of computer and information scientists and related researchers. As Lesk has pointed out, one particularly healthy sign for digital library research is that senior scholars in other computing disciplines have changed their focus in order to do digital library research (Lesk, 1999).

Several key issues for continuing digital library research are being addressed under DLI-2 funding. One of the Berkeley collaborative projects addresses the issues surrounding the scholarly dissemination of information. This is a particularly important issue, as changing models of scholarly communication gain momentum and move forward.

The international collaboration between Cornell and the UK ePrint project has contributed to the development and adaptation of the important Open Archives Initiative for Metadata Harvesting (OAI-PMH) specifications and protocols (see http://www.openarchives.org/index.html). The OAI work, which has its roots in an effort to enhance access to e-print archives, is an important component in digital library research and implementation. From both a philosophical and practical viewpoint, OAI can be regarded as a lightweight transport mechanism for exposure and dissemination of metadata, as a standards-based technology for document representation and transmission, and as a component in the changing scholarly communication landscape. The OAI protocols are being applied in a large number of federated information environments and serve as the primary metadata protocol for the NSDL project participants.

The NSDL Program

Probably the most significant development in US federal digital library support is the NSDL program. The initial development of the National Science, Technology, Engineering, and Mathematics Digital Library (NSDL) program began in late 1995 with an internal concept paper for the NSF Division of Undergraduate Education and a 1996 NSF report describing mechanisms to improve undergraduate science, technology, engineering, and mathematics (STEM) education. These reports recommended the establishment of a national digital library that would constitute an online network of learning environments for improving teaching and learning for STEM education at all levels, from kindergarten to postgraduate education.

The NSDL program envisions a system designed to meet the needs of learners, in both individual and collaborative settings, which is constructed to enable dynamic use of a broad array of materials for learning, primarily in digital format, and is actively managed to promote reliable anytime, anywhere access to quality collections and services, available both within and without the network. It seeks to become a comprehensive, online source for science, technology, engineering and mathematics education.

In 1998, two prototype projects were supported under the auspices of the DLI-2 program. These grants funded projects at Berkeley and Old Dominion University.

The NSDL program held its first formal funding cycle during fiscal year (FY) 2000. The highly competitive program has funded three rounds of grants during FY 2002 through 2002 for a total of 119 grants (out of 354 proposals) at approximately $64 million.

The NSDL has four primary program tracks. They are:

- *Core Integration*: to coordinate a distributed alliance of resource collection and service providers, and to ensure reliable and extensible access to, and usability of, the resulting network of learning environments and resources.
- *Collections*: to aggregate and actively manage a subset of the digital library's content within a coherent theme or specialty.
- *Services*: to increase the impact, reach, efficiency, and value of the digital library in its fully operational form.
- *Targeted (Applied) Research*: to have immediate impact on one or more of the other three tracks.

These grants have created collections and services for teacher and learners at all levels, and perform targeted research on digital libraries and their application to education. The NSDL has become a digital library of exemplary resource collections and services, organized in support of science education at all levels. The NSDL is emerging as a center of innovation in digital libraries as applied to education, and a community center for groups focused on digital-library-enabled science education.

The NSDL program is an unusual program for NSF in that its projects are engaged in building an enterprise much larger than the object of any one grant. The centerpiece of the NSDL program is the Core Integration project, headed by Cornell University, Columbia University, and DLESE. The Core Integration System is providing organizational and managerial functions of the digital library, including harvesting of collections' metadata with OAI as its primary harvesting technology, a search and discovery over a broad corpus of websites, a collection-wide registry describing these collections, and an OAI-compliant metadata provider service over the corpus of collections.

The NSDL Core Integration System seeks to:

- Maintain the premier gateway to the NSDL network;
- Supplement and coordinate services developed to enable effective use of, and access to, the network's content;

- Provide leadership in the development of standards for including resource collections and services in the network;
- Work with resource collection providers to establish a suite of review systems for inclusion of material;
- Coordinate the formulation of requirements – in conjunction with appropriate standards organizations and/or consortia – for interoperability, reusability, reliability, and stability of resources and services;
- Find new resource collections to join, or otherwise be affiliated with, the library.

In this way, the Core Integration System is providing overarching access services for the NSDL library and also metadata provider services for any developer wishing to develop and implement custom vertical-subject federated portals and search and discovery systems.

The IMLS Research Program

The Institute of Museum and Library Services (IMLS) is a federal grant-awarding agency that promotes leadership, innovation, and a lifetime of learning by supporting the nation's museums and libraries. Created by the Museum and Library Services Act of 1996, IMLS administers the Library Services and Technology Act and the Museum Services Act.

In terms of research grants, the primary vehicle is the National Leadership Grants for Libraries program, which awards grants of the order of $15,000 to $500,000 for up to three years.

The program supports three funding categories for libraries, three for museums and one for joint library–museum partnerships. Proposals must have national impact and provide models that can be widely adapted or replicated by others to extend the benefit of federal support. It is expected that funded projects will provide creative solutions on issues of national importance and provide leadership for other organizations.

Proposals are funded in the following areas:

- *Continuing Education, Curriculum Development and Training* supports training and education in library and information science, including traineeships, institutes, graduate fellowships and other programs.
- *Research and Demonstration* encourages strong proposals for research in library science and for demonstration projects to test potential solutions to problems in real-world situations.
- *Preservation or Digitization of Library Materials* helps to preserve and/or digitize library resources. Applicants for preservation projects should describe the significance of the materials proposed for preservation or digitization (or both) and, if applicable, any innovative approaches. Refer to program guidelines for additional requirements for digitization projects.
- *Model Programs of Library–Museum Collaboration* supports innovative projects that model how museums and libraries can work together to expand

their service to the public, with an emphasis on serving the community, using technology, or enhancing education.

The UIUC Library has secured a multi-year (2002–2005) IMLS Collection Registry and Metadata Repository grant that will utilize OAI technologies to federate metadata collections created under IMLS National Leadership Grants.

Discussion and Conclusions

Currently, US federal support for digital library programs remains strong. Indeed, the NSDL and IMLS programs have seen increases in funding in the last few years. A February 2001 report to the President and Congress developed by the President's Information Technology Advisory Committee (PITAC) entitled 'Digital Libraries: Universal Access to Human Knowledge' (http://www.itrd.gov/pubs/pitac/pitac-dl-9feb01.pdf) calls for increases in federal funding for digital library research. This report is one in a series of reports by PITAC on key contemporary issues in information technology. These focused reports examine specific aspects of the near- and long-term research and development and policies required to capture the potential of information technology to help improve the US economy and to address important problems facing the United States. The 24-member PITAC, comprising corporate and academic leaders, was established by Executive Order of the President in 1997 and renewed for a two-year term in 1999. Its charge is to provide the Federal government with expert independent guidance on maintaining America's pre-eminence in high performance computing and communications, information technology, and Next Generation Internet research and development.

The report holds that 'realizing the full potential of digital libraries will take strong leadership and a steady commitment of resources to tackle the substantial technical and policy barriers that inhibit our rapid progress toward universally accessible knowledge libraries'. The PITAC report offered four key recommendations to make digital libraries more pervasive and usable by all citizens.

- *Recommendation 1.* Support expanded digital library research in metadata and metadata use, scalability, interoperability, archival storage and preservation, intellectual property rights, privacy and security, and human use.
- *Recommendation 2.* Establish large-scale digital library Testbeds.
- *Recommendation 3.* The Federal government should provide the necessary resources to make all public Federal material persistently available in digital form on the Internet.
- *Recommendation 4.* The Federal government should play a leadership role in evolving policy to deal fairly with intellectual property rights in the digital age.

The PITAC also strongly urged the Federal government to continue its leadership role in the research and development efforts needed to extend the capabilities of digital libraries. The recommendations in the report were designed to help provide funding for the powerful vision of anytime, anywhere access to the best of human thought and culture and provide those assets for classrooms and pedagogical endeavors.

Clearly, federally sponsored digital library research projects have informed the field of digital libraries and have contributed to the development of important information services. Some have led to significant technology transfer and spinoffs (for example Yahoo and Google grew out of research performed under the Stanford DLI-1 project). The NSDL Core Integration site holds the promise of a significant portal for science education. However, significant issues remain to be addressed and it is probably not feasible that federally funded programs can or will address all of these issues.

It is also very important to note that recent significant contributions to digital library research and implementation have also been made by other non-federally funded organizations and consortiums. These include:

- commercial database vendors (Ovid, ISI),
- publishers (commercial societies such as AIP and commercial publishers such as Elsevier),
- publisher consortiums (CrossRef),
- bibliographic utilities (OCLC's work with the Dublin Core and Resource Description Framework (RDF) standards),
- the W3C (XML, XSLT),
- Academic consortia such as the Digital Library Federation and the Association for Research Libraries (OAI, the ARL Portal),
- NISO (OpenURL),
- turnkey library system vendors (Ex Libris with SFX),
- search engines (Google, WebFeat),
- computer companies (HP and D-Space), and
- database vendors (WebFeat, Oracle, Microsoft).

One possible scenario for advancing the field of digital libraries is for federally funded digital library research and the development work carried out by vendors, publishers, institutions, library consortia, and other entities to be coordinated and integrated. This is presently being done within the NSDL project, but it needs to be greatly expanded. In the day-to-day life of libraries, particularly academic libraries, librarians find themselves confronting a number of collection development and service issues as they deal with a scholarly information environment that comprises a broad array of distributed and heterogeneous online resources. This distributed web-based information environment facing academic libraries includes:

- discrete publisher and vendor full-text article repositories,
- remote and locally loaded A&I services,
- open preprint servers such as ArX,
- nascent institutional repository systems (such as D-Space),
- instructional and course management system materials (from Blackboard, WebCT, and other vendors),
- harvestable and mostly hidden web resources (based on the Open Archives Initiative or OAI protocols),

- local collections of digital objects and finding aids,
- web vertical portals and search engines, and
- local, regional, and national online catalogs and shared resource bibliographic databases.

These systems often feature different and incompatible user interfaces, search and discovery protocols, database technologies, and display and linking technologies. In order to provide quality services for users, it is necessary to construct overarching library services that link and integrate these heterogeneous resources. In particular, there is a compelling need for technologies that provide portal services and linking to and between full-text repositories.

In an effort to provide efficient and effective access to the myriad of distributed information resources, libraries, library system vendors and commercial entities have been engaging in the development of library portal software and systems that typically provide: a federated search of multiple resources, search engines, and other portals; links to full-text; and custom displays of information resources. This work will continue in parallel with any federally funded digital library work.

One particularly exciting aspect of library portal development is the introduction of broadcast or simultaneous searching of multiple information collections and resources, such as that employed by WebFeat, Ex Libris MetaLib, or Encompass. This type of federated searching contrasts with the harvested or central database approach employed by NSDL, ISI's Web of Knowledge, EI Village, and numerous OAI-based search systems, where the heterogeneous resources are loaded centrally and put into a standardized format before being searched under the same database structure and search language protocols. In conjunction with full-text linking technologies, the federated/broadcast search work provides a robust and sophisticated service for users of information resources. Several standards-based technologies, including Digital Object Identifiers (DOI) and the OpenURL, and organizations, such as CrossRef, have emerged to address some of the problems in providing effective linking.

US federally funded digital library work and the work funded by governments around the world, while typically providing a research agenda for the field, will also need to complement and be integrated with the many digital library initiatives listed above. Only then will we see significant advancements in digital library environments and improved information services for users.

References

Chowdhury, G.G. and Chowdhury, S. (1999), 'Digital Library Research: Major Issues and Trends', *Journal of Documentation*, 55(4), 409–448.

Fox, E.A. (1999), 'Digital Libraries Initiative: Update and Discussion', *Bulletin of the American Society for Information Science*, 26(1), 7–11.

Griffin, S.M. (1998), 'NSF/DARPA/NASA Digital Libraries Initiative: A Program Manager's Perspective', *D-Lib Magazine*, July/August. http://www.dlib.org/dlib/july98/07griffin.html. Accessed 15 April 2003.

Lesk, M. (1999), 'Perspectives on DLI-2 – Growing the Field,' *Bulletin of the American Society for Information Science*, 26(1), 12–13.

Mischo, W.H. and Cole, T.W. (1998). 'Processing and Access Issues for Full-Text Journals', in S. Harum and M. Twidale (eds), *Successes and Failures of Digital Libraries: Papers Presented at the 35th Annual Clinic on Library Applications of Data Processing.* Champaign: Graduate School of Library and Information Science, University of Illinois at Urbana-Champaign, 22–24 March.

Paepcke, A., Baldonado, M., Chen-Chuan K. Chang, Cousins, S., Garcia-Molina, H. (2000), 'Building the InfoBus: A Review of Technical Choices in the Stanford Digital Library Project', Stanford Database Group Publication Server, http://dbpubs.stanford.edu/pub/2000–50. Accessed 15 April 2003.

President's Information Technology Advisory Committee (2001). 'Report to the President. Digital Libraries: Universal Access to Human Knowledge,' http://www.itrd.gov/pubs/pitac/pitac-dl-9feb01.pdf, February. Accessed 15 April 2003.

Chapter 3

eLib in Retrospect:
A National Strategy for Digital
Library Development in the 1990s

Stephen Pinfield

Introduction

The UK eLib programme was launched in 1994 in an atmosphere of expectancy. Seven years, 70 projects and £20 million later, the programme came to a close. The key question is: was it successful? And if so, in what ways? What were its main achievements and, for that matter, failures? These questions (whether it was successful, and if so, how) have been debated within the information profession for a while – a substantial body of the professional literature has addressed them. The consensus seems to have emerged in the literature that eLib was (at least in part) successful, but this success is defined and qualified in different ways.

The questions 'whether?' and 'how?' are important, but there is another question that seems to have been explicitly addressed less often and yet, if anything, is more important: 'why?'. If the eLib programme was successful, why was it? What were the key factors behind its success? Why were there failures? Addressing the question 'why?' is important, since the answers could have serious implications for the way in which electronic library activities are funded and organized in the future.[1]

The questions, 'whether?', 'how?' and 'why?' are then the main themes of this chapter. But before these questions can be discussed in any meaningful way, it is first necessary to describe some of the background to the eLib programme. Tracing the historical development of eLib and defining the aims and characteristics of the programme will provide a useful context for analysing its outcomes.

Background to eLib

The story of eLib has been told a number of times (see for example Carr, 2002; Rusbridge, 1998) and will only be related here in outline. Most accounts of eLib begin (quite rightly) with the Follett report (Follett, 1993). The Follett review group (chaired by Professor Sir Brian Follett) was commissioned by the UK funding agencies for higher education (HE) to carry out a full-scale review of the academic library system. Its report, published in late 1993, was an enormously influential document which has had a profound effect on academic library strategy

19

in the UK. Not least amongst its achievements was creating the momentum for the formation of the eLib programme itself. More than ten years on, it is easy to forget that Follett was written and eLib established in a context of a perceived 'deepening crisis in academic libraries'. In an early account of eLib, Chris Rusbridge, the programme's Director for most of its life, defined this crisis as having three main aspects: 'exploding demand (fuelled by huge increases in student numbers), years of relatively stagnant funding, and hyper-inflation in the supply side, particular [*sic*] in academic journals.' (Rusbridge, 1995b).

In simple terms, the practical problems were of two kinds: space and costs. Libraries were finding it difficult to accommodate all of their collections, users and equipment; they were also finding it difficult to continue to keep up with their users' demands for information materials. To address the space problem Follett recommended that a major building programme be undertaken to extend existing libraries and build new ones. Both problems (space and costs) could also be addressed through the application of information technology. Chapter 7 of the Follett report made detailed recommendations about areas that should be further investigated, including suggestions for the level of funding for each. The areas were summarized as:

> the development of standards, pilot projects to demonstrate the potential of on-demand publishing and electronic document and article delivery, a feasibility project to promote the development of electronic journals in conjunction with relevant publishing interests, the development of a database and dataset strategy, investment in navigational tools, retrospective conversion of certain catalogues, and investment in the further development of library automation and management systems. (Follett, 1993)

The report concluded that 'the exploitation of IT is essential to create the effective library service of the future'.

Follett was well-received by the academic library community and in HE generally. The funding councils moved quickly to respond to the report and tasked the Joint Information Systems Committee (JISC) with taking forward Follett's IT-related recommendations. JISC established the Follett Implementation Group for IT (FIGIT) which, after a period of consultation, in turn set up the Electronic Libraries Programme (eLib) office and issued a structured call for project proposals to institutions. The call identified a number of programme areas most of which derived directly from Follett.

Aims of eLib

What were the aims of the eLib programme? Answering this question is crucial for assessing its success (by comparing its outcomes with its aims). And yet, unfortunately, it is more difficult to answer it than it might be assumed. It is curious that whilst FIGIT had a formal remit (quoted by Carr, 2002, p. 224), eLib, it appears, was never given a formal programme-wide mission (at least not one that was published). As Andrew Green (1997, p. 40) comments, 'the two key JISC documents announcing the establishment of eLib, Circular 2/94 and Circular 4/94, conspicuously fail to say what the effect the spending of £15 million was intended to be'. Other eLib official documentation from the time seems equally silent on this issue. The key aims of specific programme areas are defined in a number of documents (including those mentioned by Green) but the aims of the programme as a whole are not. This means that one of the obvious ways of assessing the programme's success – comparing its achievements against its stated aims – is very difficult to carry out.

It is, however, possible to piece together a view of the aims of the eLib programme by looking at the literature, particularly the publications of those who were associated with setting up and directing the programme. Two major themes emerge. The first is that eLib aimed to identify and demonstrate solutions to key technical, managerial and legal problems in the area of e-libraries at both institutional and national levels. The aim was to improve services to users in real-world situations. This aim is clearly shown in the calls for proposals and the professional literature of the time. In one of the earliest summaries of the programme, Chris Rusbridge stated that eLib's 'objectives include the use of IT to improve the delivery of electronic library services, to allow academic libraries to cope better with growth, to explore different models of intellectual property management, and to encourage new methods of scholarly publishing' (Rusbridge, 1995a, p. 231).

The second theme is that eLib also aimed to promote 'cultural change' in the academic library world and beyond. This was not so widely discussed at the beginning of the programme but became increasingly important as eLib progressed. It was, nevertheless, clearly there as an aim at the beginning. As early as 1995, Chris Rusbridge stated, 'greatest benefits will flow not from the success of any individual project, but from the changes in organisational culture and the environment' (Rusbridge, 1995b). As far as individual projects were concerned, he characterized the FIGIT view as 'the benefit lies as much in the process as in the results'.

Understanding this ambitious aim to bring about cultural change must be a crucial part of any assessment of eLib's success. In particular, it will affect the way in which the programme as a whole is assessed in relation to its individual projects. In a retrospective survey of eLib, Rusbridge (2001) suggests that 'in many ways the eLib programme was seen as distinct from the projects. We had a notion that the programme could succeed even if all the projects failed – and vice versa in both cases! This is because we were really aiming at a sea-change, a cultural shift . . .' This idea, that the programme was more than the sum of its parts, must have been one of the primary justifications for running a national programme in the first place, but it seemed to become more widely appreciated during the late 1990s as people began to think about gauging eLib's success.

Overview of the Programme

The eLib programme consisted of three interlocking phases. Phase 1 ran from 1995 to 1998, Phase 2 from 1996 to 1998, and Phase 3 from 1998 to 2001. Each phase was set in motion by a call for proposals that identified areas to be funded (JISC

Circulars 4/94, 11/95 and 3/97 respectively). Phase 1 consisted of the following programme areas (sometimes called 'strands'):

- Electronic document and article delivery.
- Electronic journals.
- Digitization.
- On-demand publishing.
- Training and awareness.
- Access to network resources.
- Supporting studies.

Phase 2 came soon afterwards and was designed to plug a number of gaps in Phase 1:

- Pre-prints and grey literature.
- Quality assurance in the electronic environment.
- Electronic reserve 'short loan' collections.

Rusbridge (1998) summarized Phases 1 and 2 under the following headings: electronic publishing, innovative approaches to learning and teaching, resources access, supporting studies, and training and awareness. Between them, Phases 1 and 2 consisted of 59 projects and cost nearly £15 million.[2] Phase 3 (12 new projects) cost over £4 million and consisted of the following strands:[3]

- Hybrid libraries.
- Large scale resource discovery (or Z39.50 clumps).
- Digital preservation.
- Projects to services.

All of these strands picked up areas identified in Phases 1 and 2 as requiring further investigation. The 'projects to services' strand explicitly identified successful projects from earlier phases which needed continuation or development funding to bring them to full maturity.

Reg Carr (1998, 2002) suggested that the different phases of eLib could be characterized in turn as 'Innovation', 'Co-operation' and 'Integration'. Writing in 1998, he said,

> the concepts overlap the phases, of course, but in general terms, Phase 1 was all about innovation, with a multiplicity of projects pushing creatively at a range of issues within a set of pre-defined programme areas. Phase 2 was characterised by filling in perceived gaps in the project array, but its emphasis was also on scalability, and there was a deliberate push to encourage more co-operative solutions as the projects began seriously to consider their viability for the longer term. And with Phase 3, eLib's attention is now centred principally on integration, with the aim being to bring together as many separate developments as possible, and to put flesh on the bones of the new integrating terminology of the 'hybrid library' and of 'clumps'. (Carr, 1998, p. 18)

Any such schematic view of eLib will inevitably be rather artificial, but this nevertheless provides a useful framework for thinking about the programme. At the very least, it makes the important point that the eLib programme as a whole developed over time. Lessons were learned, new priorities emerged and new technologies developed as the programme progressed.

Characteristics of eLib

The fact that eLib was a 'learning programme' (that it developed over time in response to emerging lessons) is one of the most important characteristics of the initiative. Perhaps the most obvious example of this was that Phase 3 was a direct response to the outcomes of Phases 1 and 2. But even within individual projects, investigators were given enough freedom to allow them to change tack if this was thought to be necessary. Sometimes project outcomes were intentionally different from those initially envisaged in project plans. The programme also developed in other important ways. Notably, it showed a growing awareness of the importance of project management techniques and it made increasing efforts to promote these in host institutions.

Learning was possible partly because eLib placed considerable emphasis on evaluation. Every project was expected to have a clear strategy for both formative and summative evaluation. Evaluation was regarded as an ongoing activity that should be in place from the outset of a project. These evaluation activities were designed to feed into further project and programme development. There were also formative and summative evaluations at the programme level. The latter were too late to inform further planning for eLib, but were useful to JISC for applying to development programme areas that succeeded eLib.

The fact that the programme was able to learn was also partly due to the way it was structured. The structure was one that might be characterized as 'loose co-ordination'. There was a small central programme office with the oversight of a large number of distributed projects. The projects were distributed in a wide range of HE institutions (several institutions often being involved in each project). The idea was that the programme office could provide direction and guidance but projects were to be responsible for their own day-to-day activities.

Each project was normally on a fairly small scale. In Phases 1 and 2, Whitelaw and Joy (2000, p. 15) calculate the average cost of each project was about £252,000. The average rose to about £341,000 in Phase 3 as eLib attempted to concentrate on a smaller number of larger projects (see Whitelaw and Joy, 2001, p. 10); but even here the numbers are relatively low, especially considering that many of the projects were run by consortia of institutions. This is certainly true when eLib is compared with, say, the US Digital Libraries Initiative (DLI), where single projects often cost the equivalent of £1 million. The philosophy in eLib was to run a large number of small projects and to see if any worthwhile results emerged from them collectively. In some cases, this did mean that there may have been more than one project investigating the same issue at the same time. The fact that the projects did not always choose the same approaches was in itself regarded as interesting and useful.

Another contrast with DLI is that, in eLib, the emphasis was very much on practical development. eLib was a research and development programme but with the accent very much on development. On the other hand, DLI was more of a 'computer science *research* programme'. (Rusbridge, 1998, emphasis added). eLib was, in this respect, part of a UK tradition identified by Peter Brophy (Brophy, 2001) of 'practice-based library research'. The emphasis was on activities that would have a direct impact on working library services and on products that could be implemented by other practitioners. As a result, the majority of partners in eLib projects were library organizations. Some academic schools were involved, as were publishers and systems suppliers, but most projects were run by and in libraries themselves. This had a profound effect on the kinds of approaches taken and the kinds of deliverables generated.

One important deliverable expected of eLib projects was dissemination. Projects were encouraged to communicate to others about their work in various ways. This did not just include describing what a project had done but also guiding others in applying the lessons that had been learned in each project's own context. Once again, every project was required to develop a clear dissemination strategy. A number of projects (particularly in Phase 3) also carried out joint dissemination activities which helped to ensure greater coordination in getting the message across.

The drive to share outcomes was such an important aspect of the way in which the eLib programme was designed because it was a *national* programme. This is the final and perhaps most important characteristic of eLib. Whilst particular projects were managed within particular institutions, it is essential to recognize that they were carrying out work as part of a national programme. Moreover, the eLib programme was itself part of a larger strategic whole in which e-library services were being developed and delivered to the UK HE community (as outlined by Pinfield, 2000). Reg Carr (1998) emphasizes this point, demonstrating that the activities of eLib were part of the larger aims of JISC and the HE funding councils.

Successes of eLib

Having discussed the background, historical development, aims and characteristics of eLib, we can now go on to examine its successes and failures. Running throughout this discussion will be the complex problem of 'what constitutes success?'

As one of the aims of eLib was to improve the delivery of library services in the electronic environment, then one sign of success would be the existence of products and services that have continued beyond the life of the eLib programme. There are a significant number of examples of these. The subject hubs, originally funded within the Access to Network Resources strand of Phase 1, are often held up as examples. These services, which identify and catalogue quality internet resources across different subjects, have continued to be funded by JISC (as well as, in some cases, receiving income from other sources) as part of its Resource Discovery Network (the policy background to this is described in Law and Dempsey, 2000). The subject hubs have also continued to develop and expand their services. The latest strategy of expansion builds on their success as catalogues of resources and is aiming to make them portals to a wider range of quality data and metadata.

The subject hubs, however, are not the only example of successful services that have continued beyond the life of eLib. Another example is HERON (Higher Education Resources On demand) which acts as a national clearing house for copyright permissions for retrospective digitization of published works. This service grew directly out of a series of successful projects in Phases 1 and 2 looking at Electronic Short Loan and On-Demand Publishing services. It has now been taken into a new era by being part-funded by a commercial provider. The Higher Education Digitization Service (HEDS) is another example of a successful ongoing service originally funded within the eLib programme. This service provides advice and support in addition to carrying out practical digitization work for HE institutions.

In the area of electronic publishing eLib had a number of successes. For example, a number of e-journals were set up, which are now well established with separate income streams (either subscriptions or other funding). Examples here are *JILT* (*Journal of Information, Law and Technology*), *Internet Archaeology* and *Sociological Research Online*. Another example is *Ariadne*. This was originally set up to publicize developments in the eLib programme itself and it is interesting to see that it has developed a life of its own, publishing articles on e-library developments quite apart from eLib. As well as journals, eLib also encouraged the development of innovative forms of publishing and communications. Examples of this, which have continued beyond the life of the programme, include Education Online (a preprint service in the area of education), WoPEc (economics working papers) and CogPrints (an e-print service in the area of cognitive science). The software that originally provided an infrastructure to CogPrints has also been funded and is now freely available from www.eprints.org to support the development of e-print repositories. The impact on scholarly communication of this development alone may prove to be profound.

Some of the projects investigating information searching and retrieval have also produced ongoing services. All of the Clumps projects have continued in some form and, in 2003, were all involved in a continuation project looking at integrating their services with those of COPAC (the joint catalogue of the Consortium of University Research Libraries). In addition, the service produced by the Agora Hybrid Library project has now been developed into a commercial product, VDX, by Fretwell-Downing, who was a partner in the original eLib project.

Still other projects such as Digimap are now ongoing services. The training and awareness project, Netskills, continues to be a very useful and popular service within HE and is an important component of the ongoing JISC training and awareness strategy. In a completely different area, the LAMDA document delivery project has also continued as a service.

Commenting on another document delivery project, Chris Rusbridge (2001) states, 'the document delivery project InfoBike may have failed in its original terms, but it mutated: first into the BIDS JournalsOnline service, which then provided the core of the spin-off company Ingenta, now a £100 million publicly quoted company! In this sense it was an extremely successful project, and one of which we can be justly proud . . .'. Other projects seem to have continued in a similarly 'mutated' form (although they may not have been as commercially successful). Most of the hybrid library projects, for example, have continued at least in part within their own institutions. One hybrid library project, HEADLINE, formed the basis of an ongoing project also funded by JISC called ANGEL. This was designed to investigate how e-library services could begin to be incorporated into wider online learning environments.

Of course, many projects were not designed to have an ongoing life. Rather, they were designed to inform the thinking of the community and create the conceptual underpinning for further development. In some respects, the hybrid library projects performed this function. However, perhaps the most important example of this within the programme was the MODELS project. MODELS was a way of generating and encapsulating the latest thinking on information delivery. It created an influential conceptual mapping of information delivery known as MIA (the MODELS Information Architecture). In many respects MIA gave rise to the clumps and hybrid library projects (although it was, in return, informed by them). It brought together information professionals from the e-library and learning technology fields alongside representatives from commercial providers in a series of intense workshops. The results of their work were widely disseminated (see for example Dempsey *et al.*, 1998). It is interesting to see that a number of commercial packages delivering cross-searching functionality now on the market reflect the thinking of these early research and development projects (MODELS, hybrid libraries and clumps). JISC strategy itself has been influenced by these projects (as well as by many other eLib activities) particularly in relation to the Distributed National Electronic Resource and the JISC Information Environment (see for example Pinfield and Dempsey, 2001).

Another project designed to inform the thinking not just of the information professionals but also of publishers and commercial suppliers was SuperJournal. This project aimed to analyse uses made of electronic journals and to investigate ways in which the journal literature could be developed in an online environment. It involved extensive input from publishers and information professionals and engagement with users and potential users.

Other projects have been influential in developing formal and informal standards in important new areas of activity. The CEDARS project, for example, was a very early player in the field of digital preservation. For several years it was the main focus of UK activity in this area (its funding was extended a number of times by JISC) and played a major part in the development of early digital preservation standards. The Clumps projects all played an important role in developing Z39.50 standards. Similarly, a number of the supporting studies commissioned by eLib were equally successful in establishing ways forward in a variety of areas.

The success of a number of eLib projects (both in generating ongoing services and in impacting upon the strategic thinking of the community) was then a major contribution to the success of the programme as a whole. However, the programme can be said to have had other major impacts quite apart from the success of particular projects. One important example of this is in the area of skills development. The eLib programme was instrumental in creating a pool of highly skilled staff. Many technical staff cut their teeth on eLib projects and they have gone on to be very useful to the community as a whole. At an organizational level, these staff have often been at the interface between libraries and computing services within their own institutions. In many cases they have acted as conduits for improved communication between these services.

Although more difficult to quantify, these kinds of developments are nevertheless important. Similarly, the whole question of the cultural impact of eLib is very difficult to measure and yet many have argued that this was the most important way in which eLib affected the UK information community in HE. Charles Oppenheim has usefully defined cultural change:

I would argue that cultural change involves:

- The lasting structural and social changes (within an organisation or set of linked organisations), PLUS
- Lasting changes to the shared ways of thinking, beliefs, values, procedures and relationships of the stakeholders within that grouping.

This definition assumes that both the formal (structural) and informal (socio-cognitive) aspects of stakeholders' work must change in some way for the 'culture' to have been fundamentally changed. The word 'lasting' is important. Changes caused by, say, the initiation of an e-lib [*sic*] project, but which do not last beyond the project's end, cannot be counted as cultural change.' (Oppenheim, 1998, p. 22)

A number of commentators have shown that it is difficult to assess the impact of eLib in these areas in a very precise way. Andrew Green (1997, p. 45), in particular, has drawn attention to a number of problems in this area. Libraries were changing anyway, there were other factors encouraging change apart from eLib, and the influence of eLib may have been 'indirect rather than direct'. Despite these problems, there is a consensus in the literature that the eLib programme caused significant cultural change or at least acted as a catalyst for it. Oppenheim (1998, p. 22) himself says, 'looking at e-lib, my perception is that it has aroused a lot of interest, and probably accelerated cultural change within the library community'. Green (1997, p. 48) is rather more effusive: 'despite some reservations I believe that when the time comes for judgment the Electronic Libraries Programme will prove to have had a powerful catalytic effect on professional library practice. Without it, our knowledge would be weaker, our standing lower, and our confidence to face the future less.' Projects such as IMPEL2 (itself a successful eLib project) have provided data to illustrate these conclusions. The summative evaluations of eLib also cite evidence in this area based on the perceptions of information professionals.

The aspects of cultural change promoted by eLib are very varied but a number of significant areas may be highlighted. eLib acted as a focus for a great deal of professional discussion and debate in the second half of the 1990s. It generated stimulating ideas about information services and the organizational structures and professional skills required to deliver them effectively. It seems to have been instrumental in promoting the wide acceptance of technology as being fundamental to the delivery of core library services. Alongside this, it also promoted the idea that librarians should be innovators – looking for opportunities to enhance imaginatively the service given to users in new and exciting ways. eLib also encouraged good practice in managing such innovation, particularly through formal or informal project management methodologies. All of this led, it is sometimes observed, to a greater confidence within the library community; confidence to play the role of leaders in their institutions and also to become more demanding customers when they deal with publishers and suppliers. And these factors were perhaps magnified by the fact that eLib projects were housed in a large number of different institutions. This meant that cultural change was more easily able to diffuse throughout the community.

Of course, much of this cultural change would probably have happened anyway, whether eLib was there or not. However, the fact that cultural change did happen in the UK within the context of a structured national programme has been important. It probably meant that it was quicker and more evenly spread than it might otherwise have been. Reg Carr (2002, p. 231) observes that eLib 'enabled the UK HE community, to a large extent "to stay in control", or at least to make coherent sense of the global information environment, and to harness many of its possibilities more effectively'.

Limitations and Failures

It is clear that the eLib programme was, in many respects, successful both in terms of identifying and demonstrating solutions to key technical, managerial and legal problems and also in promoting cultural change. However, this success was by no means unqualified. A number of important factors came into play which meant that eLib was not as successful as it might have been.

For example, there were a number of projects that sank without trace. It would perhaps be rather unfair to name these projects. Projects can fail for a whole number of reasons, many of which are not to do with the quality of the project management. Nevertheless, it needs to be observed that there is a continuum of success–failure and eLib produced projects at many points on this continuum. However, it is interesting to note that the eLib programme office was never afraid of projects failing to deliver sustainable products or services. Chris Rusbridge observed during a meeting for project managers that sometimes a project could illustrate that 'the answer is no' and this in itself may be a valuable outcome. What was important is that the lessons should be disseminated. Projects were always encouraged to be as honest about their failures as they were about their successes. But it is difficult to know whether or not this always happened.

At the programme level, it is sometimes suggested that, although eLib was a coordinated programme, in some respects it was perhaps not coordinated enough. There was considerable duplication between projects, for example. Sometimes this meant that a number of different projects were tackling the same problems and that the available resources had therefore been spread very thinly. This may not always have been the most efficient way to deal with problems, especially as, in some cases, competition seems to have developed between projects within the same strand. This issue was, however, recognized by programme managers, who in Phase 3 of eLib, explicitly sought to encourage inter-project interaction and cooperation. Phase 3 itself also featured a smaller number of larger projects compared with Phases 1 and 2. This may well have been an attempt to coordinate developments more closely.

Other areas where coordination might have been more useful were at the JISC level. It has been observed that there might have been greater coordination between the eLib programme as a whole and other similar programmes being funded by JISC, particularly JTAP (Joint Technology Applications Programme). The fact that JTAP was administered by a different JISC Committee was probably significant here. Rusbridge (2001) observed that the JISC committee structure may also have got in the way of achieving all that might have been done in the area of cultural change. A new JISC committee was established to cover training and awareness, partly as a result of the first phases of eLib highlighting it as a problem. However, the fact of the creation of a separate committee itself meant some barriers to making progress in this area were almost inevitably erected.

As well as failures of commission in eLib there were also failures of omission. There were gaps in the programme strands and their coverage. Economic issues were, for example, given little attention. As a result of JISC policy, which set itself against funding large-scale digitization activity, eLib was never in a position to create a critical mass of online material. There were also missing strategic developments in the programme. Too little was done in developing strategies for turning projects into services. Part of the problem here was the uneasy relationship eLib (and JISC) seems to have had with commercial providers. There was never a clear view of what the relationship should be with the profit-making sector.

Finally in this section, it should perhaps be observed that Follett and eLib were both set up in a context of the crisis of space and costs. It is an irony that, although successful in many ways, eLib did not provide any magic bullets in these areas. 'One of the lessons of eLib as a whole ... is that electronic media do not save money or library space and are not likely to in the near future' (Whitelaw and Joy, 2001, p. 50). This does not perhaps indicate that eLib was a failure but rather that any expectations that it would solve the problems proved unrealistic.

Why was eLib successful?

Having qualified the success of eLib in various ways, it still needs to be emphasized that it was fundamentally a successful programme. It effectively addressed many key technical, managerial and cultural issues and did so in ways that had a real impact on the library and information community in HE. The remaining question is 'Why?' Whilst more work needs to be done on this question, a number of preliminary suggestions may be made. They are divided here into two main categories. First, there are contextual factors – those which were outside the eLib programme but which provided eLib with an environment in which it could grow. Secondly, there are factors to do with the programme itself and the way it was structured and managed.

Perhaps the most important contextual factor was the Follett report itself. Follett in many ways expressed the concerns of the library community in the early 1990s, but also identified possible solutions. It provided a sense of direction. In doing so, it helped to turn a sense of crisis into a sense of urgency. Reg Carr summarizes the successes of the Follett report, which had become clear by 1997:

> ... it had focused attention on the challenges facing academic libraries in the fast-moving transition into the world of digital information; had provided a coherent national framework for addressing those challenges; had leveraged considerable additional funds into HE library and information services for digital library developments; and had become an important central plank for the five-year forward strategy of the JISC itself. (Carr, 2002, p. 229)

Most importantly, it provided what Lorcan Dempsey described as a 'motivating scenario' for a large number of projects.

The timing of eLib was also right. The programme got moving just as the World Wide Web was beginning to make its influence felt in UK HE. It is interesting that the Follett report, written in 1993, did not make any mention of the web. A year later, as the projects were being set up, the potential of the web was becoming clearer. Even then, many projects considered other options, but certainly by late 1995 it was obvious that all eLib projects would be concentrating on web-based services. In many cases the projects then became an early showcase for the web in the UK library community and helped to raise an awareness of its potential in delivering information services. The combination of the flexibility provided by the new World Wide Web and also the solid infrastructure provided by the well-established Joint Academic Network (JANET) gave eLib a head start.

The technical infrastructure was important, but there was also a supportive policy infrastructure in place. The eLib programme was part of a larger strategic whole. It was seen in many ways as the development arm of JISC's content-based services. Carr (2002, p. 229) comments that, 'by 1997 ... the eLib programme was already firmly embedded in the longer term development plans of the JISC'. In practical terms, this meant that the eLib programme was seen as important enough to be given the time and the money to carry out its work. The fact that eLib became an important staging-post in the development of the Distributed National Electronic Resource (DNER) and the JISC Information Environment initiatives shows this was the right decision.

High-level JISC support was crucial in the eLib success but so was grassroots institutional buy-in. eLib was widely supported in the HE information community from the beginning. Following the Follett report, FIGIT took care to consult institutions about the range of projects that should be undertaken, making their support more likely and more widespread. FIGIT was also careful to ensure that a variety of institutions were represented amongst project partners. In fact, over the course of the eLib programme, the vast majority of UK HE institutions were involved in projects in some way or another. This meant that the national programme was able to have local impact. Host institutions took their part in the programme seriously and worked hard to ensure that their projects delivered.

One element of the programme was particularly popular in institutional library and information services – its practical emphasis. The programme encouraged projects to think about how their work could have an impact on real-world services in a practical way. This meant that information professionals in institutions could see that eLib was working, whether they were directly involved or not. This was especially true since the programme office encouraged projects to work iteratively and to have things to show quickly. The adage that 'demonstration is better than description' came to be used in Phase 3 in particular (see Pinfield, 2001), but reflects the attitude that ran throughout the programme.

Such attitudes were characteristic of the programme largely because of the way it was structured and managed. The structure involving a central programme office, and distributed projects gave eLib its particular flavour. Most of the time this seems to have created a successful balance between central direction on the one hand and local innovation on the other. Individual projects were given enough freedom to experiment where necessary but they always had the discipline of regular reporting and accountability. The fact that the later Research Support Libraries Programme (RSLP), also funded by the Higher Education Funding Councils, adopted the same model demonstrates that it was considered to be successful at the time.

As well as reporting to the programme office on progress, projects were also expected to report on their evaluation activities. The emphasis placed on evaluation within eLib was also important in its success. Indeed, it was this which allowed projects to develop iteratively. They incorporated regular formative evaluation activities right from the beginning. Projects also collaborated with programme level evaluation, both formative and summative, as a way of informing overall development.

Like evaluation, dissemination was also a central element of the programme and contributed to its success. There was an emphasis on sharing lessons learned and products in practical ways. Projects were active in contributing to the professional literature, taking part in conferences, organizing practitioner workshops and other forms of publicity. This meant that the learning outcomes from the programme were diffused throughout the community rapidly. Whilst perhaps more could have been done practically to assist non-project partners in implementation, dissemination (as explained earlier) was nevertheless significantly successful.

History is made by a combination of impersonal forces and individual actions, and eLib was no exception. The final key reason for the programme's success was the work of particular people. At the programme level, a number of important figures had the vision and determination to get the programme moving, and also the management and communication skills to ensure it was successful. Individuals such as Lynne Brindley (chair of FIGIT), Derek Law (an active member of FIGIT), Reg Carr (chair of the JISC Committee with responsibility for eLib), Chris Rusbridge (Director of eLib), Lorcan Dempsey (leading advocate of the programme), as well as Brian Follett himself, helped to ensure the success of the programme. At project level, there was also a large number of imaginative and determined project directors, managers and staff who devised project proposals, managed project development, and communicated project outcomes in effective ways. These people worked hard on their projects, in particular, and on eLib, in general. In the end, the success of eLib was very much down to them.

Conclusion

The fact that eLib was a success (albeit a qualified one) indicates that it is a model upon which future e-library research and development activity can be based, at least in the UK. It is good to see that since eLib closed, follow-on programmes have been set up by JISC and other agencies and managed in similar ways. They include RSLP, the DNER and Information Environment, the 5/99 programme, the Focus on Access to Institutional Resources programme, and others. These initiatives have built on the foundations of eLib in interesting and useful ways. Like eLib, they have aimed to diffuse benefits throughout the whole of the HE community and beyond. They have also tried to tie developments into the strategic directions of JISC and the funding councils (and UK HE generally) in ways that will mean the activities are more likely to be sustainable. In many ways eLib was the first of these sorts of programmes. They are its legacy and a testament of its success.

Acknowledgements

Thanks to Lorcan Dempsey, Chris Rusbridge, and particularly Reg Carr for helpful comments.

Notes

1   The terms 'electronic library', 'e-library', and 'digital library' are used in this chapter interchangeably.
2   For detailed figures, see Whitelaw and Joy (2000, p. 15).
3   For detailed figures, see Whitelaw and Joy (2001, p. iii).

References

Articles and Reports

Brophy, P. (2001),'The historical context of eLib: practice based library research in the UK', *Library Management*, 22(1/2), 15–18.
Carr, R. (1998), 'Integrate, co-operate, innovate: an introduction', *The New Review of Information and Library Research*, 4, 17–26.
Carr, R. (2002), 'Towards the academic digital library in the UK: a national perspective', in S.K. Hannesdottir, (ed.), *Global Issues in 21st Century Research Librarianship* (Helsinki: NORDINFO), pp. 221–233.
Dempsey, L., Russell, R., Murray, R., and Heseltine, R. (1998), 'Managing access to a distributed library resource: report from the fifth MODELS workshop', *Program*, 32(3), 265–282.
Follett, B. (chair) (1993), *Joint Funding Council's Libraries Review Group: Report*, (Bristol: Higher Education Funding Council for England). Available at: http://www.niss.ac.uk/education/hefc/follett/.

Green, A. (1997),'Towards the digital library: how relevant is eLib to practitioners?', *The New Review of Academic Librarianship*, 3, 39–48.

Joint Information Systems Committee (1994), *Circular 4/94 – FIGIT Framework* (Bristol: JISC). Available at http://www.jisc.ac.uk/pub/c4_94.html.

Joint Information Systems Committee (1995), *Circular 11/95 – Electronic Libraries Programme (eLib):Targeted Call for New Proposals* (Bristol: JISC). Available at http://www.jisc.ac.uk/pub/c11_95.html.

Joint Information Systems Committee (1997), *Circular 3/97 Electronic Information Development Programme: eLib Phase 3* (Bristol: JISC). Available at http://www.jisc.ac.uk/pub97/c3_97.html.

Law, D. and Dempsey, L. (2000), 'A policy context: eLib and the emergence of the subject gateways', *Ariadne*; (25) September. Available at http://www.ariadne.ac.uk/issue25/subject-gateways/.

Pinfield, S. (2000), 'The relationship between national and institutional electronic library developments in the UK: an overview'. *The New Review of Academic Librarianship*, 6, 3–20. Revised version published in T.V. Ershova and Y.E. Hohlov (eds) *Libraries in the Information Society*, (Munich: K.G. Saur, 2002), IFLA Publications 102, pp. 134–148.

Pinfield, S. (2001), 'Beyond eLib: lessons from Phase 3 of the Electronic Libraries Programme', report to JISC. Available at http://www.ukoln.ac.uk/services/elib/papers/other/pinfield-elib/elibreport.html.

Pinfield, S. and Dempsey, L. (2001), 'The Distributed National Electronic Resource (DNER) and the hybrid library', *Ariadne*, (26) January. Available at http://www.ariadne.ac.uk/issue26/dner/.

Rusbridge, C. (1995a), 'The Electronic Libraries Programme', *Serials*, 8(3), 231–240.

Rusbridge, C. (1995b), 'The UK Electronic Libraries Programme'. *D-Lib Magazine*, 1(6), December. Available at http://www.dlib.org/dlib/december95/briefings/12uk.html.

Rusbridge, C. (1998), 'Towards the hybrid library', *D-Lib Magazine*, 4(7), July/August. Available at http://www.dlib.org/dlib/july98/rusbridge/07rusbridge.html.

Rusbridge, C. (2001), 'After eLib', *Ariadne*, (26) January. Available at http://www.ariadne.ac.uk/issue26/chris/.

Whitelaw, A. and Joy, G. (2000) *Summative Evaluation of Phases 1 and 2 of the eLib Initiative: Final Report* (Guildford: ESYS). Available at http://www.ukoln.ac.uk/services/elib/papers/other/intro.html#elib-evaluation.

Whitelaw, A. and Joy, G. (2001), *Summative Evaluation of Phase 3 of the eLib Initiative: Final Report* (Guildford: ESYS). Available at http://www.ukoln.ac.uk/services/elib/papers/other/intro.html#elib-evaluation.

Websites

ANGEL http://www.angel.ac.uk/
Ariadne http://www.ariadne.ac.uk/
CEDARS http://www.leeds.ac.uk/cedars/
CogPrints http://cogprints.ecs.soton.ac.uk/
COPAC http://www.copac.ac.uk
eLib http://www.ukoln.ac.uk/services/elib/
eprints.org http://www.eprints.org/
Digimap http://edina.ac.uk/digimap/
HEADLINE http://www.headline.ac.uk/
HERON http://www.heron.ac.uk/
Higher Education Digitisation Service http://heds.herts.ac.uk/

IMPEL2 http://ilm.unn.ac.uk/impel
InfoBike http://www.bids.ac.uk/elib/infobike/homepage.html
Internet Archaeology http://intarch.ac.uk/
JANET http://www.ja.net/
JILT http://elj.warwick.ac.uk/Jilt/
JISC http://www.jisc.ac.uk/
JTAP http://www.jtap.ac.uk/
LAMDA http://lamdaweb.mcc.ac.uk/
MODELS http://www.ukoln.ac.uk/dlis/models/
Netskills http://www.netskills.ac.uk/
Resource Discovery Network http://www.rdn.ac.uk/
Sociological Research Online http://www.socresonline.org.uk/
SuperJournal http://www.superjournal.ac.uk/sj/
WoPEc http://netec.mcc.ac.uk/WoPEc.html

PART 1
POLICY AND PLANNING

Chapter 4

How to Pay for Digital Libraries

Mike Lesk

Introduction

Jim Gray, the Turing Award winner, once said to me, 'may all your problems be technical'. We know how to build digital libraries, but we don't know how to make them economically sustainable.

Today, there is a vast number of users of digital libraries. The Library of Congress website gets 2 million requests a day for files. In 2000, the Library sent out 700 million items (totaling 9 terabytes) whereas the reading rooms only delivered 1.6 million items to the readers (perhaps one terabyte total, if each were a typical book).[1] Other online digital files also have vast numbers of users; every US faculty member is familiar with the problem of persuading students to use the traditional library as well as the web for writing papers. But most of these searchers and readers are not paying anything. Since computers, network connections, staff, and the creation of content cost money, how are digital libraries to continue to exist?

The web, of course, continues to grow, and the cost of computing equipment continues to decline. Figure 4.1 shows the increase in the size of the web, and Figure 4.2 shows the cost of disk space;[2] both are on a log-scale. The rate

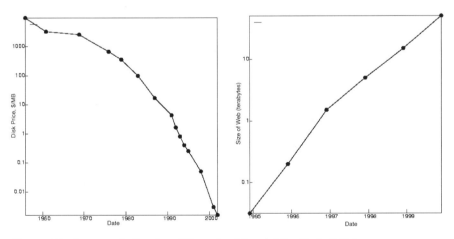

Figure 4.1   Increase in the size of the web   Figure 4.2   Cost of disk space

of change continues to be dramatic. We can now easily store a digital library; for the first time in my life, people say that they have empty space on their disk drives.

Traditionally, communities (universities or governments) paid for basic library services for their members, with some special services (e.g. photocopying) being fee-based. The web, however, is worldwide. Every university librarian is being asked 'why should our university pay to maintain such-and-such a web service, when most of the users are not our students, faculty, or alumni?'

The situation is aggravated by the desire of some publishers to bypass libraries. Every business now admires the ability of the airlines to charge different prices for the same commodity, and thus get more money from those more able to pay. Publishers would like, ideally, to identify each reader of their publications and extract the maximum payment from each one. Why, instead, let them pool their resources, buy only one copy for a library, and hide their marketing demographics?

Organizationally, we do not know who will provide information to scholars in the future. Technological transitions often mean a change in the organization that provides the service: Western Union does not run e-mail, the railroads do not fly airplanes, and Winsor & Newton does not make photographic film. Will 'digital libraries' be run by traditional library organizations or by publishers, or by somebody else? There is no shortage of people that want to be in this niche: publishers, bookstores, wholesalers, telecommunications companies, computer centers, and new start-ups (although enthusiasm is down from the days of 1999–2000). Nor do we know whether there will continue to be as many libraries as there are now. In a world where every town's restaurants, drugstores, and clothing stores are merely instances of national chains, the independently run public and college libraries seem almost an anachronism.

The organizational solution depends on the economic one. How will digital information delivery be funded?

Among the possibilities are:

- Communities pay the full cost (what we do today).
- Readers pay by the month or year (subscription fees).
- Readers pay by the item received (by transaction).
- Authors pay (page charges).
- Advertising pays.
- Others (bounties, cost avoidance, publicity values).

Each of these items can be weighed and, unfortunately, found wanting.

Community Support

Steve Harnad[3] has argued at great length that digital publication is so cheap that community support for free information ought to be affordable. ARL statistics, very roughly, would suggest that the yearly cost of a research library per book is in the range of $3–8, and that per staff member a library might have 7000–20,000 books.[4] If we assume that a book is about 0.5 MB on average, that means a typical cost is at least $5 per MB, and that each staff member keeps track of not more than 10 GB. By contrast, the San Diego Supercomputer Center manages disks, even replicated for safety, at something like $3000 per terabyte or one-third of a cent per megabyte. The Internet Archive also has prices in the cents per megabyte range and with thousands of gigabytes per staff member.

A fairer comparison to these data facilities might be an offsite deposit library, such as the Northern Regional Library facility of the University of California, which keeps track of some 2 million books with about 20 staff, or some 50 GB per person. Similarly, the Center for Research Libraries has about 4 million books and an annual budget around $4 million, or about $1 per book and $2/MB. Even these numbers, although about a factor of 5 better than a library providing the usual academic services, are a factor of 100 larger than computer storage. So digital storage sounds really cheap, as it should with the raw capital cost of disk space running at $179 for 120GB in the summer of 2002, or 0.15 cents per megabyte.[5] That's a tenth of a cent a book-equivalent, whereas building a book storage building, even as a warehouse, runs about $2/book. However, it's not that simple.

The numbers above suggest that a repository library is 1/5 the cost of a normal university library. This means that most of the cost of a library is in services – cataloging, reference, circulation and the like – and not in the cost of keeping the building heated and painted and answering the occasional request to fetch a book. Nobody who works in a library will be surprised by that. Unfortunately, the implication is that you cannot save all that much money by reducing the cost of storage via digitization. If 80% of a library's cost is in services, not storage, even reducing the storage cost to zero leaves the library needing 80% of its budget.

Well, maybe digital libraries won't provide any services. Google can be used instead of a catalog, acquisitions can be done with robot web crawlers, and people looking for reference help can be told to get lost. For expert researchers, that might be of use in some situations. It's not a strategy likely to be thought appropriate or adequate for a university that has a responsibility to teach students. We'll have to hope that it is not widely adopted in response to financial pressures.

There are some savings possible in services. Libraries can share digital files more easily than paper copies, so some of the acquisitions tasks might be shared. And some of the digital material replaces paper material and comes with its own cataloging and the like; for example JSTOR has been deliberately designed to substitute for back-issue files of traditional serials. JSTOR estimates that libraries could save $140 million/year by substituting its service for traditional paper storage (Bowen, 2001). So far, relatively few libraries have discarded journal issues because JSTOR holds them, but many do move the journals to cheaper storage.

Unfortunately the attempts to share also destroy locality. If the resources provided are not used solely by the community paying for them, why should the community pay? In the past, the number of visitors from one library to another has been relatively small, and whether or not they were charged fees, the impact on the library budget was small. Today, the majority of the users of a university site may be outsiders, and they are likely to come from all over the world. For example, the British resource site BUBL (digital library resources for the UK) got only 15 per cent of its identifiable accesses in July 2002 from UK sites.

So why should any university provide a good rather than minimal digital library service? This is the 'tragedy of the commons' once again, on a global scale. The danger is that each university will try to cut its library budget, hoping the students will find what they need elsewhere. Fortunately, the library community is very strong in both its public service ethic and its inertia, which should keep things going until the economists can figure a way out.

Subscription Sales

Another possibility is that digital library services can be provided on a cost-recovery basis. Certainly many publishers are trying this. So far, success is limited. The poster child for internet subscriptions is the online *Wall Street Journal*. Figure 4.3 shows the number of subscriptions for the *Wall Street Journal* and for the runner-up, *Consumer Reports* (Richtel, 2002).

The *Wall Street Journal* has more paper subscribers (over 2 million), and so does *Consumer Reports* (over 4 million). The paper prices are higher ($175/year for the *Wall Street Journal*, and $26/year for *Consumer Reports*), so the discrepancy in revenue is even larger than the discrepancy in subscription counts, but this is still a substantial online subscriber base. If everyone paid full price (there are discounts available in both paper and online modes), the *Wall Street Journal* would get about 15 per cent as much from online as from paper, and *Consumer Reports* almost 20 per cent.

A key choice publishers must make is whether to price for individuals or libraries. Clearly, both the *Wall Street Journal Interactive Edition* ($79/year, less if you subscribe on paper as well), and *Consumer Reports* ($24/year) are priced to permit individuals to subscribe. But other publications such as JSTOR or Elsevier's '*Science Direct*' are priced only for libraries. Reed Elsevier reports that, in 2001,

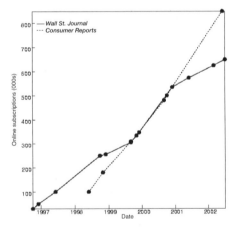

Figure 4.3   Levels of subscriptions for online *Wall Street Journal* and *Consumer Reports*

ScienceDirect sales were up 50 per cent, and that revenue in 2002 from online sales will top $1.5 billion, so the library subscription model is working here, thanks to elaborate definitions of who is allowed to access material (Morais, 2002).

An example that may be more relevant from the standpoint of scholarly publishing is the ACM Digital Library, which offers access to all the ACM journals and proceedings online for approximately $100/year. This is again an individual price, affordable by many individual members of the ACM (a US professional society for computer scientists). The ACM digital library reached 47,000 subscribers in 2001, more than 1/3 of the ACM membership (some of these are getting a student discount). ACM paper subscriptions have dropped about 1/3; however, they had been dropping anyway. ACM was caught in a cycle of an increasing number of Computer Science (CS) researchers wanting places to put their articles, stimulating the creation of new journals, and spreading the readership ever thinner. ACM found itself printing more articles but fewer copies of each one as the membership distributed its purchases over the additional publications. With luck, the digital library will be a partial answer to this since there is no problem with 'small production runs' – articles of interest to only a small specialized group (such as the tenure committee at the author's institution) are just fine in digital form.

There was a time when internet connectivity was free; there were services hoping to give away connection time in exchange for the right to send ads, or as a hook to sell more complex communications packages. These all died in the marketplace, and people now expect to pay for connectivity. Many for-sale online publications have also died off, after the hype of the dot-com boom collapsed. Yet, there are now some hopeful signs.

A survey of the Online Publishers Association reported in the *New York Times* on 1 August 2002 estimated that consumers spent $675 million on digital goods and services, with 12.4 million people paying for some form of content. Business and financial sites collected $214.3 million. The total content sales in the first quarter of 2002 were $300 million, almost as much as in the first half of 2001, which means that the area is growing strongly.

On balance the subscription model for individuals has not been very successful. It appears that libraries, or some equivalent buying club, remain the most obvious method for people in universities and research institutions to get their information.

Transaction Payments

Buying all the parts for a car costs more than buying the whole car. Many publishers used to dream of selling individual articles and so getting more money than for selling whole magazines. However, this hasn't worked out. Many newspapers now sell their back articles through Newsbank, for example, but with prices at $2.50 an article or more, usage is low. There are several possible explanations of why this business model has not succeeded:

- the price is too high for the demand;
- there is enough free stuff out there;
- librarians and readers are risk-averse.

A price of $2.50 for a single article from a newspaper that may have cost 35 cents for the whole issue on publication day certainly seems high. Of course this is a small amount of money if the information is of commercial value, but not that many older news stories have great value. 'Yesterday's newspaper is like yesterday's fish', an old saying goes.

There was a substantial effort in the late 1990s to develop 'micropayment' systems. These would have been able to charge a few cents for things; First Virtual was perhaps the best known. However, none of these seem to have caught on. First Virtual Holdings started in 1994, became MessageMedia in 1998, and was acquired by DoubleClick in 2002. Cybercash also began operations in 1994 and was bought by Verisign in 2001 as part of a bankruptcy auction (Milunovich, 2002).

A sort of Gresham's law also operates because of the amount of free information on the web: why pay for a newspaper article if some free site will provide what appears to be the right information? Few newspapers have the kind of widespread name recognition that will cause people to seek them out (the *New York Times*, of course, being one of the best known); magazines with general public credibility are even rarer.

Book publishing on the web, for downloading, is also a much hyped but little used methodology. In 2000, Stephen King tried publishing a book online in installments as shareware (payment on the honor system), with a threat to stop providing new chapters unless 75 per cent of the downloaders paid for it. He quit after six chapters, claiming that only 46 per cent had paid for the last installment, with about 40,000 copies sent out. Few other e-publishers sell any comparable numbers. There was a rash of 'e-book' publicity and products in 2001, which has died in the marketplace. Whether it will return when better devices with larger screens and lighter weight appear is unknown (Rose, 2002).

In addition, many parties in this transaction are risk-averse, and don't like the uncertainty of buy-by-the-item. Journal publishers, for example, have traditionally avoided many conventional business problems by collecting in advance for subscriptions. If the check bounces, you just don't send the magazine. You get six month's float on the money, and you don't need elaborate record-keeping to send out bills. By contrast, selling individual stories carries a need to count usage, compute bills, and chase down customers who don't pay. On the buying side, libraries often get their budget once a year and don't like setting aside money for bills that cannot be accurately estimated. Users are also often wary of expenses that can mount up quickly. All these considerations push the business away from pay-per-item and towards pay-per-month.

It seems unlikely, therefore, that the eventual support of digital libraries will come from selling individual items by the byte. Perhaps the comparison is to photocopy machines: yes, there are a few of them being used in libraries with coin slots, or similarly in shops, but the bulk of the photocopy machines sold are in offices or homes and are not selling a per-page service.

Author-pays

Years ago, Brown and Traub argued that page charges, assessed against authors, would greatly help the finances of journals. By collecting the initial cost of each page from the author, and the incremental costs from the reader, the journal would be economically secure as the number of subscribers or pages changed. Since the incremental cost of papers posted online is virtually zero, the idea of assessing all costs against the authors is attractive. In fact, that's what happens today – most websites are paid for by the author's employer. Should that be institutionalized in some way, with professional journals charging the authors to pay for their websites, and then not caring who reads them?

Page charges, however, were not a success in the scientific journal field. Many authors, given the choice of professional society journals with page charges and commercial journals without page charges, were happy to publish in commercial journals (which, in some cases, also offered faster publication or a better chance of having the paper accepted). It may well be that any money saved on page charges was paid back double in subscription fees, but that was the library's problem, whereas page charges were usually paid by the department or research grant. Since the authors route the papers to the journals, it seems likely that the same problem would reappear in the digital world.

Frequently, the organizers of meetings on this subject suggest that 'authorities' impose rules on where scientists can publish. They may appeal to university presidents, government funding agencies, or whoever for a rule that requires publication in professional society journals or online. The practising scientists are likely to resent such rules, however, and they are politically difficult to impose; university presidents have enough trouble telling the faculty where to park their cars, let alone where to publish their papers. An economic solution is almost certain to be more effective, appealing to the author's self-interest. For example, Steve Lawrence of NEC showed that online articles are cited more often than paper-only articles (Lawrence, 2001). Perhaps this may motivate authors to go to self-publishing on the web in the future. Unfortunately, scholarly respect is not the same thing as actually being read. Remember the famous quip 'deans can't read, they can only count'; now, the increasing length of scholarly monographs have led some to say 'deans can't read, they can only weigh'.

Another problem with page charges is the shifting of costs among institutions. Although we tend to talk about the 'scholarly community' and suggest that the readers and authors of journals are the same people, it's not a perfect match. In particular, for scientific journals, there are both university and commercial organizations providing papers and subscriptions. The universities provide a larger share of the papers than they do of the subscriptions. Thus, shifting costs from readers to authors would shift costs from commercial organizations to universities, and the universities are probably less able to bear the burden.

A large part of the difficulty is with prestige. Authors of scientific papers normally publish for credit, promotion and renown, not money. It has proven difficult to persuade authors to send their best papers to an online journal; they fear not being suitably rewarded during tenure decisions, for example. It ought to be possible to quell such fears by using the prestige of either major universities or major scientists. So far, unfortunately, the tenure committees and university presses have in general, been even more conservative than the faculty, and the most desired publications are still on paper, even if the ones most read are on the web.

Despite this history, late 2002 saw a major new effort in the biomedical area to create an online journal funded by page charges, the Public Library of Science.[6] Several major scientists, including Harold Varmus, are supporting this attempt to create an online journal with the prestige of *Science, Nature* or *Cell*. The Gordon and Betty Moore foundation has provided $9 million of initial funding, and the first journal *PLoS Biology* appeared in 2003 with *PLoS Medicine* due in mid-2004. Each article is expected to pay $1,500; funding from the Soros Foundation is available to help authors in countries where this charge might be prohibitive. Reading, downloading or printing the journals will be free. Time will tell whether this attempt will succeed.

Advertising

Although advertising has rarely been important in the economics of scholarly journals, it certainly determines the financial health of more popular publications and of broadcast television. Is it possible that advertising could support digital libraries? There's certainly enough total money out there. Just to look at some minor categories, cable TV advertising and Yellow Pages advertising in 2000 were each over $12 billion. Online advertising, although smaller at about a third of that, is still comparable to total university library budgets.

Figure 4.4 shows the rise of online advertising spending. There is wide disagreement about these numbers; the historical statistics below are from the Internet Advertising Bureau and the future predictions come from firms such as

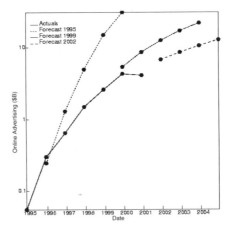

Figure 4.4   Trends in online advertising spending

Jupiter and Forrester. The chart shows both what has actually happened and the predictions made in 1995, 1999 and the 2002; you can thus decide whether you wish to believe the current predictions.

The market for internet advertising has been stagnant of late. The most recent quarterly report, showing $1.47 billion of adverts in the third quarter of 2002, was a 1% advance on the previous quarter and an 18% decline from a year earlier.[7] Online advertising dropped for six quarters in 2001–2002, partly because so much of it was placed by other dot-coms which no longer exist. Advertisers have become discouraged as fewer than 1 per cent of people who view an ad click on it.

Unfortunately, despite the $4 billion total (or more), it is all focused on a few websites, particularly the very popular ones. The potential for specificity in web advertising is not used as fully as it might be; few sites – other than the leading search engines and portals – get much advertising. It is hard to imagine enough advertising going to libraries to make a difference. Even in the boom years most small journals, for example, did not attract many ads to their websites, and it is unlikely that libraries, even if they sought out ads more actively, would get many. As the Internet advertising market has matured, ad placement has mostly gone to a few heavily used sites.

Thinking historically, very few scholarly journals got a large fraction of their budget from advertising, with only a few ads for books and employment positions on their back pages. Libraries have not historically sold advertising, and have not seen much opportunity there. The main 'advertising' in a library has traditionally been for donors: buildings, reading rooms, and book purchase funds are named for individuals the way sports arenas are named for corporations. And one problem with computer technology is that its transitory nature and the rate at which it becomes obsolete make donors reluctant to fund it, since whatever their name is on may evaporate in a few years. On balance, it seems unlikely that digital libraries will find much advertising support.

Other

Grant Support

The Andrew W. Mellon Foundation is particularly well known for its funding for activities such as JSTOR and ArtStor. JSTOR, having been started with Mellon funding, is now an independent not-for-profit institution. Although many other foundations (Kellogg, Soros, and the Packard Humanities Institute come to mind) support libraries, it is not reasonable to expect that operational funding for digital libraries will come from these sources. Some projects are supported by government funding (in the US, typically the National Endowment for the Humanities or the National Science Foundation), but again these tend to be specific research projects rather than long-term support.

Cost Avoidance

Many companies have gone to putting information on websites as an alternative to customer service operations. Similarly, much material intended, at least partly, as publicity or advertising, even if traditionally sold, may well be placed on websites. For example, you can buy the San Francisco Muni Transit map for $2.50, or you can find it on the web for free. The transit system's finances are based on ridership, not map sales, and they are happy to provide free access to information as a way of encouraging transit use. Similarly, many government agencies now publish their information on the web rather than, or in addition to, printing it on paper; in general, these agencies were only trying to do cost-recovery anyway. Some professional societies may turn to free online distribution for similar reasons. This argument, of course, will not apply to commercial publishers.

Advertising the Print Medium

The National Academy Press has, for a few years, been putting all its new books on the web for free access, and providing the complete text of each book. To the surprise of many, the result has been an increase in print sales. Similarly, the Brookings Institute has put 100 of its books online free, and the paper sales of those books have doubled. This result is perhaps similar to the experience of record companies, which found years ago that having their records played free on the radio increased sales. In fact, recording companies were willing to slip cash to disk jockeys to select their records, producing occasional 'payola' scandals.

   Web availability has also encouraged readership of out-of-copyright items. The University of Virginia is distributing almost seven e-books a minute, with more than 6 million shipped so far (in the first 21 months of operation). Perhaps it is not surprising to see *Alice in Wonderland* and *Huckleberry Finn* near the top of their best-seller list; but in one month they sent out more than 2000 copies of the works of Andrew Dickson White. One wonders if he sold that well during his lifetime (although he was President of both Cornell University and the American Historical Assocation in the 19th century).

Reputation and Publicity

Just as prestigious publishing arms such as Harvard University Press add to the reputation of a university, a good website may help as well. University libraries certainly compete to have good websites; in fact, this is making some trouble for system design, because of tensions over apparent credit between the library digitizing a work, the library running the web server that has it, and the library portal used by a student. Each participant would like to be perceived as the helpful and important entity; thus there has been a rise of 'branding' of university catalogs, for example. I don't know of any example of a library giving its card catalog a 'trade name', but we now have all sorts of systems named Melvyl, Hollis, Virgo, and the like.

Bounties

Once, AOL was willing to pay content providers for online content, which they hoped would attract users to their system. These payments disappeared when free web content became available, and were never very large anyway (*Time* magazine received ten times as much money for advertising AOL to its readers as it got for providing content to AOL users). It seems unlikely that any reasonable business model will be resuscitated from this idea.

Dedicated Taxes

In some countries, various fees or taxes are devoted to content production. For example, Germany taxes blank audiotape, and sends the money to the society of composers. The UK has a licence fee for television owners which helps support the BBC. One could imagine similar arrangements for online information, whether phrased as a tax on disk drives or modems or whatever. One example proposed in the United States is the suggested 'endowment' of the Digital Promise Coalition. It suggests that money from a spectrum sale of the digital spectrum for next generation telecommunications be placed in a fund whose income would be used to create or make accessible digital information.

My personal view of the political chances of any new tax or fund in the United States is low. Dedicated taxes are not popular for many reasons, and the collapse of the telecom boom makes spectrum sales less lucrative than previously hoped.

Government Financial Support in General

It is more possible that government funding on a national level could support digital information in some way without a dedicated tax or fund. The US government already has such organizations as IMLS (the Institute for Museum and Library Services). The most immediate program of importance is the National Digital Library effort at the Library of Congress. This has a potential budget of $175 million and is making plans to expand on the earlier American Memory effort.

Perhaps more important in the long run are activities related to education. For example, the National Science Foundation is investing some $60 million to create a national digital resource to support education in the sciences, mathematics, engineering and technology. The NSF has also joined with the United Kingdom to support research in the use of digital libraries to teach specific subjects in higher education. In the longer run, the US Department of Education might take an interest in the development of digital techniques for the improvement of education. We do not know yet to what extent the educational applications are going to involve the re-use of existing resources, that is, digitizing material now in libraries, or the creation of entirely new kinds of courseware or other teaching aids.

Pledge Breaks on the Internet

Public radio and television are, like the web, an example of the free distribution of information to citizens. The US does not have a 'licence fee' for their support and, to make an analogy between digital information online and on the air, one could imagine some variety of online begging. Shareware, for example, works this way. Some libraries do have places on their website where they explain how the public can make donations to encourage the work, but as of now these are relatively low-key, and not very important financially. Again, one is skeptical that this will be an important source of money.

Conclusions

Libraries are facing major changes. Now 84 per cent of libraries have online catalogs of their holdings, and 91 per cent have some kind of electronic reference tools (this may be only a single CD-ROM). The effect of OPACs was, first of all, to increase circulation, but now walk-in activities are declining as students use the web. Figure 4.5, taken from ARL statistics, shows the change relative to 1995 in reference queries, circulation, and inter-library loan (ILL). Only inter-library loan is going up – these are the requests for things that can not be replaced by local digital copies, since the library does not even have a local paper copy. The other metrics are now going down; the additional walk-ins prompted by the on-line catalogs are now giving way to people who don't come at all because they prefer searching web to using print. Librarians noticed that when perhaps 1/3 of their catalog was online, students quit bothering to search the older cards. Perhaps, in the same way, if students can find on the web 1/3 of

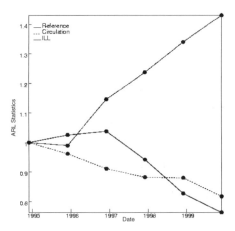

Figure 4.5   Changes in the levels of reference queries, circulation and inter-library loan activity since 1995

what they ought to have for a paper, they will settle for that rather than go to the library.

It is likely that there will be a split between the collection of information and the user services (reference, ILL, and simply the provision of reading rooms on campuses) in the organization of libraries. Increasingly, information is likely to come from servers at publishers, societies, and bigger libraries. Some local services, such as circulation and study spaces, are inherently local; others, such as reference, could in principle be remote, and we may see those move to consortia. Corporations sometimes move 'customer support' off-shore, for example, to India. However, few US libraries are owned by organizations that would feel politically comfortable in doing off-shore reference services.

For the primary funding of digital library operations, there seem to be two likely choices: individual purchases and/or community purchases. At the moment, both of these have large resources, which support paper libraries, and which might be redirected.

Libraries are actively engaged in digital library creation. Many libraries have programs for digitizing special collections, such as the Harvard University Libraries with their 'digital initiative', a five-year program investing some $12 million. The Digital Library Federation combines many institutions with such programs, and encourages the further development and sharing of such projects, paid for out of traditional library resources and research grants.

Many libraries are also creating new material, often as part of university educational programs. One of the most ambitious is Fathom, which is a joint effort of many institutions including, in the UK, the British Library, British Museum, London School of Economics and the Natural History Museum and, in the US, Columbia University, the University of Chicago, the University of Michigan, and the New York Public Library. See www.fathom.com for the full list of institutions. MIT's Open Courseware initiative plans to make materials used in teaching at MIT freely available around the world. At present, Fathom charges for its material; the MIT site is free.

Perhaps the most direct way in which libraries in general are supporting digital materials is through their acquisitions budgets. The fraction of their expenditures spent on electronic materials is increasing. In 1998, US academic libraries spent $153 million on electronic materials and $1,363 million on paper materials (out of a total of $1.6 billion), or about 10 per cent. Advanced libraries may be at 30 per cent and specialized libraries, for example in biotechnology companies, could reach 80 per cent. The share of purchase funds going to electronics at one library, the State University of New York (SUNY) is shown in Figure 4.6.

If institutional libraries are good, multi-institutional libraries may be better. The arguments that cause university faculty to pool their needs to gain access to resources also work to suggest that universities should work together to gain access to even larger resources. Brian Hawkins suggested some years ago that libraries merge their purchasing power to gain leverage in the negotiations over electronic rights, and the United Kingdom has a single purchasing agent for electronic materials in UKOLN.

An alternative economic model for digital libraries is the direct sale of technical material to individual researchers. The most promising example of a working

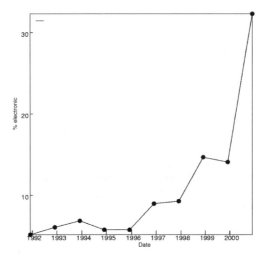

Figure 4.6   Share of purchase funds spent on electronic materials at the State University of New York

system so far seems to be the ACM Digital Library. It has both individual and institution subscription rates, has a large number of readers/customers, and could well be the model of a successful future digital library (DL) system. Another example is JSTOR, which is now financially independent of the Mellon Foundation, but has no individual subscribers; all users are associated with some institution. Neither JSTOR nor ACM, however, have any illusions about getting billions of dollars out of their online services.

It may be some time before commercial publishers admit that no economic model is likely to make scientific and scholarly publishing as lucrative as video games, and that out-of-print material is mostly worthless. Libraries keep older material around not because it is lucrative, but because it is not.

In summary, what we see today is a mixture of free distribution, library funding, and some individual purchases. We don't know yet whether the future will be dominated by

(a)   authors paying, probably by institutions supporting the distribution of their faculty publications;
(b)   readers paying through their libraries, with traditional publishers continuing but now delivering electronics;
(c)   readers paying individually, so that publishers bypass libraries; or
(d)   outsiders paying, so that some government agency or foundation provides much of the basic infrastructure and information.

My personal guess is that (d) is unlikely for political reasons, and that (c) is also unlikely despite the success of some professional societies. Whether universities decide that they would, on balance, rather do (a) than (b) is still a toss-up. Self-publishing would recover control for the universities, and probably save money (by pushing more work onto the authors); but it would require new administrative and economic structures in the universities. It is a choice between inertia and cost-savings, and so far it looks like inertia is winning.

Notes

1   Library of Congress circulation numbers are in the table in Section I, page 12 of the Library of Congress Consolidated Financial Statements, available on the web at http://lcweb.loc.gov/fsd/fin/pdfs/fy0101.pdf; the online usage statistics are on the www.loc.gov/stats webpage.
2   The chart of web size is a collection of numbers reported by Lycos (for the early years), the group at NEC that monitored web size, and the Internet Archive. See in particular 'How big is the web? How much of the web do the search engines index? How up to date are the search engines?' by Steve Lawrence and Lee Giles, at http://www.neci.nec.com/'lawrence/websize, which is an updated version of a paper they published in *Science* ('Searching the World Wide Web', by Steve Lawrence and C. Lee Giles, *Science*, vol. 280, pp. 98–100, 1998). The chart of disk prices comes from years of buying disks and collecting advertisements.
3   Steve Harnad's writings about online publication are available at his website http://www.ecs.soton.ac.uk/'harnad/intpub.html.
4   The ARL statistics are at http://www.arl.org/stats/arlstat/index.html in various formats.
5   The SDSC number is a private communication from Reagan Moore; the annual report of CRL is at http://wwwcrl.uchicago.edu/info/aboutcrl/ARFY01.pdf, and the price of disk drives is readily available from www.dirtcheapdrives.com. We await the arrival of the already announced 300 GB drives (Maxtor) and the resulting continued decrease of price per byte.
6   See http://www.publiclibraryofscience.org.
7   See the Internet Advertising Bureau site, quoting Price Waterhouse Coopers: http://www.iab.net/news/pr_2002_12_19.asp.

References

Bowen, W.G. (2001), 'The Academic Library In a Digitized, Commercialized Age: Lessons from JSTOR', January, http://www.jstor.org/about/bowen.html.
Lawrence, S. (2001), 'Online or Invisible?', Nature 411 (6837), 521. http://www.neci.nec.com/'lawrence/papers/online-nature01/.
Milunovich, S. (2002), 'Micropayment's big potential', *Red Herring*, 5 November.
Morais, R. (2002), 'Double Dutch No Longer', *Forbes*, 11 November.
Richtel, M.A. (2002), 'Shift Registers in Willingness to Pay for Internet Content', *The New York Times*, 1 August.
Rose, M.R. (2002) '2001 was a hard read for e-books', *Wired News* http://www.wired.com/news/culture/0,1284,49297,00.html.

Chapter 5

Content and Services Issues for Digital Libraries

Derek Law

Introduction

Most of the attention regarding digital libraries has gone on the technical developments that do, and will make them feasible, whether permanent locators, version control, metadata or cross-platform searching. Thus far, much less attention has been given to the areas of e-collection building and online services. What little thinking has gone on is limited in vision, can be partial and even part of a lopsided political agenda (Sun, 2003). A recent review of the history of 'Informatization' over the last 40 years gives collections barely a mention (Duff, 2003). But the sheer volume of electronic materials is growing rapidly (OCLC, 2003) and requires thought to be given to policy on collection building as well as the technology and practices which will allow it to happen. Present academic research builds on the collections of the past: it therefore behoves us to build collections for the future. It has been claimed in the context of Open Archives that 'the biggest challenge is getting content' (Pinfield, 2003). In the context of e-collection building, the challenge is perhaps that of building collections of coherent content.

Building Research Collections for the Future

In the past, building collections was relatively straightforward. The papers of distinguished academics were collected from their studies after death; manuscripts and books were purchased from rare book and manuscript dealers, contacts were cultivated in the hope of donations. The very stability of the paper record allowed patience and often multiple opportunities to determine where papers gravitated to. Nor were the collections only paper, but sometimes also physical objects. The University of Hull famously added Philip Larkin's lawnmower to its library collections (*The Guardian*, 2002).

The issues are much more daunting when it comes to electronic materials and largely revolve around media formats and preservation, as described in Chapter 7, by Lazinger. However, we do precious little in terms of what would have constituted collections in the past. E-drafts of documents and paper, e-correspondence between researchers, personal files on a PC rather than in a filing cabinet, and the electronic equivalent of lab books, are all falling through the net. While we feed off the collections of the past we generally fail to reflect on how the so-called 'born digital' collections of the future will look. Nor do we consider how the material will be held. The absence of agreed repository standards must be a major cause of concern. Ironically, as in so many things, one can see a potential solution in looking back to the experience of the past to develop thinking on the future. The Maori tradition is an oral one and they have developed a quite specific set of criteria to guide the selection of the keepers of that oral tradition (Winiata, 2002):

(1) Receive the information with utmost accuracy.
(2) Store the information with integrity beyond doubt.
(3) Retrieve the information without amendment.
(4) Apply appropriate judgement in the use of the information.
(5) Pass the information on appropriately.

These points seem a perfect guide to the preservation requirements of tomorrow's e-collections.

A Typology of Collections

Thinking on collections has most fruitfully taken place within the context of the Digital Library Federation (http://www.diglib.org/dlfhomepage.htm) and has produced interesting work, for example on strategies for developing sustainable and scalable digital library collections. Greenstein (2000) proposes four types of collection:

- local digitization projects that produce surrogates for analogue information objects;
- data creation projects that produce information resources that have no analogue equivalent and are in this respect 'born digital';
- the selection of existing third-party data resources for inclusion in a collection either through their outright acquisition or by acquiring access under some licensing arrangement; and
- the development of internet gateways comprising locally maintained pages or databases of web-links to third-party networked information.

This typology allows an exploration of the nature and extent of what is, should be, and could be made available.

Digitized Surrogate Resources

It is a commonplace that not all existing collections will be digitized. Scale, copyright and value are argued to make such conversion implausible. It is certainly the case that, at present, we tend to see projects delivering selected subsets of collections rather than the whole. Digitized resources can be further sub-categorized beyond Greenstein's single overarching category, because the motives for digitization are very varied. Improved access, preservation, aggregation of scattered material, and more are all reasons for creating digital collections, as the following examples of the sub-categories show.

Surrogates of Rare Items: The British Library

An excellent example of this is the British Library's Treasures collection (http:// www.bl.uk/collections/treasures.html), where rare treasures are made more accessible to the public (and indeed to scholars). This collection contains such heterogeneous material as the Magna Carta, the Lindisfarne Gospels, the Gutenberg Bible and the notebooks of Leonardo Da Vinci. What these great documents have in common is their rarity and their public prominence. The e-collection acts as a surrogate to allow these great iconic treasures to be open to all.

Surrogates for Whole or Part Collections: The Springburn Virtual Library

During the summer of 2000 it became apparent that the Springburn Community Museum faced closure for financial reasons. Although the collections were to be transferred to the Mitchell Library in Glasgow, this much loved and popular local resource would be separated from its community. A project was put in place to ensure that the museum's rich collection of local photographs would still be accessible to the local public over the internet. Funding was secured to digitize a representative selection of materials from the collections and to lay the foundations for the Springburn Virtual Museum. Images were chosen to convey the social and economic history of Springburn, notably community and tenement life and the important local railway industry; see http://gdl.cdlr.strath.ac.uk/springburn/. As a result, a community threatened with the loss of a resource has had at least a subset of it made more accessible to all.

Digitized Surrogate Collections Assembled from Multiple Repositories: The Valley of the Shadow

The much admired Valley of the Shadow Project focuses in great detail on the experience of two communities, one Northern and one Southern, through the American Civil War, as an exemplar to give an understanding of the experience of the nation as a whole. It consists of a hypermedia archive of sources for Augusta County, Virginia, and Franklin County, Pennsylvania. A rich variety of materials has been assembled – newspapers, letters, diaries, photographs, maps, church records, population census, agricultural census, and military records. It encourages users to interact with materials rather than simply access them; see http:// www.iath.virginia.edu/vshadow2/

A collection with a quite different focus and ambition is the Great Britain Historical GIS Project (www.gbhgis.org), which aims to have systematic information on the history of every locality in Britain, using everything from Ordnance Survey maps to Victorian gazetteers and Defoe's *A Journey through the Whole Island of Britain*. It can be searched using postcodes and aims to allow everyone to access information relevant to their own area.

Collections Assembled Specifically to be Digitized

The Aspect project (http://gdl.cdlr.strath.ac.uk/aspect/) was set up to create a digital archive of the ephemera – leaflets, flyers, postcards, newsletters – produced by candidates and political parties for the first Scottish parliamentary election in May 1999. The archive is based on the collection of election ephemera held by the Andersonian Library at the University of Strathclyde, which is acknowledged to be an important and unique record of a key event in Scottish history. The creation of a digital archive will significantly improve the accessibility and usability of the information contained within the collection whilst conserving the original materials, which may be subject to deterioration through loss and damage. Thus, a collection being built for use by future researchers is being made immediately available, using digitization as a deliberate strategy in acquisition.

Born Digital Resources

The number and scale of these is growing from scholarly journals to new fiction, from datasets and satellite images to digital video and computer-generated graphics. Many are being preserved. But examples of born digital collections are rare. It is arguable that these remain individual items rather than forming a coherently built collection. Perhaps the nearest to this is the various collections of learning objects being assembled in many universities. For example, Boezerooy (2003) gives a comprehensive overview of the Australian experience which demonstrates that these exist but are not always created with library advice or assistance or indeed even with long term preservation in mind.

Third Party Data Sources

In the UK, JISC began its work of building the Distributed National Electronic Resource in 1990 (Law, 1994) and now has a hugely rich collection of resources licensed to the community (JISC, 2003). That consortial licensing model has been widely followed. The International Coalition of Library Consortia (ICOLC) first met in 1997 and has grown to be a self-help group of some 150 consortia from all over the world. It considers issues of common concern, principally in the context of higher education and research. Without necessarily supporting it however, ICOLC (http://www.library.yale.edu/consortia/) in effect works within the present pattern of scholarly communication to make material as available as possible.

The electronic environment offers up new and as yet unexplored models of data acquisition, whether for a single institution or in consortia. The intention expressed by Singapore in its seminal planning for the Intelligent Island (Chun Wei Choo, 1997) is to create an information entrepôt and hub for the region. It is easy to build on this concept to develop the concept of information arbitrage (Law, 2001), the notion of buying and selling information around the world, taking advantage of the time shift to buy data cheaply at offpeak times when they are little used in a country. Similar thinking has informed the development of 7×24 reference services, as described later in this chapter.

Quite novel models have also been proposed to allow freer access to the scholarly research literature. Most of the debate has centred on the ailing STM model more fully explored by Harnad in Chapter 6. The model he has advocated for many years has moved from the fringe of debate to the mainstream. Most recently, the so-called Budapest Declaration, under the aegis of the Soros Foundation declared that:

> We invite governments, universities, libraries, journal editors, publishers, foundations, learned societies, professional associations, and individual scholars who share our vision to join us in the task of removing the barriers to open access and building a future in which research and education in every part of the world are that much more free to flourish. (http://www.soros.org/openaccess/read.shtml)

Most of the debate has focused on the perceived failure of the STM (Scientific, Technical and Medical) model of scholarly communication where the highest priced journals exist. Many other initiatives, such as Biomed Central (http://www.biomedcentral.com/) and SPARC (http://www.arl.org/sparc/) have demonstrated the concern felt in the wider scholarly community at the present state of scholarly communication and the need to change that. We appear to have developed a monster that has steadily lost sight of the fact that publishing exists to support research and not the opposite. In this debate, however, little thought has been given to the Humanities and Social Sciences, where huge numbers of journals and researchers exist and where journals are often effectively produced as a labour of love from within university departments. Here, some steps are being taken actively to persuade and assist small scholarly publishers to shift their content to electronic formats. The role then is to mediate the transfer to an e-environment and not simply to acquire content. Such an initiative is the SAPIENS project (Scottish Academic Periodicals: Implementing an Effective Networked Service) involving six Scottish universities and the National Library of Scotland (http://sapiens.cdlr.strath.ac.uk/). It aims to:

- examine the case for a centralized Scottish electronic journal service that might enable and encourage smaller publishers to make existing and new journals available in electronic form;
- design and build a demonstrator service, which will deliver current journals from a representative selection of publishers via a common gateway; and
- develop and launch an operational service, together with a marketing strategy to ensure that it is self-sustaining within a year of the end of the project.

Librarians here, as elsewhere, have developed a catalytic role in helping to make available the content required by library users.

Mirroring and Caching

This is a somewhat neglected subset of third-party licensing. A mirror site, in essence, contains a locally held copy of data from another site or sites and is a mechanism for reducing costly internet traffic. An excellent early example of this is the Visible Human dataset. This was originally constructed in the United States with the support of the National Library of Medicine (NLM). It contains images of a 39-year old convicted murderer who, prior to his execution, donated his corpse to medical science. The dataset was subsequently expanded with the addition of the images of a female at greater resolution than used for the male. The bodies have been 'sliced' to create the images. NLM did not want to see copies of the dataset mounted outside the USA, quite properly fearing that issues such as version control and quality assurance were not sufficiently settled in the mid-1990s to give comfort of proper data management. For the UK, this proved a problem since this wonderful resource was heavily used in medical teaching and consumed great quantities of bandwidth as images were slowly downloaded. Mirroring was the obvious solution. Discussions began with NLM and, after protracted discussions, the final sticking point (according to folklore!) was the need for guarantees on what would happen to the data if the host institution disappeared. At that point, in 1997, JISC accepted an offer from the University of Glasgow to act as the host (http://vhp.gla.ac.uk/), not least on the grounds that it had already existed for half a century before Columbus sailed the ocean blue. Whether or not the tale is true, it does demonstrate that mirroring can be just as complicated an exercise as licensing commercial data. Certainly in the UK, as network charging begins to influence decisions, it seems reasonable to expect a greater interest in mirroring as a method of reducing traffic as much as improving accessibility.

The same is true of caching data. This is one of the black arts of computing but does have a significant impact on costs, traffic and availability. This stems from the well-known library principle that the books most likely to be used are those that have been used already. Thus, a URL used once in an organization is much more likely to be sought again than one never used. So the cache (local, regional or even national) stores recently retrieved URLs for a specified period of time, in case they are searched for again. The speed of retrieval is thus much enhanced. The UK National Cache has been studied in depth (Sparks *et al.*, 1999) in terms of performance and value for money and this is very informative in indicating the impact that an institutional caching strategy might have.

Internet Gateways

Such gateways have now existed for several years, whether as generalist services such as BUBL 'Free User-Friendly Access to Selected Internet Resources Covering all Subject Areas, with a Special Focus on Library and Information Science' (http://bubl.ac.uk/) or subject specific services such as EEVL for the engineering community (http://www.eevl.ac.uk/). Typically, these are university based 'free' services, funded by third parties, often government agencies. These are based on the notion that no single institution can manage with discrimination all the information on the internet and that the labour can sensibly be divided. The UK experience began with several projects under the access to networked resources strand of the Follett Report (Law and Dempsey, 2000). These were intended to cover a range of subject areas: OMNI (medical and bioscience), ADAM (art and design), EEVL (engineering) and RUDI (urban design), all began the task of building databases of internet resources in their respective subject areas from scratch, while SOSIG extended a pre-existing project. Funding was also provided to support the gateways by funding ROADS, which aimed to develop software that could be used by the gateways to create the resource databases and serve them to users via the web. The success of these initial projects led the JISC to develop the Resource Discovery Network (RDN), which uses this approach to cover all subject disciplines (Dempsey, 2000). The usage of the RDN gateways has been disappointingly low and this national approach may have to be reappraised.

One major issue appears not to have been addressed so far. There is a bland assumption that there is an almost infinite supply of bandwidth and that issues of access and slow-to-load pages will disappear: that view is not necessarily shared by all. At the same time there is an equally unthinking assumption that resources are either good or bad. However, there is a more sophisticated but so far neglected approach which asks whether the Pareto Principle might also apply to online resources. This well known principle, sometimes known as the 80/20 rule, is used in many contexts. In the information field it suggests that 80 per cent of the usage comes from 20 per cent of the documents or collections.

It is typically assumed that access should be given to the best or most complete or most authoritative material, but these terms are never explored or defined. Networked environments add the complication of accessibility in a quite novel way. For example, in many parts of Europe, the quality of connectivity to the United States drops dramatically after the golden hours of the European morning, once American users wake up and begin to log on. So is a similar or smaller resource (but just as accurate) available 24 hours a day to be preferred to a larger resource effectively available for, say, only two-thirds of the day? We need to consider whether juggling the variables of time, comprehensiveness and accessibility can produce more effective and efficient services. As always, the key to making the Pareto Principle both workable and acceptable is choosing the right 20 per cent! There is a need for a much more sophisticated appraisal of all the factors surrounding internet gateway access than has perhaps been the case thus far.

Shared Services

Internet gateways are perhaps closer to services than collections, although they will undoubtedly help to define the perception of the library in the future. If libraries can provide online services, which are seen as independent, authoritative and right, they seem certain to see off competition from those less skilled. In an inversion of Gresham's Law, Law's First Law [1] states that 'Good Information Systems will drive out bad'. The development of electronic services in libraries dates back to the creation of the first automated systems in the 1960s and the area of e-services is well understood and much discussed, for example by Pantry and Griffiths (2002).

Thinking is only just beginning on how using the network to share services can be exploited – although interlending and document supply is a long-standing triumph of professional cooperation much enhanced by new technologies, as is shared cataloguing.

The development of shared programmes for information skills training is perhaps an old-fashioned but important starting point for sharing. A growing number of locally prepared but networked based products is available.

Much interest has been shown in shared reference services where a timeshift allows 7×24 coverage for those staff and students who prefer anti-social habits to the normal working day. For example, the University of Technology in Sydney and the University of Strathclyde in Glasgow are piloting such a shared service where each answers reference enquiries from the other's users during the questioner's night – daytime in the other country.

Conclusions

To some extent the issue of e-collections will define the future of libraries. At one extreme there is Brewster Kahle who has adopted the universal library philosophy of the great nineteenth century libraries, considering the internet to be the library, and has a very unsentimental view of past glories such as the Alexandrine Library: 'Great library – too bad it was burnt' (Kaushik, 2003). Less comprehensive virtual libraries will require the application of the traditional skills of selection of content as well as its preservation, if not physical space; while the argument for the library as a physical place even in a digital future has been strongly argued by the UK's Library and Information Commission (Library and Information Commission, 1999). Whatever the future holds for libraries in terms of physical location, e-collections will need to be built. It is then our existing professional skills in selection, acquisition and cataloguing that place librarians as the best qualified group to organize content – provided the challenge is recognized and accepted.

Note

1   The creation of Law's First Law is as much an attempt to seek attention as succinctness. There is also Law's Second Law, which emphasizes the importance of offering information skills training through the library. It states that 'User friendly systems aren't'.

References

Boezerooy, P. (2003), 'Keeping up with our neighbours: ICT developments in Australian Higher Education', LTSN Generic Centre [n.p.].

Chun Wei Choo (1997), 'IT2000: Singapore's Vision of an Intelligent Island', in: P. Droege (ed.), *Intelligent Environments* (Amsterdam: North-Holland).

Dempsey, L. (2000), 'The subject gateways: experiences and issues based on the emergence of the Resource Discovery Network', *Online Information Review*, 24(1), 2000, 8–23. Also available at http://www.rdn.ac.uk/publications/ior-2000–02-dempsey/.

Duff, A.S. (2003), 'Four "e"pochs: the story of informatization', *Library Review* 52(2), 58–64.

Greenstein, D. (2000), 'Strategies for developing sustainable and scalable digital library collections', http://www.diglib.org/collections/collstrat.htm.

Guardian (2002), *The Education Guardian* Thursday 9 May 2002 [news item] http://education.guardian.co.uk/higher/humanities/story/0,9850,712877,00.html.

JISC (2003), 'e-collections: exploiting the opportunities' [JISC collections folder] (Bristol; JISC) www.jisc.ac.uk/collections/.

Kaushik, R. (2003), 'Spreading The Digital Word', *ExtremeTech*, 29, April. http://www.extremetech.com/article2/0,3973,1047454,00.asp.

Law, D. (1994), 'The development of a national policy for dataset provision in the UK: a historical perspective', *Journal of Information Networking*, 1(2), 103–116.

Law, D. (2002), 'The Library in the Market: Information arbitrage as the new face of an old service', *IATUL Proceedings*, 11 (New Series) 2001 (Delft: Delft University of Technology), 2002.

Law, D. and Dempsey, L. (2000), 'A Policy Context – e-Lib and the emergence of subject gateways', *Ariadne*, (25) 5 pp. http://www.ariadne.ac.uk/issue25/subject-gateways.

Library and Information Commission (1999), *2020 Vision* http://www.lic.gov.uk/publications/policyreports/2020.pdf.

OCLC (2003) Five year information format trends. OCLC, March www.oclc.org/info/trends/.

Pantry, S. and Griffiths, P. (2002), *Creating a Successful E-Information Service* (London: Facet).

Pinfield, S. (2003), 'Open Archives and UK Institutions', *D-Lib Magazine*, 9 (3).

Sparks, M., Neisser, G. and Hanby, R. (1999) 'An Initial Statistical Analysis of the Performance of the UK National JANET Cache http://wwwcache.ja.net/papers/initial_analysis/.

Sun (2003) 'Sun Microsystems Educational Consultation Forum. Creating the Distributed National Research Library', paper ECF04 February, 2003.

Winiata, W. (2002), 'Ka purea e ngā a hau a Tāwhirimātea: Ngā Wharepukapuka o Ngā Tau Ruamano', Keynote address, LIANZA Conference, Wellington. http://www.confer.co.nz/lianza2002/PDFS/Whatarangi%20Winiata.pdf.

Chapter 6

Open Access to Peer-Reviewed Research Through Author/Institution Self-Archiving: Maximizing Research Impact by Maximizing Online Access

Stevan Harnad

Five Essential Post-Gutenberg Distinctions

In order to understand what has changed for scientific and scholarly research publication in the transition from the Gutenberg (on-paper) to the Post-Gutenberg (online) era, we first have to make five critical distinctions. If we fail to make any one of these distinctions, it will be impossible to make sense of the unique new possibilities opened up by the online era of 'Scholarly Skywriting' (Harnad, 1990) in the 'Post-Gutenberg Galaxy' (Harnad, 1991).

Distinguish the Non-give-away Literature from the Give-away Literature

This is the most important Post-Gutenberg distinction of all. It is what makes this small, refereed research literature anomalous (~20,000 refereed journals, ~2,000,000 articles annually) and fundamentally unlike the bulk of the written literature: its authors do not seek, nor do they receive, royalties or fees for their writings. Their texts are author give-aways (Harnad 1995a). The only thing these authors seek is research 'impact' (Harnad and Carr, 2000; Harnad, 2003d; Harnad *et al.*, 2003), which comes from accessing the eyes and minds of all potentially interested fellow-researchers everywhere, now, and any time in the future, so they can read, use, cite, apply, and build upon our work. It is this research impact that in turn generates researchers' real rewards: promotions, tenure, research-funding, prizes, prestige – and making one's mark on the course of human knowledge.

The litmus test for whether a piece of writing falls in the small give-away sector of the literature or the much larger non-give-away sector is: 'Does the author seek a royalty or fee in exchange for his writings?' If the answer is *yes* (as it is for virtually all books – cf. Harnad *et al.* 2000 – and newspaper or magazine articles), then the writing is non-give-away; if the answer is *no*, then it is give-away.

None of what follows here is applicable to non-give-away writing, yet the royalty-based, non-give-away model is the one that most people have in mind when they think of writing. So it is not surprising that that small fraction of writing that the more general model does not fit should seem anomalous, and give rise to some confusion at the beginning of the online age.

Distinguish Income (Arising from Article Sales) from Impact (Arising from Article Use)

Unlike all other authors, researchers derive their income not from the sale of their research reports but from the scholarly/scientific impact of their reported findings, that is, how much they are read, used, cited, applied and built-upon by other researchers. Hence, all toll-based access-barriers are income-barriers for research and researchers (Harnad, 1998a), restricting their potential impact to only those (institutions, mainly) who can and do pay the access-tolls. As most institutions cannot afford the access-tolls to most refereed research journals, this means that most research papers cannot be accessed by most researchers (Harnad, 1998b). Currently, all that potential impact is simply lost.

Note that, although researchers do not derive income from the sale of their refereed research papers ('imprint income'), they do derive income from the impact of those papers ('impact income'). The simple reason why researchers, unlike non-give-away authors, do not seek imprint-income for their refereed research is that the access-tolls for collecting imprint-income are barriers to impact-income (research grants, salaries, promotion, tenure, prizes), which is by far the more important reward for researchers, most of whose refereed papers are so esoteric (Harnad, 1995b) as to have no imprint-income market at all.

Distinguish between Copyright Protection from Theft-of-Authorship (Plagiarism) and Copyright Protection from Theft-of-Text (Piracy)

These two very different aspects of copyright protection have always been conflated (Harnad, 1999b), because it is the much larger and more representative *non-give-away* literature that has always been the model for copyright law and copyright concerns. But copyright protection from theft-of-authorship (plagiarism), which is essential for both give-away and non-give-away authors, has nothing at all to do with copyright protection from theft-of-text (piracy), which non-give-away authors want but give-away authors do not want. One can have full protection from plagiarism without seeking any protection from piracy.

Distinguish Self-publishing (Vanity Press) from Self-archiving (of Published, Refereed Research)

The essential difference between unrefereed research and refereed research is quality-control (peer review, Harnad, 1998/2000) and its certification (by an established peer-reviewed journal of known quality). Although researchers have always wished to give away their refereed research findings, they still wish them to be refereed, revised (if necessary), and then certified as having met established quality standards. Hence, the self-archiving of refereed research should in no way be confused with self-publishing, for it includes as its most important component, the online self-archiving, free for all, of peer-reviewed, *published* research papers.

Distinguish Unrefereed Preprints from Refereed Postprints

Eprint ('eprints' = preprints + postprints) archives, consisting of research papers self-archived online by their authors, are not, and have never been, merely 'preprint archives' for unrefereed research. Authors can self-archive therein all the embryological stages of the research they wish to report, from pre-refereeing, preprints, through successive revisions, until the refereed, journal-certified postprint, and thence still further, to any subsequent corrected, revised, or otherwise updated drafts (post-postprints), as well as any commentaries or responses linked to them. These are all just way-stations along the scholarly skywriting continuum (Harnad, 1990). See http://www.eprints.org/self-faq/

The Optimal and Inevitable for Researchers

- The entire full-text refereed corpus online.
- On every researcher's desktop, everywhere.
- 24 hours a day.
- All papers citation-interlinked.
- Fully searchable, navigable, retrievable, impact-rankable.
- For free, for all, forever.

All of this will come to pass. The only real question is 'How Soon?' And will we still be *compos mentis* and fit to benefit from it, or will it only be for the Napster generation? Future historians, posterity, and our own still-born potential scholarly impact are already poised to chide us with hindsight (Harnad, 1999b). What can the research community do to hasten the optimal and inevitable? Here are some recent concepts that may help.

Two Useful Acronyms, One New Distinction, and One New Ally

Subscription/Site-Licence/Pay-Per-View Tolls: The Impact/Access-Barriers

Subscription/Licence/Pay-Per-View (S/L/P) tolls are the access-barriers, hence the impact-barriers, constraining researchers and their give-away research. Tolls are the journal publisher's means of recovering costs and making a fair profit. High costs were inescapable in the expensive and inefficient on-paper Gutenberg era; but today, in the online Post-Gutenberg era, continuing to do it all the old Gutenberg way, with its high costs, must be clearly seen (in the special case of this minority give-away literature only: not the majority royalty/fee-based literature!) as the optional add-on that it has become, rather than as the obligatory feature that it used to be.

Be wary about the language of obligatory 'value-added', with which the peer-reviewed literature 'must', by implication, continue to be inextricably bundled together. The only essential service still provided by journal publishers (for this anomalous, author-give-away literature in the Post-Gutenberg era) is peer review itself (Harnad, 1998/2000). The rest – on-paper versions, online PDF page images, deluxe online enhancements (mark-up, citation-linking, etc) – are all potentially valuable features, to be sure, but only as take-it-or-leave-it options. In the online era there is no longer any necessity, hence no longer any justification, for continuing to hold the refereed research itself hostage to access-tolls bundled with whatever add-ons they happen to pay for. Beware also of any attempt to trade off S for L or L for P in Subscription/Licence/Pay-Per-View: pick your poison, all three forms of toll are access-barriers, hence impact-barriers, and hence all three must go – or rather, they must all now become only the price-tags for the add-on, deluxe options that they buy for the researcher and his institution, but no longer also for the peer-reviewed essentials, which can now be self-archived for free for all.

Quality-Control and Certification: Peer Review

Peer review itself is not a deluxe add-on for research and researchers, for certification is an essential (Harnard, 1998/2000). Without peer review, the research literature would be neither reliable nor navigable, its quality uncontrolled, unfiltered, unsignposted, unknown, unaccountable. But the peers who review it for the journals are the researchers themselves, and they review it for free, just as the researchers report it for free. So it must be made quite clear that the only real quality-control cost is that of implementing the peer review, not actually performing it.

Estimates (for example, Odlyzko, 1998) as well as the real experience of online-only journals (for example, *Journal of High Energy Physics*, http://jhep.cern.ch/; *Psycoloquy*, http://www.cogsci.soton.ac.uk/psycoloquy/) have shown that the peer-review implementation cost is quite low – about 1/3 (c. $500) of the total amount that the world's institutional libraries (or rather, the small subset of them that can afford any given journal at all!) are currently paying every year per article, jointly, in access tolls (c. $1500). Once the 2/3 toll-based add-ons become optional, the essential 1/3 peer review cost could easily be paid out of the 3/3 toll savings – if and when the world's libraries should ever decide they no longer need the add-ons. (The other 2/3 savings can be used to buy other things, for example, books, which are not, and never will be, author give-aways.)

Separating (i) Peer-Review Service-Provision from (ii) Eprint Access-Provision (and from (iii) Optional Add-ons)

Researchers need not, and should not, wait until journal publishers voluntarily decide to separate the provision of the essential peer-review service from all the other optional add-on products (on-paper version, publisher's PDF version, deluxe enhancements) before their give-away refereed research can at last be freed of all access- and impact-barriers. All researchers can free their own refereed research now, virtually overnight, by taking the matter into their own hands; they can self-archive it in their institutional Eprint Archives: http://www.eprints.org. Access to the eprints of their refereed research is then immediately freed of all toll-barriers, forever, and its research impact is at last maximized (Harnad, 2003d).

Interoperability: The Open Archive Initiative (OAI)

Papers self-archived by their authors in their institutional Eprint Archives can be accessed by anyone, anywhere, with no need to know their actual location, because all Eprint Archives are compliant with the Open Archives Initiative (OAI) meta-data tagging protocol for interoperability: http://www.openarchives.org.

Because of their OAI-compliance, the papers in all registered Eprint Archives can be harvested and searched by Open Archive Services such as Cite-Base (http://citebase.eprints.org/help/), the Cross Archive Searching Service (http://arc.cs.odu.edu/), and OAISter (http://oaister.umdl.umich.edu/o/oaister/) providing seamless access to all the eprints, across all the Eprint Archives, as if they were all in one global, virtual archive.

The 'Subversive Proposal' (Updated for the OAI Era)

Enough to Free Entire Refereed Corpus, Forever, Immediately

Eight steps will be described here. The first four are not hypothetical in any way; they are guaranteed to free the entire refereed research literature (~20,000 journals annually) from its access/impact-barriers right away. The only thing that researchers and their institutions need to do is to take these first four steps. The remaining four steps are hypothetical predictions, but nothing hinges on them: The refereed literature will already be free for everyone as a result of steps (i)–(iv), irrespective of the outcome of predictions (v)–(viii).

Universities install and register OAI-compliant Eprint Archives (http://www.eprints.org) The Eprints software is free and GNU open-source. It, in turn, uses only free software; it is quick and easy to install and maintain; it is OAI-compliant and will be kept compliant with every OAI upgrade (http://www.openarchives.org/). Eprint Archives are all interoperable with one another and can hence be harvested and searched (for example, http://arc.cs.odu.edu/) as if they were all in one global 'virtual' archive of the entire research literature, both pre- and post-refereeing.

Authors self-archive their pre-refereeing preprints and post-refereeing postprints in their own university's Eprint Archives This is the most important step; it is insufficient to create the Eprint Archives. All researchers must self-archive their papers therein if the literature is to be freed of its access- and impact-barriers. Self-archiving is quick and easy; it need only be done once per paper, and the result is permanent, and permanently and automatically uploadable to upgrades of the Eprint Archives and the OAI-protocol.

Universities subsidize a first start-up wave of self-archiving by proxy where needed Self-archiving is quick and easy, but there is no need for it to be held back if any researcher feels too busy, tired, old or otherwise unable to do it for him or herself: library staff or students can be paid to 'self-archive' the first wave of papers by proxy on their behalf. The cost will be negligibly low per paper, and the benefits will be huge; moreover, there will be no need for a second wave of help once the palpable benefits (access and impact) of freeing the literature begin to be felt by the research community. Self-archiving will become second-nature to all researchers as the objective digitometric indicators of its effects on citations and usage become available online (Harnad 2001e; Lawrence, 2001a, 2001b) (for example, cite-base or Research Index).

The give-away corpus is freed from all access/impact barriers online Once a critical mass of researchers has self-archived, the refereed research literature is at last free of all access- and impact-barriers, as it was always destined to be.

Hypothetical sequel

Steps (i)–(iv) are sufficient to free the refereed research literature. We can also guess at what may happen after that, but these are really just guesses. Nor does anything depend on their being correct. For even if there is no change whatsoever – even if universities continue to spend exactly the same amounts on their access-toll budgets as they do now – the refereed literature will have been freed of all access/impact barriers forever. However, it is likely that there will be some changes as a consequence of opening access to the refereed literature by author/institution self-archiving. The following is what those changes might be.

Users will prefer the free version? It is likely that once a free, online version of the refereed research literature is available, not only those researchers who could not access it at all before, because of toll-barriers at their institution, but virtually all researchers will prefer to use the free online versions. Note that it is quite possible that there will always continue to be a market for the toll-based options (on-paper version, publisher's online PDF, deluxe enhancements) even though most users use the free versions. Nothing hinges on this.

Publisher toll revenues shrink, library toll savings grow? But if researchers do prefer to use the free online literature, it is possible that libraries may begin to cancel journals, and as institutional toll savings grow, journal publisher toll revenues will shrink. The extent of the cancellation will depend on the extent to which there remains a market for the toll-based add-ons, and for how long.
   If the toll-based market stays large enough, nothing else need change.

Publishers downsize to become providers of peer-review service plus optional add-ons products? It will depend entirely on the size of the remaining market for the toll-based options whether, and to what extent, journal publishers will have to cut costs and downsize to providing only the essentials. The only essential, indispensable service is peer review.

Peer-review service costs on outgoing research funded out of toll-savings on incoming research? If publishers can continue to cover costs and make a decent profit from the toll-based *optional add-ons* market, without needing to downsize to peer-review service-provision alone, nothing much changes. However, if publishers do need to abandon providing the toll-based products and to scale down instead, to providing only the peer-review service, then universities, having saved 100 per cent of their annual access-toll budgets, will have plenty of annual windfall savings from which to pay for their own researchers' continuing (and essential) annual journal-submission peer-review costs (1/3). The rest of their savings (2/3) they can spend as they like (for example, on books – plus a bit for Eprint Archive maintenance).

Post-Gutenberg Copyright Concerns

There is a great deal of concern about copyright in the digital age, and some of it may not be easily resolvable (for example, what to do about the pirating of software and music). But none of that need detain us here, because digital piracy is only a problem for non-give-away work, whereas we are concerned here only with give-away work. (Again, failing to make the give-away/non-give-away distinction leads only to confusion, and the misapplication of the much bigger and more representative non-give-away model to the anomalous and much smaller give-away corpus, which it does not fit.)

The following digital copyright concerns are relevant to the non-give-away literature only.

Protecting Intellectual Property (Royalties)

This is as much of a concern to authors of books as to authors of screenplays, music and computer programs. It is also a concern to performers who have made digital audio or video disks of their work. They do not wish to see that work stolen; they want their fair share of the gate-receipts in return for their talent and efforts in producing the work. But the producers of refereed research reports do not wish to have protection from 'theft' of this kind; on the contrary, they wish to encourage it. They have no royalties to gain from preventing it; they have only research impact to lose from access-denial of any kind.

Allowing Fair Use (User Issue)

'Fair Use' is another worthy concern. It has to do with certain sanctioned uses of non-give-away material, such as all or parts of books, magazine articles, and so on, often for teaching purposes. The producers of these works do not wish to lose their potential royalty/fee-income from these works. The producers of refereed research reports, in contrast, wish to give their work away; hence fair-use issues are moot for this special give-away literature. Copyright law is very different in the US and the UK (and elsewhere). It is therefore very important to check the relevant law and current practice.

Preventing Theft of Text (Piracy)

The producers of refereed research reports do not wish to prevent the 'theft' of their texts; they wish to facilitate it as much as possible. (In the on-paper era they used to purchase and mail reprints to requesters at their own expense!)

The following digital copyright concern is relevant to all literature, both give-away and non-give-away.

Preventing Theft of Authorship (Plagiarism)

No author wants any other author to claim to have been the author of his work. This concern is shared by all authors, give-away and non-give-away. However, it has nothing whatsoever to do with concerns about theft-of-text, and should not be conflated with such concerns in any way: give-away work need not be held hostage to non-give-away concerns about theft-of-text under the umbrella of 'protecting' it from theft-of-authorship. (Unfortunately, some journal publishers still try to use their copyright transfer agreements for this purpose, although their numbers are shrinking: see http://www.lboro.ac.uk/departments/ls/disresearch/romeo/Romeo Publisher Policies.htm.)

The following digital copyright concern is relevant to the give-away literature only.

Guaranteeing Author Give-Away Rights

Apart from the protection from plagiarism and the assurance of priority that all authors seek, the only other 'protection' the give-away author of refereed research reports seeks is protection of his give-away rights! (The intuitive model for this is advertisements: what advertiser wants to lose his right to give away his ads for free, diminishing their potential impact by charging for access to them!)

There is now no need for the authors of refereed research to worry about exercising their give-away rights, for they can do it, legally, even under the most restrictive copyright agreement, by using the following strategy.

How to Get Around Restrictive Copyright Legally

('Preprint+corrigenda strategy')

Self-archive the Pre-refereeing Preprint

Self-archiving the preprint is the critical first step. Before it has even been submitted to a journal, your intellectual property is incontestably your own, and not bound by any future copyright transfer agreement. So archive the preprints (as physicists have done for 12 years now, with over 250,000 papers, and cognitive scientists have done for 5 years now, with over 1,500 papers). This is a good way to establish priority, elicit informal feedback, and keep a public record of the embryology of knowledge.

[Note that some journals have, apart from copyright policies, which are a legal matter, 'embargo policies', which are merely policy matters (non-legal). Invoking the 'Ingelfinger (Embargo) Rule', some journals state that they will not referee (let alone publish) papers that have previously been 'made public' in any way, whether through conferences, press releases, or online self-archiving. The Ingelfinger Rule, apart from being directly at odds with the interests of research and researchers and having no intrinsic justification whatsoever – other than as a way of protecting journals' current revenue streams – is not a legal matter, and unenforceable. So researchers are best advised to ignore it completely (Harnad, 2000a, 2000b), exactly as the authors of the 250,000 papers in the Physics Archive have been doing for 12 years now. The 'Ingelfinger Rule' is under review by journals in any case; *Nature* http://npg.nature.com/pdf/05_news.pdf has already dropped it, *Science* may soon follow suit too.]

Submit the Preprint for Refereeing (Revise and so on)

Nothing changes in author publication practices; nothing needs to be given up. Submit your preprint to the refereed journal of your choice, and revise it as usual in accordance with the directive of the Editor and the advice of the referees.

Upon Acceptance, Try to Fix the Copyright Transfer Agreement to Allow Self- archiving

Copyright transfer agreements take many forms. Whatever the wording is, if it does not explicitly permit online self-archiving, modify it so that it does. Here is a sample way to word it (http://cogprints.soton.ac.uk/copyright.html):

> I hereby transfer to [publisher or journal] all rights to sell or lease the text (on-paper and online) of my paper [paper-title]. I retain only the right to self-archive it publicly online on my institution's website.

About 20 per cent of journals already formally support self-archiving of the refereed postprint: http://www.lboro.ac.uk/departments/ls/disresearch/romeo/Romeo %20Publishing%20Policies.htm. Most other publishers (perhaps another 70 per cent) will also accept this clause, but only if you explicitly propose it yourself (they will not formulate it on their own initiative).

If the Above is Successful, Self-archive the Refereed Postprint

Hence, for about 90 per cent of journals, once you have done the above, you can go ahead and self-archive your paper. Some journals (perhaps 10 per cent), however, will respond that they decline to publish your paper unless you sign their copyright transfer agreement verbatim. In such cases, sign their agreement and proceed to the next step.

If the Above is Unsuccessful, Archive the 'Corrigenda'

Your pre-refereeing preprint has already been publicly self-archived since prior to submission, and is not covered by the copyright agreement, which pertains to the revised final ('value-added') draft. Hence, all you need to do is to self-archive a further file, linked to the archived preprint, which simply lists the corrections that the reader may wish to make in order to conform the preprint to the refereed, accepted version.

Everyone chuckles at this point, but the reason it is so easy is precisely because this is the author give-away literature. No non-give-away author would ever dream of doing such a thing (that is, archiving the prepublication draft for free, along with the corrigenda). And copyright agreements (and copyright law) are designed and conceived to meet the much more representative interests of non-give-away authors and their much larger body of royalty/fee-based work. Hence, this simple and legal expedient for the special, tiny, anomalous, give-away literature has no constituency anywhere else.

Yet this simple, risible strategy is also feasible, and legal (Oppenheim, 2001) – and sufficient to free the entire current refereed corpus of all access/impact barriers immediately!

What You Can do Now to Free the Refereed Literature Online

Researchers: Self-archive all Present, Future (and Past) Papers

The freeing of their present and future refereed research from all access- and impact-barriers forever is now entirely in the hands of researchers. Posterity is looking over our shoulders, and will not judge us flatteringly if we continue to delay the optimal and inevitable needlessly, now that it is clearly within our reach. Physicists have already shown the way, but at their current self-archiving rate, even they will take another decade to free the entire Physics literature (http://www.ecs.soton.ac.uk/'harnad/Temp/self-archiving.htm Slide 25) – with the Cognitive Sciences (http://cogprints.soton.ac.uk) being slower still, and most of the remaining disciplines not even started.

This is why it is hoped that (with the help of the eprints.org institutional archive-creating software) distributed, institution-based self-archiving, as a powerful and natural complement to central, discipline-based self-archiving, will now broaden and accelerate the self-archiving initiative, putting us all over the top at last, with the entire distributed corpus integrated by the glue of interoperability (http://www.openarchives.org).

As to the past (retrospective) literature: the preprint+corrigenda strategy will not work there, but as the retrospective journal literature brings virtually no revenue, most publishers will agree to author self-archiving after a sufficient period (6 months to 2 years) has elapsed. Moreover, for the really old literature, it is not clear that online self-archiving was covered by the old copyright agreements at all. And if all else fails for the retrospective literature, a variant of the pre-print+corrigenda strategy will still work. Simply do a revised second edition!

Update the references, rearrange the text (and add more text and data if you wish). For the record, the enhanced draft can be accompanied by a 'de-corrigenda' file, stating which of the enhancements were not in the published version. (And of course the starting point for the revised, enhanced second edition, if you no longer have the digital text in your word processor, can be scanned and OCR'd from the journal; by thus distributing the task, authors can do for their own work for-free what JSTOR http://www.jstor.org/ is only able to do for the work of others for-fee.)

Universities: Install Eprint Archives, Mandate Them; Help in Author Start-up

Universities should create institutional Eprint Archives (for example, CalTech) for all their researchers. They should also mandate that they be filled. It is already becoming normal practice for faculty to keep and update their institutional CVs online on the web; it should be made standard practice by both research institutions and research funders as well as research analyzers and assessors that all CV entries for refereed journal articles are linked to their archived full-text version in the university's Eprint Archive. There is a model and free software for adopting such a standardized CV at http://paracite.eprints.org/cgi-bin/rae_front.cgi.

Universities need to mandate the self-archiving of all peer-reviewed research output in order to maximize its research impact for exactly the same reasons as they currently mandate publishing it (and indeed as the quite natural Post-Gutenberg extension of 'publish or perish': 'publish with maximized research impact, through self-archiving'). For a model university/departmental self-archiving policy statement, see: http://www.ecs.soton.ac.uk/'harnad/Temp/archpolnew.html.

Universities should be encouraged to provide a modest start-up budget to pay library experts or students to undertake self-archiving for researchers who cannot, or will not, undertake the task themselves. It would be a small amount of money very well-invested. It will only be needed to get the first wave over the top; from then on, the momentum from the enhanced access and impact will maintain itself, and self-archiving will become as standard a practice as email.

However, what needs energetic initial promotion and support is the first wave. If (i) the enhanced visibility, accessibility and usability (Lawrence 2001a, 2001b) of their own research output and its resulting enhanced impact on the research of others, plus (ii) the enhanced access of their own researchers to the research output of others are not incentive enough for universities to promote and support the self-archiving initiative energetically, they should also consider that it will be an investment in (iii) a potential solution to their serials budget crisis and hence the possible recovery of 2/3 of their annual serials (toll) budget. (Note that the success of the self-archiving initiative is predicated on the same Golden Rule on which both refereeing and research themselves are predicated: if we all do our own part for one another, we all benefit from it: 'Self-archive unto others as ye would have them self-archive unto you'; Harnad, 2003d).

Libraries: Maintain the University Eprint Archives; Help in Author Start-up

Libraries are the most natural allies of researchers in the self-archiving initiative to free the refereed journal literature. Not only are they groaning under the yoke of the growing serials budget crisis, but librarians are also eager to establish a new digital niche for themselves, once the journal corpus is online: maintaining the Eprint Archives, and facilitating the all-important start-up wave of self-archiving (by being ready to do 'proxy' self-archiving on behalf of authors who feel they cannot do it for themselves), will be a critical role for libraries to play.

(1)   Offer trained digital librarian help in showing faculty how to self-archive their papers in the university Eprint Archive (it is very easy).

(2)   Offer trained digital librarian help in doing 'proxy' self-archiving, on behalf of any authors who feel that they are personally unable (too busy or technically incapable) to self-archive for themselves. Authors need only supply their digital full-texts in word-processor form: the digital archiving assistants can do the rest (usually only a few dozen key/mouse-strokes per paper). The proxy self-archiving will only be needed to set the first wave of self-archiving reliably in motion. The rewards of self-archiving – in terms of visibility, accessibility and impact – will maintain the momentum once the archive has reached critical mass. And even students can do for faculty the few keystrokes needed for each new paper thereafter.

(3)   Digital librarians, collaborating with web system staff, should be involved in ensuring the proper maintenance, backup, mirroring, upgrading, and migration that ensures the perpetual preservation of the university Eprint Archives. Mirroring and migration should be handled in collaboration with counterparts at all other institutions supporting OAI-compliant Eprint Archives.

Libraries can also facilitate a stable transition through their collective, consortial power (SPARC: http://www.arl.org/sparc), providing leveraged support for publishers who are prepared to commit themselves to a schedule for downsizing to the essentials only (the peer review service, to the author/institution). Individually they can also be preparing in advance for the restructuring that will come if their toll savings grow; about 1/3 of their annual savings will need to be redirected to cover their university's own authors' peer-review charges per outgoing paper. The remaining 2/3 is theirs to use in any way they see fit!

Students: Stay the course! Surf! *The Future is Optimal, Inevitable and Yours!*

Students are well-advised to keep doing what they do naturally: favour material that is freely accessible on the web. This will not net them very much of the non-give-away literature, but it will put consumer pressure on the give-away research literature, especially as these students come of age, and become researchers in their turn.

Publishers: Support Self-archiving

(1) Publishers should explicitly allow and encourage authors to self-archive their *pre-refereeing preprints.*
    One potential model is *Nature*'s embargo statement:

> *Nature* does not wish to hinder communication between scientists ... Neither conferences nor preprint servers constitute prior publication.

Another potential model is Elsevier's preprint statement:

> As an [Elsevier] author you [have the] right to retain a preprint version of the article on a public electronic server such as the World Wide Web.

(2) Publishers should also explicitly allow and encourage authors to self-archive their *peer-reviewed postprints.*
    One potential model is the American Physical Society's copyright statement:

> The author(s) shall have the following rights ... The right to post and update the Article on e-print servers as long as files prepared and/or formatted by APS or its vendors are not used for that purpose. Any such posting made or updated after the acceptance of the Article for publication shall include a link to the online abstract in the APS journal or to the entry page of the journal.

Another potential model is the The Association of Learned and Professional Society Publishers' (ALPSP) model license:

> You ... retain the right to use your own article (provided you acknowledge the published original in standard bibliographic citation form) in the following ways as long as you do not sell it [or give it away] in ways that would conflict directly with our commercial business interests. You are free to use your article ... mounted on your own or your institution's website; [posted to free public servers of preprints and/or articles in your subject area] ...

See also: Rights MEtadata for Open archiving (ROMEO) index http://www.lboro.ac.uk/departments/ls/disresearch/romeo/ and FOS policy statements by learned societies and professional associations http://www.earlham.edu/'peters/fos/lists.htm#statements.

In this critical transitional time between the paper and online eras, refereed journal publishers are best-advised to concede graciously on self-archiving, as the American Physical Society (APS) and so many other publishers are doing, rather than attempting instead to use copyright or embargo policy to prevent or retard self-archiving. Such measures are not only (a) in clear and direct conflict with the interests of research and researchers, but (b) they are destined to fail, (c) they can already be legally circumvented, and (d) they only serve to make publishers look bad.

A much better policy is to accept and support what is undeniably the optimal outcome for research, researchers, and their institutions in the online era, namely, their research impact maximized through toll-free access for *all* its would-be users (and no longer just those whose institutions can afford the access tolls). This means beginning to look seriously at alternative business models, including the possibility of eventually separating the provision of the essential peer-review *service* to the author-institution (peer review implementation charges, per submitted paper) from the provision of all other add-on toll-based *products* (for example, on-paper version, online version, other added-values) to the reader-institution, which should be sold as options, rather than being used to try to keep holding the essentials (the refereed final draft) hostage to impact-blocking access-tolls. There will still be a permanent niche for journal publishers. What remains to be seen is whether that will entail downsizing to peer-review service-provision alone, or whether there will also continue to be a market for toll-based add-ons even after the peer-reviewed drafts are publicly available toll-free through the Eprint Archives.

Government/Society: Mandate Public Archiving of Public Research Worldwide

Government and society should support the self-archiving initiative, reminding themselves that most of this give-away research has been supported by public funds, with the support explicitly conditional on making the research findings public (http://www.sciencemag.org/cgi/content/full/281/5382/1459). In the Post-Gutenberg world, there is no longer any need for that public accessibility to be blocked by toll-barriers (Harnad *et al.*, 2003).

The beneficiaries will not just be research and researchers, but society itself, inasmuch as research is supported because of its potential benefits to society. Researchers in developing countries and at the less affluent universities and research institutions of developed countries will benefit even more from toll-free access to the research literature than will the better-off institutions, but it is instructive to remind ourselves that even the most affluent institutional libraries cannot afford most of the refereed journals! None have access to more than a small subset of the entire annual corpus (http://fisher.lib.virginia.edu/arl/index.html). So open access to it all will benefit all institutions (Odlyzko, 1999a, 1999b). On the other side of barrier-free access to the work of others, all researchers, even the most affluent, will benefit from the barrier-free impact of their own work on the work of others. Moreover, a toll-free, interoperable, digital research literature will not only radically enhance access, navigation (for example, citation-linking) and impact, hence research productivity and quality, but it will also spawn new ways of monitoring and measuring that impact, productivity and quality (for example, download impact, links, immediacy, comments, and the higher-order dynamics of a citation-linked corpus that can be analyzed from preprint to post-postprint, to yield an 'embryology of knowledge' (see Harnad and Carr, 2000; http://www.ecs. soton.ac.uk/'harnad/Temp/self-archiving.htm).

Prima-facie FaQs for Overcoming Zeno's Paralysis

Researchers and their university administrators and librarians have so far been held back from self-archiving by certain prima facie worries, all of which are easily shown to be groundless. These worries are rather like 'Zeno's Paradox': 'I cannot walk across this room, because before I can walk across it, I must first walk half-way across it, and that takes time; but before I can walk half-way across it, I must walk half-half-way across it, and that too takes time; and so on; so how can I ever even get started?' This condition might better be called 'Zeno's Paralysis' (http://www.ecs.soton.ac.uk/'harnad/Hypermail/Amsci/0819.html). Each of the worries can easily be shown to be groundless (and *has* been shown to be groundless, by myself and many others, many times). Yet the very same prima facie worries keep appearing elsewhere, like mushrooms, no matter how decisively they are uprooted in each instance. It will be a matter for future historians to explain the puzzle of why we were needlessly held back for so long from the optimal and inevitable even when it was well within reach, by these gratuitous worries (despite the 'Los Alamos Lemma', http://www.ecs.soton.ac.uk/'harnad/Hypermail/Amsci/0470.html, which is that whatever alleged obstacle was not sufficient to deter physicists from self-archiving 130,000 papers to date should not be holding back the rest of us either!).

Rebuttals to the most common of these prima facie worries about self-archiving are given below; in future they can be used as FAQs to reply by number. Most are brief and to the point, because there are no long, complex, hidden issues in any of these cases. Hence, it is best to get to the point in the simplest, most direct way possible. There is also a good deal of overlap and redundancy between them.

FAQ 1   Preservation

> I worry about self-archiving because archived eprints may not continue to exist or to be accessible in perpetuum online, the way they were on-paper.

This worry is misplaced. It is not really a worry about self-archiving at all, but about the *online medium* itself. As such, it needs to be directed toward the primary database in question, which is the toll-access refereed journal literature, currently in the hands of publishers and libraries, and most of it already in both paper and digital form. If you are worried about the preservation of the online version, it is to its publishers and subscribing/licensing librarians that your worry needs to be addressed. The preprints and postprints that are being self-archived by their authors in their institutional eprint archives today are intended to maximize impact by providing immediate open access; they are merely open-access *supplements* to that toll-based primary literature at this time, not *substitutes* for it.

To put even this misdirected worry into perspective, we must remember that print-on-paper is not permanent either. The only relevant parameter is the *probability* of future access. The on-paper probability, such as it is, is achieved by generating (a) multiple copies that are (b) geographically distributed (c) in a (relatively) robust medium and can be made (d) visible to the human eye.

All four of these properties can be achieved (and have been) on-line too, and the resulting preservation probability can be made as good as, or even better than, the current probability on-paper.

That should be the end of the story: for once this concern is no longer grounded in actual, objective probabilities, but only in prior habits and attendant intuitions, then we are talking about biases and superstitions and not about actual risks.

There are a few side issues. People worry about global power-failures, or global dictatorships. They should remind themselves that these are matters of probability too, and have their equivalents in paper.

People also, by analogy with current unreadable documents in obsolete word-processors or peripherals, worry about whether the digital code, even if preserved, will always be accessible and visible to the eye.

The answer is again in probability. The reason print-on-paper has been faithfully preserved across generations (when it has been) is that the literate world's collective interests were vested in ensuring that it should do so. This same continuity of collective interests will exist for the digital corpus too, for the same reasons, except that digital code will be much *easier* to keep migrating to every successive new technology than print on-paper to every successive building or regime ever was.

(And there is always the option for those who are still not confident enough in the technology, despite the odds, of printing out hard copies as back-up: Indeed, that is a good way to put the magnitude of one's preservation worries to the test: who will still feel the need to keep hard copies, and of how much of the corpus, once it's all online and accessible to everyone, everywhere, at all times?)

In short, setting up active preservation programs implemented by digital librarians is indeed important and necessary; but it would be completely irrational to interpret the need for robust preservation programs as a reason for any hesitation or delay whatsoever about proceeding with self-archiving right now – *a fortiori*, because, for the time being, self-archiving is merely a *supplement* to, not a *substitute* for, the existing modes of preservation, on paper and online. If and when the day should ever come when primary journal publishers decide to downsize and become peer-review service-providers only, cutting costs by offloading the access and archiving burden entirely onto the network of institutional archives, then that institutional network will be quite ready, willing and able to take over the distributed digital preservation burden for its collective research legacy. But that time is not now, hence this worry (about self-archiving now) is misplaced.

FAQ 2   Authentication

> I worry about self-archiving because you can never be sure whether you are reading the definitive version of an eprint online, the way you can be sure on-paper.

Again, the rational way to put this into context and proportion is to remind ourselves that the authenticity of an on-paper version is just a matter of probability too, and that the very same factors that maximize that probability on-paper can also maximize it online. Indeed, if we wish, we can make both the probability and the verifiability of authenticity online much higher than it currently is on-paper through techniques such as public hash/time-stamping and encryption.

Nor should the authentication issue be confused with the issue of Peer-Review (FAQ 7) or Journal Certification (FAQ 5) (separate questions), nor with the question of 'version control' (FAQ 23). There will be self-archived preprints, revised drafts, final accepted, published drafts (postprints), updated, corrected post-postprints, peer comments, author replies, revised second editions. In all of this, the refereed, accepted final draft is one crucial 'milestone', but not the only one, in the embryology of knowledge (and not even always the best one) (Harnad, 1990).

Finally, there are some of the 'authentication' worries arising from conflating self-archiving and self-publication (section 1.4). To say it in longhand: the main objective of the self-archiving initiative is the freeing of the *refereed* drafts from access/impact barriers. The refereed draft has already been 'authenticated' by the journal that peer-reviewed it. Do not confuse that authentication with some worry about whether this self-archived draft is indeed what the author purports it to be. The only thing the author is 'self-certifying' in this case is that this is indeed the *journal-certified* final draft. There is, of course, always a possibility that it is *not* the journal-certified final draft; but that was also true when the author sent you an on-paper reprint. The probabilities can, as usual, be tightened to make them as high as we feel comfortable with in either case (especially with *institution-CV-based* self-archiving, see section 7.2). In addition, as in the case of preservation (FAQ 1), self-archiving is at this stage merely a *supplement*, not a *substitute* for existing forms of authentication.

Again, there are no rational authentication concerns to deter us from self-archiving immediately.

FAQ 3   Corruption

> I worry about self-archiving because eprints can be altered or otherwise corrupted on-line in ways they could not be corrupted on-paper.

If the 'authentication' worry (FAQ 2) is the worry about 'self-corruption' by the author who has self-archived his own paper, this second 'corruption' worry is about 'allo-corruption' by parties other than the author.

Again, the answer is that simple and effective means are available to ensure that an online draft is uncorrupted with as high a probability as we feel we need. This too is therefore a non-problem. (Nor should it, again, be conflated with self-publication issues, which are irrelevant to the self-archiving of refereed, journal-published papers.) Whatever level of incorruptibility we feel we need, we can also have it for self-archived papers.

Consequently, corruptibility worries provide no rational basis for deterring us from self-archiving immediately.

FAQ 4   Navigation (info-glut)

> I worry about self-archiving because there is already too much to read, and it is already too hard to navigate it on paper; adding eprints will just make this situation even worse.

This worry deserves even less space than the others. It is incontestable that the information glut (http://www.sims.berkeley.edu/how-much-info/summary.html) is far more navigable and manageable online than on-paper.

The primary objective of self-archiving is to free the refereed journal literature from impact-blocking access-tolls online. That literature is *already* being published on-paper. (If you think it should not be, it is with the journals and their referees that you need to take issue, not with self-archiving or the online medium!) When it is all accessible toll-free online, there is no need for anyone to feel any more (or less) obliged to read the refereed literature than they did on-paper. Keeping it either offline or toll-based is certainly no cure for the information glut (if there is one); it merely makes the existing access-tolls the arbitrary arbiters of whether or not one reads something, rather than the reader's own rational judgement. (And unrefereed preprints can of course always be ignored altogether, if the reader wishes, online just as on-paper.) In short, there is no rational deterrent at all to immediate self-archiving from concerns about navigation or information glut.

FAQ 5   Certification

> I worry about self-archiving because papers are not certified online, the way they are in a journal on-paper.

This worry is again based on conflating publication and archiving (see section 1.4): the journal publisher (and referees) provide the certification; the archive merely provides access. The author, in self-archiving, 'self-certifies' his or her refereed, published draft as indeed being the self-same draft that the journal refereed and published (and certified). This being the case is, as usual, a matter of probability, whether online or on-paper. And that probability can be made as high as we feel we need.

Again, there is no rational deterrent to immediate self-archiving in the certification worry.

FAQ 6   Evaluation

> I worry about self-archiving because there is no evaluative process online as there is on-paper.

Again, a conflation of publishing and archiving (section 1.4): journal editors and their referees evaluate drafts and revisions, and if/when they are satisfied that their journal's quality standards have been met, they certify the final draft as having met them (peer review). The author self-archives the peer-reviewed postprints (and unrefereed preprints, and perhaps revised post-postprints), tagging them correspondingly. We can decide how high a probability we need that the peer-reviewed draft is indeed the peer-reviewed draft, but that is not the problem of evaluation, but just the question of Authentication (FAQ 2) again.

There is therefore no rational deterrent to immediate self-archiving anywhere in the evaluation worry.

FAQ 7   Peer review

> I worry about self-archiving because online eprints are not refereed, as they are on-paper: what will become of peer review?

Again, a conflation of publishing and archiving, as well as of preprints and postprints. The author self-archives both pre-refereeing preprints and refereed postprints (and so on), and each is clearly tagged as such. The peer review continues to be performed by the referees, as it always was. Peer-review is medium-independent.

Peer review is not without its flaws, but improving peer review first requires careful testing of alternative systems, and demonstrating empirically that these alternatives are at least as effective as classical peer review in maintaining the quality of the refereed literature (such as it is). No alternatives have yet been tested or demonstrated effective. Hence, current peer review reform or elimination proposals are merely speculative hypotheses at this time, and red herrings insofar as the freeing of the peer-reviewed literature is concerned. The self-archiving initiative is directed at freeing the current peer-reviewed literature, such as it is, from the impact/access barriers of access-tolls, now. It is not directed at freeing the literature from peer review, or at testing or implementing untested alternatives to peer review (Cf. http://library.caltech.edu/publications/ScholarsForum/ 042399sharnad.htm and http://www.cogsci.soton.ac.uk/'harnad/Ebiomed/com0509. htm#harn45).

The benefits of freeing the refereed literature now are a sure thing; the benefits (if any) from future alternatives to peer review (if any) are purely hypothetical, and certainly nothing to hold back from self-archiving. (See: 'Peer review reform hypothesis-testing' [http://www.ecs.soton.ac.uk/'harnad/Hypermail/Amsci/0479.html], 'A note of caution about "Reforming the system"' [http://www.ecs.soton.ac.uk/ 'harnad/Hypermail/Amsci/1169.html], 'Self-selected vetting vs. peer review: supplement or substitute?' [http://www.ecs.soton.ac.uk/'harnad/Hypermail/Amsci/ 2340.html].)

Again, there is no rational deterrent to immediate self-archiving in the peer-review worry.

FAQ 8   Paying the piper

> I worry about self-archiving because someone surely has to pay for all this: you can't get something for nothing!

There are many fallacies embedded in this worry, among them misunderstandings about the nature of global networked communication. Internet connectivity is now a standard part of the infrastructure of most of the world's universities and research institutions. If you are not equally worried about who pays for your emails, websites, and web-browsing, you should not be worrying about your self-archiving either. Moreover, paying access-tolls is not paying the pertinent piper here anyway!

The refereed research literature is minuscule compared with the rest of the traffic on the web (http://www.sims.berkeley.edu/research/projects/how-much-info/sum-mary.html). It is the flea on the tail of the dog. Worry about the storage and bandwidth for the growing daily creation and use of audio, video, and multimedia (most of it non-research use!) by researchers at universities and research institutions before even beginning to fret about the refereed flea. As usual, there is also some of the archiving/publishing conflation here (section 1.4), thinking that we must find some sort of counterpart for the printing/distribution costs, somewhere. But there isn't any. The cost per-paper of permanent online archiving is virtually zero, yet everyone, everywhere, has access to it all, forever. This is a Gutenberg expense that has simply vanished in the Post-Gutenberg Galaxy, leaving only the Cheshire Cat's grin.

There is indeed one essential publishing cost that still needs to be paid, but it has nothing to do with internet use: it is the cost of implementing peer review. That cost, however, is only 1/3 of the access-tolls currently being paid, and hence could easily be paid out of the annual toll savings (see section 3.2).

The last of the 'who-pays-the-piper' worries is, I think, a variant of the Capitalism (FAQ 14) worry. The best way to dispel it is to note that refereed publishing in the Post-Gutenberg world, once the literature has been made openly accessible through self-archiving, is likely (apart from whatever optional add-on products and services there may still be a market for) to downsize into a *service* (peer review), provided to the author-institution, instead of the toll-based *product* (the text) that was provided to the reader/institution in the Gutenberg era.

Nothing hinges on this, however, for as long as the world wants to keep paying for the toll-based product, even after the refereed literature has been self-archived, the piper will be fully paid, yet the literature will be free of all its access/impact barriers.

Hence, there is no rational deterrent to immediate self-archiving in the who-pays-the-piper worries.

FAQ 9   Downsizing

> I worry about self-archiving because it may force journal publishers to shrink to a non-sustainable size, and then where would we be?

No one can predict with certainty the evolutionary path that scientific/scholarly journal publishing will take once the refereed corpus is accessible online, toll-free, through self-archiving. The toll-based market for the on-paper version, for the publisher's online version or for other enhanced options may continue indefinitely, or it might shrink but re-stabilize at a lower level, or it might disappear altogether – and this could happen relatively slowly or relatively quickly.

It is not clear in advance which of the current established journal publishers will want to continue doing what, under what conditions. The bottom line is that the only remaining *essential* service will be peer review. If and when that is the only service for which there remains a market, many current journal publishers will be able and willing to downsize to that niche; those that are not able or willing will terminate journal operations, in which case their titles (that is, each journal's editor, editorial board, referees, and authorship) will simply migrate to new on-line-only open-access journal publishers who are ready to adapt to the new niche (for example, the Institute of Physics's *New Journal of Physics* and *BioMed Central*).

Once again, there is no rational deterrent to immediate self-archiving in worries about publisher downsizing.

FAQ 10   Copyright

> I worry about self-archiving because it is illegal, it violates copyright agreements, and can jeopardize career and livelihood.

Please see the sections on copyright (section 5) and on legal ways to self-archive despite restrictive copyright transfer agreements (section 6).

In brief, more and more journals already support self-archiving (http://www.ecs.soton.ac.uk/'harnad/Temp/rcoptable.gif) and among those who do not yet formally support it, many will agree to author self-archiving if the author asks; for those journals that still don't, self-archiving the preprint before submission and a 'corrigenda' file after acceptance is sufficient, and completely legal. What career and livelihood depend on is peer review and impact, and all self-archiving authors continue to enjoy both; neither one needs to be sacrificed for the other.

No rational deterrent to immediate self-archiving can be found in copyright worries.

FAQ 11   Plagiarism

> I worry about self-archiving because it is so much easier to steal someone else's text online, and publish it as one's own, than it is to do so on-paper.

This is again a matter of probability. Yes, 'it is much easier to steal someone else's text online, and publish it as one's own, than it is to do so on-paper', but it is also much easier to detect such thefts online; and it is possible to do both (steal and detect) on-paper too.

Depending on how important we find it to do so, we can make escape from detection so improbable online that it becomes harder to plagiarize on-line than on-paper. It is not clear, however, whether it is even all that important to do so. Worries about plagiarism are usual based on the archiving/publishing conflation (section 1.4): once one's findings have been refereed and published, it is hard for anyone else to derive any benefit from them at the expense of the author (the peer-reviewed version settles all subsequent authorship disputes).

Pre-refereeing preprints are another story; they are dealt with partly in the prior discussion of Authentication (FAQ 2) above, and partly under Priority (FAQ 12), below.

For refereed postprints, however, refraining from self-archiving them because of worries about plagiarism would be no more rational than refraining from publishing them on-paper in the first place, for the very same reason.

There is no rational deterrent to immediate self-archiving in plagiarism worries.

FAQ 12   Priority

> I worry about self-archiving because one cannot establish priority online as one can on-paper.

Establishing priority is again a matter of probability, but it can readily be made much more definitive and reliable (and earlier) online than on-paper if we wish;

see Authentication (FAQ 2). Crucially, for the all-important refereed postprints, priority has already been established by publishing them, and self-archiving is merely to maximize access and impact.

Again, this is no rational deterrent to immediate self-archiving in priority worries.

FAQ 13   Censorship

> I worry about self-archiving because censors could decide what can and cannot appear online.

This worry too is probably based in part on the usual archiving/publishing conflation (section 1.4) (casting the web and the archive in the role of a publisher who refuses to publish your work).

It is true that one's online literary goods are at the mercy of the archives and archivists. But one's analog on-paper literary goods were likewise at the mercy of the libraries. They could have chosen to 'censor' our work too.

Again, it is just a matter of deciding how tight we wish to make the probabilities in this medium. Mirroring, caching/harvesting and distributed coding already go some way toward taking the risk away from any potentially sinister local hands. And for refereed, published postprints, this argument (against enhancing their access) makes no sense at all.

No rational deterrent to immediate self-archiving can be found in worries about censorship.

FAQ 14   Capitalism

> I worry about self-archiving because access-tolls are hallmarks of capitalism, market economics, supply and demand, free enterprise. Give-aways smack either of socialism, or market interference, or non-sustainability.

This too is merely a superstition. There are plenty of perfectly capitalistic precedents for give-aways, *advertising* being the most prominent one. If the thought of advertisers curtailing the potential impact of their ads by charging potential customers for access to them makes no sense, then it makes just as little sense to curtail the potential impact of research findings by charging potential users for access to them.

Nor is there any market interference in self-archiving one's own refereed research: if institutions and individuals want to pay for access-tolls to the on-paper version, or the publisher's PDF, or further options, they can still do so; but there is no longer any need or justification for continuing to hold the essentials (the peer-reviewed draft) hostage to those toll-based options in the Post-Gutenberg era, any more than there was any need or justification for continuing to hold the essentials of long-distance communication hostage to postal transport costs in the era of telephony. (Rather than capitalism being under assault from self-archiving, trying to prevent researchers from benefiting from this new, more efficient and economical way of disseminating and maximizing the impact of their refereed research smacks of protectionism.)

Two variants on the capitalism-worry arise from skepticism about the eventual transition from providing a toll-based product to the reader-institution to providing a peer-review service to the author-institution. Note that, strictly speaking, it is not even necessary to answer these worries, as this eventual transition is hypothetical, whereas freeing the refereed literature now through self-archiving is not; but here are replies anyway.

Question 1: Won't paying directly for the peer-review service lead to inflated peer-review costs by the most prestigious journals?

Question 2: Won't peer-review revenues lower standards, so that lower-quality work is accepted in order to get more peer-review revenue?

The answer to both is similar: referees referee for free, and journal quality and prestige (and impact) depend on *rejection* rates. Trying to inflate revenue by lowering acceptance thresholds simply lowers quality, thereby favoring the competition, with its higher standards. This is a built-in counter-weight. Likewise, for raising peer-review rates: as referees referee for free, there is no reason one journal should charge more than another, and if they do, they risk driving not only the authors but also the unpaid referees to the competition. The competitive commodity in this anomalous give-away domain is quality, and nothing else.

A proposal has occasionally been voiced to preserve access-toll-barriers by buying authors off from self-archiving, by offering to share the revenue with them (royalty payments). But the trade-off between imprint-income and impact-income (for example, http://www.hero.ac.uk/rae/) is so disproportionate for this anomalous domain that there is not faintly enough money available to make (refereed-research) authors prefer sacrificing their potential impact in exchange.

Therefore, there is no rational deterrent to immediate self-archiving in worries about capitalism.

FAQ 15   Readability

> I worry about self-archiving because it is inconvenient to read texts on screen, and hard on the eyes. It is also not suitable for bed, beach or bathroom reading.

At the moment it is undeniable that for extended, discursive reading, on-paper is still preferable to online. This will no doubt change, but even now it is no reason whatsoever for not self-archiving. First, a large proportion of the scientific and scholarly use of the refereed research literature consists of browsing and searching, not linear reading, and for this, online navigation is already incomparably superior. Second, there is still that vast potential readership to consider, whose access to your research in *any* form is currently blocked by unaffordable access tolls (Odlyzko, 1999a, 1999b; http://www.arl.org/stats/index.html); for that entire disenfranchised population, it is either online or not at all. Finally, even for linear reading, the archived version can always be printed off.

Again, there is no rational deterrent to immediate self-archiving in worries about readability.

FAQ 16   Graphics

I worry about self-archiving because online graphics have coarser resolution than on-paper and require too much storage capacity and transmission time.

Graphics too will no doubt improve. With a few exceptions, such as fine arts and histology, digital graphics are already good enough. Users can always decide whether or not they feel they need to access the deluxe hard copy; there is no need to make a pre-emptive decision on their behalf, as the on-line version is in any case a *supplement*, not a *substitute*, for the time being.

Graphics are quite a natural test-bed to see whether there is still any market left for any toll-based add-ons. In many cases, web illustrations are already considerably better than paper, with the potential for higher resolution and greater dynamic range, especially as links. This is particularly true for illustrations in fields where the data are collected digitally in the first place, such as Astronomy.

No rational deterrent to immediate self-archiving can be found, therefore, in worries about graphics.

FAQ 17   Publishers' future

I worry about self-archiving because of what it might do to journal publishers' future.

See the replies about Paying the Piper (FAQ 8), Downsizing (FAQ 9), and Capitalism (FAQ 14). Those journal publishers who are willing and able to scale down to their new Post-Gutenberg niche if and when it should ever become necessary can do so. New online-only open-access journal publishers (for example, the Institute of Physics's *New Journal of Physics* and *BioMed Central*) are ready to take over the titles in the cases where they are not. The remaining peer-review service costs per submitted paper can be paid for by the author-institution out of 10–30 per cent of its annual 100 per cent access toll-savings. In addition, refereed journal publication is only a small portion of publication, most of the rest of which, being non-give-away, will proceed online much the way it does on-paper.

No rational deterrent to immediate self-archiving exists in worries about publishers' future.

FAQ 18   Libraries'/Librarians' future

I worry about self-archiving because of what it might do to libraries' and librarians' future.

The refereed serials literature is all going online anyway, irrespective of the speed or success of the self-archiving initiative. If this requires restructuring of some librarian skills and functions, this will take place in any case. Some have thought that managing digital serials collections will fill the gap, but it is not clear how much management those will need, apart from paying the annual access toll-bills! Author/Institution Eprint Archives, on the other hand, will call for more digital librarian skills, in everything from helping researchers to do the self-archiving, to maintaining the institution's Eprint Archive and seeing to its continued interoperability with the rest of the world's Eprint Archives, its upgrading, and its preservation.

Moreover, in implementing and maintaining the institutional Eprint Archives, Libraries will be investing in the solution of their serials crisis. Of the 100 per cent annual access-toll budget that this can potentially save, after 10–30 per cent of it has been redirected to cover author-institution peer-review costs, the remaining 70–90 per cent can be used to fund other librarians' activities, including the purchase of non-give-away materials such as books (whether on-paper or online).

There is no rational deterrent to immediate self-archiving in worries about libraries'/librarians' future.

FAQ 19   Learned Societies' future

I worry about self-archiving because of what it might do to Learned Societies' future.

Learned Societies are potential allies in, and beneficiaries of, the self-archiving initiative. First, they are us. Whatever is good for research, and for research impact, is therefore also good for Learned Societies.

Many of them, however, are also journal publishers, and hence may one day face downsizing pains. Unlike commercial publishers, however, their first and last allegiance will of course be to research and researchers, that is, to us. We will hear rationalizations about needing the access-toll revenues to fund 'good works' such as meetings, scholarships and lobbying. But it will quickly become evident that, on the one hand, some of these good works are not essentials either, and certainly nothing that we would want to sacrifice research impact for; and the subset of these good works that really is essential (for example, meetings) will prove to be able to fund itself in other ways, rather than needing to be subsidized at the expense of research impact. (Imagine explicitly asking the society membership, once the causal connection between access and impact (Lawrence, 2001a, b) becomes common knowledge: 'Are you willing to continue subsidizing your society's good works with your own lost research impact, by foregoing open-access and letting toll-access continue to decide who can and cannot use your [give-away] research?')

Learned Societies (and perhaps also University Presses) are also natural candidates for taking over the serials titles of commercial journal publishers who prefer to discontinue journal operations rather than scale down to just becoming peer-review service providers.

There is no rational deterrent to immediate self-archiving in worries about Learned Societies' future.

FAQ 20   University conspiracy

I worry about self-archiving because I worry that universities may have other plans for their researchers' writings, such as Eprint Archive Access-Tolls.

This worry seems to be based on some (one hopes) over-suspicious views about university administrators and their motives.

We should not forget that the give-away refereed literature is esoteric, with virtually no 'market' per paper. So whereas there might be a basis for suspicion about what our hard-pressed universities might like to do if they could get their hands on our exoteric, *non*-give-away work (royalty-bearing books and textbooks), there is not much they could do to squeeze revenue out of our no-market, give-away refereed research reports even if they wanted to. On the contrary, our universities, like ourselves, co-benefit far more from the potential impact-income of our research output – maximized by removing all access-barriers – than from any potential imprint-income that could be squeezed out of it by, in effect, co-opting the 'P' from the publishers' S/L/P (Subscription/License/Pay-Per-View) access-tolls and using it to charge institutional archive access-tolls.

Moreover, our universities' potential access-toll savings, and relief from their serials crises, are completely dependent on freeing access to our research. Any sign of university-levied archive-access tolls would simply serve to keep the current access tolls in place (simply changing the hand on the udder of the toll-based cash-cow).

No rational deterrent to immediate self-archiving exists, therefore, in worries about University conspiracy.

FAQ 21   Serendipity

> I worry about self-archiving because of those lucky happenstances that happen only when browsing index cards, library shelves, and journal contents.

This worry, despite its charm, does not deserve much space: With time, it will become evident that on-screen digital searching and browsing can be every bit as serendipitous as on-paper analog searching and browsing; chance adjacency effects are every bit as potent either way. The searching and browsing will simply be less exhausting to the limbs and fingers.

Hence, no rational deterrent to immediate self-archiving exists in worries about loss of serendipity.

FAQ 22   Tenure/Promotion

> I worry about self-archiving because it does not count as refereed publication, and might even interfere with the chances for refereed publication.

Yet another instance of the archiving/publishing conflation (see section 1.4). The self-archiving initiative is aimed at freeing peer-reviewed publications from access toll-based access/impact barriers (not from peer review). Unrefereed preprints do not count as publications online any more than they do on-paper (Garfield, 1999).

The other half of this worry is probably a variant of the Copyright (FAQ 10) concerns (q.v.), as well as concerns about Embargo policies (Harnad, 2000a, 2000b), both of which are groundless.

Once again, there is no rational deterrent to immediate self-archiving in worries about tenure/promotion.

FAQ 23   Version control

> I worry about self-archiving because there may be many versions and there is no way to be sure which is which, and whether it is the right one.

There will be self-archived preprints, revised drafts, final accepted, published drafts (postprints), updated, corrected post-postprints, peer comments, author replies, revised second editions. OAI-compliant Eprint Archives will tag each version with a unique identifier. All versions will be retrieved by a cross-archive OAI search, and the 'hits' can then be identified and compared by the user to select the most recent, official or definitive draft, exactly as if they had all been found in the same index catalog.

FAQ 24   Napster

> I worry about self-archiving because it seems to be stealing, like Napster or Gnutella.

Author-end give-aways of their *own* digital products via self-archiving is the antithesis of consumer-end rip-offs of *others'* non-give-away digital products via Napster (www.napster.com) or Gnutella (gnutella.wego.com): http://www.ecs. soton.ac.uk/'harnad/Temp/newscientist.htm

It is very important to distinguish clearly and distance the two, because any inadvertent or willful conflation of the self-archiving initiative with Napster can only retard the progress of the self-archiving initiative toward the optimal and inevitable.

('Information is free' is nonsense. There is and always has been both *give-away* and *non-give-away* information. Steal the latter and you simply kill the incentive to provide it in the first place.)

FAQ 25   Mark-Up

> I worry about self-archiving because it would jeopardize proper mark-up.

Mark-up (the tagging of all functional parts of a document, such as titles, headings, sections, figures, tables, paragraphs, and any other potentially identifiable and manipulable sub-parts) is becoming increasingly important in digital documents. The most general mark-up 'language' is called SGML, and the subset of SGML that has been provisionally adopted for digital documents on the web is called XML. Most authors today use either Word, PDF, HTML, or TEX to create and render their documents. The documents thus produced do not have mark-up that is rich enough or flexible enough to allow important functions such as reference linking, flexible re-formatting, and reliable, intact migration to future formats for permanent preservation. The richer mark-up is currently provided by publishers and it must be done by hand and is therefore costly.

Hence, an Eprint archive of documents self-archived without XML mark-up is only a short-term archive. A long-term archive requires the rich mark-up provided by publishers. However, if present-day user preference for the free open-access documents prevents publishers from being able to recover their mark-up costs, will both the benefits of mark-up and the long-term functionality of the archived documents be lost?

The solution to this problem is the following.

(1) For now, self-archiving is not a *substitute* for what publishers do and provide, but a *supplement* to it, providing a parallel open-access version of the peer-reviewed text for any user whose institution cannot afford access to the publisher's toll-access version. The publisher's marked-up version will have more functionality, for those who can afford to pay for it, but the peer-reviewed full-text will at last be accessible to everyone, already maximizing its research impact today. This is the immediate short-term goal of self-archiving.

(2) Once the short-term goal of open access is attained, several alternative futures become possible, and no one yet knows which of them will actually take place. The two main alternatives are as follows.

     (a) Nothing else changes. The self-archived version is accessible to all would-be users for free, and the publisher's marked-up version continues to be accessible only to those who can afford to pay. The publisher's revenues continue to pay for the mark-up, and its benefits are reserved for those who can afford to pay for them, as before, but the full-text without the mark-up (in WORD, HTML, PDF, or TEX) is available to everyone else.

          It should be clear that if (a) is the eventual outcome, then that is no reason to hold us back from immediate self-archiving, as we have everything to gain from it (maximized access), and nothing to lose. The status quo continues, in parallel, along with the immediate effects of open access.

          There is another possibility, however, and perhaps a more likely one:

     (b) User preference for the open-access version reduces demand for the publisher's marked-up version to such an extent that its costs can no longer be covered from access tolls as they had been in the past. How is mark-up to be provided and paid for now?

          If (b) is the eventual outcome, then because open-access will prevail, the cost-recovery can no longer be on the reader/institution end, in the form of access tolls. However, the reader/institutions also happen to be the author/institutions. Hence they are in a position to redirect a portion of their annual windfall toll savings to cover the remaining essential costs per *outgoing* paper rather than per *incoming* paper, as now. The collective cost currently paid by all subscribing institutions combined averages $1,500 *per incoming paper*. If all subscribing institutions instead get back their portions of these costs, then the $500 per paper cost of peer review can easily be paid out of these annual windfall savings, with plenty of savings to spare. The cost per-paper of physical archiving is negligible: how much would mark-up cost, per paper, over and above peer review?

No one knows exactly, yet, but it is likely that a good deal of the task of mark-up can be offloaded onto the authors, just as digital text preparation has been, with the development of user-friendly XML mark-up tools. WORD will soon generate automatic XML versions, just as it now generates automatic HTML (and they will no doubt prove equally inadequate, needing to be supplemented by some Windows-based hand-manipulation by the author). But overall, it is likely that the pressure of necessity will inspire increasingly effective and easy-to-use author-based mark-up capability.

The pressure of necessity that drives these adaptive changes, however, will come from the existence of the free open-access version. So mark-up concerns provide no reason to hold us back from immediate self-archiving.

FAQ 26   Classification

I worry about self-archiving because we would first need a subject classification system.

There are (at least) two ways to think of University Digital Archives, both of them important and valid, but definitely not the same.

(a)   The *University Digital Archive* as the university digital library – or, more specifically, the university digital library for all of the university's own scholarly, scientific and pedagogic output. (This includes journal articles, books, teaching materials, and any other digital content the university produces and wishes to include in its digital output.) See SPARC's position paper on institutional repositories and MIT's DSpace.

There is no question that a rigorous system of classification and tagging – to make such a total university digital output navigable and integrable and interoperable with corresponding digital output from other universities in similar University Digital Archives – would be extremely important to have, indeed a prerequisite for the usefulness and usability of such a university digital output library.

(b)   The *University Eprint Archive* as a means of providing open access to all of the university's peer-reviewed research output (before and after peer review). Almost without exception, this is the work that also appears in the peer-reviewed journals sooner or later (indeed, that is how it gets peer-reviewed).

It should be clear that (b) is a very special subset of (a). But it should be equally clear that that special subset does not have any particular or pressing classification problem! These are not books. They are journal articles. Our journal articles are not indexed in our university library card catalogs (only the journals in which they appear are). When we want to search the journal literature, we do not look to any university classification system: we go to indexing services such as INSPEC, MEDLINE, ISI, and so on. (Those do have their own classification systems, but it is unlikely that any of those classifications could out-perform Google-style Boolean search on an inverted full-text index, especially if aided by citation-frequency-based, hit-based, recency-based, or relevance-based ranking of search output, as done, for example, by citebase: http://citebase.eprints.org/help/index.php.)

It is important to make it clear that the peer-reviewed research corpus – and those University Eprint Archives for which that particular corpus is the main target literature at this time – do not have a classification problem, and need not and should not wait for any solution to any classification problem before getting on with the infinitely more pressing task of getting themselves filled with their university's research output – so that they can at last start plugging the chronic leak in its potential impact!

Agenda (a) (the university digital output library) is very important and worth pursuing; it is also an extremely valuable collaborator to agenda (b) (open access to peer-reviewed research through institutional self-archiving) – but only if the two agendas facilitate rather than restrain one another (as any implication that agenda (b) has classification problems to solve would most definitely do).

FAQ 27   Secrecy

> I worry about self-archiving because it would compromise the secrecy of patents and sponsored research.

Self-archiving is only for research results one wishes to make public, just as publishing is. Whatever one does not wish to publish, one does not self-archive. (Eprint Archives also have the option of depositing a text for internal use only, not accessible to the public, if/when this is judged useful.)

FAQ 28   Affordability

> I worry about self-archiving because it will interfere with making toll-access more affordable.

The immediate purpose of self-archiving is to maximize research impact, not to make toll-access more affordable. Research impact has been lost (by research and researchers) since the beginning of refereed research publication because of the high costs of providing paper access. The online medium now makes it possible to stop losing this impact. Of course, universally affordable toll-access would have the same effect (if it were truly universal – that is, the universities of all potential users of all refereed research could afford to access it all). It would be splendid if journal publishers could provide universally affordable toll-access, and they are certainly encouraged to work toward doing so. But in the meantime, it is quite understandable that today's researchers prefer not to wait (for when and if universally affordable toll-access arrives). They will self-archive to maximize their research impact now (while they are still alive and *compos mentis*).

Some may think the competition to the toll-access version from the open-access version will keep toll-access less affordable; some may think it will have the opposite effect, encouraging cost-cutting and downsizing to the essentials, making it more affordable. If the price of the value-added toll-access version becomes affordable enough, and the demand for its added-value is sufficient to sustain the market, then it is demand for the open-access version that will shrink, and along with it the incentive to self-archive, for the universal affordability will make any further impact loss negligible.

That is not where we are right now, however, and researchers would be rather foolish to wait patiently to see how things may or may not eventually turn out if they were to continue to renounce their potential daily impact even today, when it is no longer necessary.

FAQ 29   (your prima-FaQ here . . .)

Appendix: Some Relevant Chronology and URLs

(see also Peter Suber's fuller timeline at the Free Online Scholarship site: http://www.earlham.edu/'peters/fos/timeline.htm)

Psycoloquy (Refereed On-Line-Only Journal) (1989)
http://www.cogsci.soton.ac.uk/psycoloquy

'Scholarly Skywriting' (1990)
http://cogsci.soton.ac.uk/'harnad/Papers/Harnad/harnad90.skywriting.html

Physics Archive (1991)
http://arxiv.org

'Post-Gutenberg Galaxy' (1991)
http://www.cogsci.soton.ac.uk/'harnad/Papers/Harnad/harnad91.postgutenberg.html

'Interactive Publication' (1992)
http://www.cogsci.soton.ac.uk/'harnad/Papers/Harnad/harnad92.interactivpub.html

Self-Archiving ('Subversive') Proposal (1994)
http://www.arl.org/scomm/subversive/toc.html

'Tragic Loss' (Odlyzko) (1995)
http://www.research.att.com/'amo/doc/tragic.loss.txt

'Last Writes' (Hibbitts) (1996)
http://www.law.pitt.edu/hibbitts/lastrev.htm

NCSTRL: Networked Computer Science Technical Reference Library (1996)
http://cs-tr.cs.cornell.edu

University Provosts' Initiative (1997)
http://library.caltech.edu/publications/ScholarsForum/

CogPrints: Cognitive Sciences Archive (1997)
http://cogprints.soton.ac.uk

Journal of High Energy Physics (Refereed On-Line-Only Journal) (1998)
http://jhep.cern.ch/

Science Policy Forum (1998)
http://www.sciencemag.org/cgi/content/full/281/5382/1459

American Scientist Forum (1998)
http://amsci-forum.amsci.org/archives/september98-forum.html
http://www.cogsci.soton.ac.uk/'harnad/Hypermail/Amsci/subject.html

*OpCit:*Open Citation Linking Project (1999)
http://opcit.eprints.org

E-biomed: Varmus (NIH) Proposal (1999)
http://www.nih.gov/about/director/pubmedcentral/pubmedcentral.htm

Open Archives Initiative (1999)
http://www.openarchives.org

Cross-Archive Searching Service (2000)
http://arc.cs.odu.edu

Eprints: Free OAI-compliant Eprint-Archive-creating software (2001)
http://www.eprints.org

FOS: Free Online Scholarship Movement (2001)
http://www.earlham.edu/'peters/fos/timeline.htm

BOAI: Budapest Open Access Initiative (2002)
http://www.soros.org/openaccess

Citebase: Scientometric Search Engine:
http://citebase.eprints.org/

UK RAE Reform Proposal
http://www.ariadne.ac.uk/issue35/harnad/

Harnad Home Pages
http://www.ecs.soton.ac.uk/'harnad/
http://www.princeton.edu/'harnad/

References and Further Reading

Carr, L., Hitchcock, S., Hall, W. and Harnad, S. (2000) 'A usage based analysis of CoRR' [A commentary on 'CoRR: a Computing Research Repository' by Joseph Y. Halpern], *ACM SIGDOC Journal of Computer Documentation.* May 2000. http://www.cogsci. soton.ac.uk/˜harnad/Papers/Harnad/harnad00.halpern.htm.

Duranceau, E. and Harnad, S. (1999), 'Electronic Journal Forum: Resetting Our Intuition Pumps for the Online-Only Era: A Conversation With Stevan Harnad', *Serials Review*, 25(1), 109–115 http://www.cogsci.soton.ac.uk/˜harnad/Papers/Harnad/harnad99.ejforum. html.

Garfield, E. (1955), 'Citation Indexes for Science: A New Dimension in Documentation through Association of Ideas', *Science*, 122, 108–111 http://www.garfield.library. upenn.edu/papers/science_v122(3159)p108y1955.html; http://www.garfield.library.upenn. edu/papers/cseimpactfactor05092000.html.

Garfield, E. (1999), 'Commentary: Acknowledged Web Posting Is Not Prior Publication', *The Scientist*, 13(12). http://www.the-scientist.com/yr1999/June/comm_990607.html.

Harnad, S. (1990), 'Scholarly Skywriting and the Prepublication Continuum of Scientific Inquiry', *Psychological Science*, 1, 342–343 (reprinted in *Current Contents*, 45, 9–13, 11 November 1991) http://cogsci.soton.ac.uk/˜harnad/Papers/Harnad/harnad90.skywriting. html.

Harnad, S. (1991), 'Post-Gutenberg Galaxy: The Fourth Revolution in the Means of Production of Knowledge', *Public-Access Computer Systems Review*, 2(1), 39–53 http:// cogsci.soton.ac.uk/harnad/Papers/Harnad/harnad91.postgutenberg.html.

Harnad, S. (1992), 'Interactive Publication: Extending American Physical Society's Discipline-Specific Model for Electronic Publishing', *Serials Review*, Special Issue on Economics Models for Electronic Publishing, pp. 58–61. http://cogsci.soton.ac.uk/harnad/ Papers/Harnad/harnad92.interactivpub.html.

Harnad, S. (1994), 'A Subversive Proposal', in: A. Okerson and J. O'Donnell (eds) *Scholarly Journals at the Crossroads: A Subversive Proposal for Electronic Publishing*, (Washington, DC: Association of Research Libraries), June 1995. http://www.arl.org/scomm/ subversive/toc.html.

Harnad, S. (1995a), 'The PostGutenberg Galaxy: How to Get There From Here', *Information Society*, 11(4), 285–292. Also appeared in: *Times Higher Education Supplement*. Multimedia, p. vi, 12 May 1995. http://cogsci.soton.ac.uk/˜harnad/THES/thes.html.

Harnad, S. (1995b), 'Sorting the Esoterica from the Exoterica: There's Plenty of Room in Cyberspace: Response to Fuller', *Information Society*, 11(4), 305–324. Also appeared in: *Times Higher Education Supplement*. Multimedia. p. vi, 9 June 1995. http://cogsci.soton. ac.uk/˜harnad/THES/harful1.html.

Harnad, S. (1995c), 'Interactive Cognition: Exploring the Potential of Electronic Quote/ Commenting', in: B. Gorayska and J.L. Mey (eds) *Cognitive Technology: In Search of a Humane Interface*, (Elsevier) pp. 397–414. http://cogsci.soton.ac.uk/harnad/Papers/Harnad/harnad95.interactive.cognition.html.

Harnad, S. (1995d), 'Electronic Scholarly Publication: Quo Vadis?', *Serials Review*, 21(1), 70–72 (Reprinted in *Managing Information*, 2(3), 1995). http://cogsci.soton.ac.uk/harnad/ Papers/Harnad/harnad95.quo.vadis.html.

Harnad, S. (1996), 'Implementing Peer Review on the Net: Scientific Quality Control in Scholarly Electronic Journals', in: R. Peek, and G. Newby, (eds) *Scholarly Publishing: The Electronic Frontier* (Cambridge MA: MIT Press) pp. 103–108. http://cogsci.soton. ac.uk/˜harnad/Papers/Harnad/harnad96.peer.review.html.

Harnad, S. (1997a), 'How to Fast-Forward Serials to the Inevitable and the Optimal for

Scholars and Scientists', *Serials Librarian*, 30, 73–81. http://www.cogsci.soton.ac.uk/
'harnad/Papers/Harnad/harnad97.learned.serials.html (Reprinted in C. Christiansen and C.
Leatham (eds) *Pioneering New Serials Frontiers: From Petroglyphs to CyberSerials*
(1997), (New York: Haworth Press), and in French translation as *Comment Accelerer
l'Ineluctable Evolution des Revues Erudites* vers la Solution Optimale pour les Chercheurs et la Recherche http://www.enssib.fr/eco-doc/harnadinteg.html.

Harnad, S (1997b) 'The Paper House of Cards (And Why It is Taking So Long to Collapse)',
Ariadne, 8, 6–7. Longer version http://cogsci.soton.ac.uk/harnad/Papers/Harnad/harnad97.
paper.house.ariadne.html.

Harnad, S. (1997c), 'Learned Inquiry and the Net: The Role of Peer Review, Peer Commentary and Copyright', *Learned Publishing*, 11(4), 283–292. Short version appeared in
1997 in *Antiquity* 71, 1042–1048. Excerpts also appeared in the *University of Toronto
Bulletin*, 51(6), p. 12. http://citd.scar.utoronto.ca/EPub/talks/Harnad_Snider.html; http://
www.cogsci.soton.ac.uk/'harnad/Papers/Harnad/harnad98.toronto.learnedpub.html.

Harnad, S. (1998a), 'For Whom the Gate Tolls? Free the Online-Only Refereed Literature',
American Scientist Forum, http://amsci-forum.amsci.org/archives/september98-forum.html
http://www.cogsci.soton.ac.uk/'harnad/amlet.html.

Harnad, S. (1998b), 'On-Line Journals and Financial Fire-Walls', *Nature*, 395(6698),
127–128 http://www.cogsci.soton.ac.uk/'harnad/nature.html.

Harnad, S. (1998/2000) 'The invisible hand of peer review', *Nature* [online] (5 November
1998) http://helix.nature.com/webmatters/invisible/invisible.html. Longer version in *Exploit
Interactive* 5 (2000). http://www.exploit-lib.org/issue5/peer-review/; http://www.cogsci.
soton.ac.uk/'harnad/nature2.html.

Harnad, S. (1999a), 'The Future of Scholarly Skywriting', in: A. Scammell, (ed.) I in the
Sky: Visions of the information future, *Aslib*, November 1999. http://www.cogsci.
soton.ac.uk/'harnad/Papers/Harnad/harnad99.aslib.html.

Harnad, S. (1999b), 'Free at Last: The Future of Peer-Reviewed Journals', *D-Lib Magazine*,
5(12), December 1999. http://www.dlib.org/dlib/december99/12harnad.html.

Harnad, S. (1999c), 'Advancing Science By Self-Archiving Refereed Research', *Science
dEbates* [online], 31 July 1999. http://www.sciencemag.org/cgi/eletters/285/5425/197#
EL12.

Harnad, S. (2000a), 'E-Knowledge: Freeing the Refereed Journal Corpus Online', *Computer
Law & Security Report*, 16(2), 78–87. [Rebuttal to Bloom Editorial in *Science* and
Relman Editorial in *New England Journal of Medicine*.] http://www.cogsci.soton.ac.uk/
'harnad/Papers/Harnad/harnad00.scinejm.htm.

Harnad, S. (2000b), 'Ingelfinger Over-Ruled: The Role of the Web in the Future of Refereed
Medical Journal Publishing, *The Lancet Perspectives*, 256 (December Supplement), s16.
http://www.cogsci.soton.ac.uk/'harnad/Papers/Harnad/harnad00.lancet.htm.

Harnad, S. (2001a), 'AAAS's Response: Too Little, Too Late', *Science dEbates* [online], 2
April 2001. http://www.sciencemag.org/cgi/eletters/291/5512/2318b. Fuller version: http://
www.cogsci.soton.ac.uk/'harnad/Tp/science2.htm.

Harnad, S. (2001b), 'The Self-Archiving Initiative', *Nature*, 410, 1024–1025. http://www.
cogsci.soton.ac.uk/'harnad/Tp/nature4.htm. *Nature WebDebates* version: http://www.nature.
com/nature/debates/e-access/Articles/harnad.html. Fuller version: http://www.cogsci.soton.
ac.uk/'harnad/Tp/selfarch.htm.

Harnad, S. (2001c), 'The Self-Archiving Alternative', *Nature WebDebates*. http://www.nature.
com/nature/debates/e-access/index.html; http://www.cogsci.soton.ac.uk/'harnad/Tp/nature3.
htm.

Harnad, S. (2001d), 'The (Refereed) Literature-Liberation Movement', *New Scientist*. http://
www.cogsci.soton.ac.uk/'harnad/Temp/newsci1.htm. Fuller version: http://www.cogsci.
soton.ac.uk/'harnad/Temp/newscientist.htm.

Harnad, S. (2001e), 'Research Access, Impact and Assessment', *Times Higher Education Supplement*. http://www.cogsci.soton.ac.uk/'harnad/Tp/thes1.html.

Harnad, S. (2003a), 'Electronic Preprints and Postprints', *Encyclopedia of Library and Information Science*, (Marcel Dekker). http://www.ecs.soton.ac.uk/'harnad/Temp/eprints.htm.

Harnad, S. (2003b), 'Online Archives for Peer-Reviewed Journal Publications', in: J. Feather and P. Sturges (eds), *International Encyclopedia of Library and Information Science*. (Routledge). http://www.ecs.soton.ac.uk/'harnad/Temp/archives.htm.

Harnad, S. (2003c), 'Back to the Oral Tradition Through Skywriting at the Speed of Thought', *Interdisciplines*. http://www.interdisciplines.org/defispublicationweb/papers/6.

Harnad, S. (2003d), 'Self-Archive Unto Others as Ye Would Have Them Self-Archive Unto You', *The Australian Higher Education Supplement*. http://www.ecs.soton.ac.uk/'harnad/Temp/unto-others.html.

Harnad, S. and Carr, L. (2000), 'Integrating, Navigating and Analyzing Eprint Archives Through Open Citation Linking (the OpCit Project)', *Current Science* 79(5), 629–638. http://www.cogsci.soton.ac.uk/'harnad/Papers/Harnad/harnad00.citation.htm. http://www.iisc.ernet.in/'currsci/sep102000/629.pdf.

Harnad, S. and Hemus, M. (1997), 'All or None: There Are No Stable Hybrid or Half-Way Solutions for Launching the Learned Periodical Literature in the PostGutenberg Galaxy', in: I. Butterworth, (ed.) *The Impact of Electronic Publishing on the Academic Community* (London: Portland Press). http://cogsci.soton.ac.uk/'harnad/Papers/Harnad/harnad97.hybrid.pub.html.

Harnad, S., Varian, H. and Parks, R. (2000), 'Academic publishing in the online era: What Will Be For-Fee And What Will Be For-Free?', *Culture Machine*, 2 (online journal) http://www.cogsci.soton.ac.uk/'harnad/Temp/Varian/new1.htm. http://culturemachine.tees.ac.uk/frm_f1.htm.

Harnad, S., Carr, L., Brody, T. and Oppenheim, C. (2003), 'Mandated online RAE CVs Linked to University Eprint Archives: Improving the UK Research Assessment Exercise whilst making it cheaper and easier', *Ariadne*, http://www.ecs.soton.ac.uk/'harnad/Temp/Ariadne-RAE.html.

Harnad, S., Carr, L. and Brody, T. (2001), 'How and Why To Free All Refereed Research', from *access- and impact-barriers online, now*. http://www.cogsci.soton.ac.uk/'harnad/Tp/science.htm.

Hayes, P., Harnad, S., Perlis, D. and Block, N. (1992), 'Virtual Symposium on Virtual Mind, *Minds and Machines*, 2(3), 217–238. http://cogsci.soton.ac.uk/harnad/Papers/Harnad/harnad92.virtualmind.html.

Hitchcock, S., Carr, L., Jiao, Z., Bergmark, D., Hall, W., Lagoze, C. and Harnad, S. (2000), 'Developing services for open eprint archives: globalisation, integration and the impact of links', *Proceedings of the 5th ACM Conference on Digital Libraries*, San Antonio, Texas, June 2000. http://www.cogsci.soton.ac.uk/'harnad/Papers/Harnad/harnad00.acm.htm.

Hitchcock, S., Brody, T., Gutteridge, C., Carr, L., Hall, W., Harnad, S., Bergmark, D. and Lagoze, C. (2002), 'Open Citation Linking: The Way Forward', *D-Lib Magazine*, 8, (10). http://www.dlib.org/dlib/october02/hitchcock/10hitchcock.html.

Hitchcock, S., Woukeu, A., Brody, T., Carr, L., Hall, W., and Harnad, S. (2003), 'Evaluating Citebase, an open access Web-based citation-ranked search and impact discovery service', http://opcit.eprints.org/evaluation/Citebase-evaluation/evaluation-report.html.

Lawrence, S. (2001a), 'Online or Invisible?', *Nature*, 411(6837), 521. http://www.neci.nec.com/'lawrence/papers/online-nature01/.

Lawrence, S. (2001b), 'Free online availability substantially increases a paper's impact', *Nature Web Debates*, http://www.nature.com/nature/debates/e-access/Articles/lawrence.html.

Light, P., Light, V., Nesbitt, E. and Harnad, S. (2000), 'Up for Debate: CMC as a support for course related discussion in a campus university setting', in: R. Joiner (ed.), *Rethinking Collaborative Learning* (London: Routledge). http://www.cogsci.soton.ac.uk/'harnad/Papers/Harnad/harnad00.skyteaching.html.

Odlyzko, A.M. (1998), 'The economics of electronic journals', in: R. Ekman and R. Quandt, (eds), *Technology and Scholarly Communication* (University of California Press). http://www.dtc.umn.edu/'odlyzko/doc/eworld.html.

Odlyzko, A.M. (1999a), 'Competition and cooperation: Libraries and publishers in the transition to electronic scholarly journals', *Journal of Electronic Publishing*, 4(4) *Journal of Scholarly Publishing*, 30(4), pp. 163–185.

Odlyzko, A.M. (1999b): A definitive version of his views appeared as: R Stephen Berry and Anne Simon Moffat (eds), *The Transition from Paper: Where Are We Going and How Will We Get There?*. Published online in 2001 by the American Academy of Arts & Science. http://www.press.umich.edu/jep/04–04/odlyzko0404.html http://www.research.att.com/'amo/doc/competition.cooperation.pdf.

Odlyzko, A.M. (2002), 'The rapid evolution of scholarly communication', *Learned Publishing*, 15, 7–19. http://rosina.catchword.com/vl=11319436/cl=24/fm=docpdf/nw=1/rpsv/catchword/alpsp/09531513/v15n1/s2/p7; http://www.si.umich.edu/PEAK-2000/odlyzko.pdf.

Oppenheim, C. (2001), 'The legal and regulatory environment for electronic information', *Infonortics*. http://www.infonortics.com/publications/legal4.html.

Chapter 7

Issues of Policy and Practice in Digital Preservation

Susan S. Lazinger[1]

Introduction

Electronic texts, unlike the fixed texts of print data, are subject to inadvertent destruction of both the physical medium on which they exist and the intellectual content of their information. Electronic texts, so easy to edit, manipulate, revise, and improve, have lost their assurance of permanence. There are many ways to destroy electronic data inadvertently. First, the *medium* is at risk. Then there is the bigger problem of *intellectual* preservation. Data may be destroyed inadvertently. Many types of accidental changes may occur: a document can be damaged accidentally or as a result of the nature of the electronic resource (for example, a dynamic database, by its nature, is frequently updated, erasing previous data in the updating). Unauthorized tampering with one's own work, for example to cover one's tracks or destroy evidence, or with the work of another person, can also destroy electronic data. Lack of metadata and systems documentation, electronic data in forms that cannot be preserved because the software or hardware becomes obsolete or the digital resources have been *designed* to prevent any copying, and finally a lack of empowering mechanisms to institutions willing and able to be caretakers of our electronic resources all threaten our digital heritage.

At an international conference on digital preservation and long-term accessibility of digital materials, held in York, UK, in December 2000, Lynne Brindley, Chief Executive of the British Library, delivered a keynote speech in which she observed that preservation management of our digital resources is essential not only for all the reasons cited above, but also for important economic reasons:

> Large sums of money are becoming available for creating electronic images and for creating exciting, innovative ways of using images. For very sound economic reasons, that investment, those digital assets need to be managed . . . However central access is to all our activities, it remains the case that, as in our analogue world, there is no access without preservation.

The benign neglect of our ancestors in their caretaking of printed materials will no longer work in the digital environment, she warns. If we are to pass on our digital heritage to our descendants, as our ancestors passed on their printed heritage to us, preservation decisions must be integrated with the creation process itself.

Selection of Material for Preservation

The first act of digital preservation is identifying or selecting which material merits the effort of preservation. The fluidity and dynamic nature that digital data add to preservation raise questions such as which version of a resource is the 'genuine' one. Furthermore, the time frame within which selection choices must be made is shortened due to the problems of media instability and technological obsolescence. Dynamic databases, which change from moment to moment, add a further complication to the process of digital archiving because they can only be preserved through samples or snapshots. Digital resources also require decisions not only about what items to keep, but also which elements of the resource should be preserved. Features such as links to other documents and interactivity will be lost unless decisions are made to keep them. In the final analysis, the question is not only *what* should be preserved, but *how much* of each digital item should be preserved. Digital preservation thus may involve saving not only the resource, but also contextual information such as information on the medium (which may need to be changed frequently) and metadata about the contents. Finally, the issues involved in digital archiving are different for 'born-digital' materials than they are for materials that have been digitized, because the original print source of digitized materials is usually both documented and preserved. Born-digital material, on the other hand, is in danger of disappearing without a trace unless it is properly identified, documented for future access and preserved technologically.

Defining the digital resource, given this complex environment, is not simple. The Task Force on Archiving of Digital Information emphasizes that the central goal of digital preservation must be to preserve information integrity. It defines five components that constitute the integrity of digital documents: *content* (intellectual substance contained in information objects), *fixity* (content fixed in a discrete object as opposed to continuously updated documents), *reference* (reliable systems for locating and citing), *provenance* (a record of the document's origin and chain of custody), and *context* (a document's interaction with elements in the wider digital environment).

In addition, digital objects can be classified according to various typologies. The first major division of digital objects is into two main groups: *digitized* material, converted from documents or other media into electronic format, and *natively digital* (also referred to as 'born digital') material, which was created in digital form. Both groups can be further divided according to their characteristics and forms. Typologies of electronic publications in the literature on electronic data archiving are numerous and varied.

Answers to the question of what to preserve, like the definitions and typologies of digital resources, are also numerous and varied. Collection policies and selection criteria of individual research institutions and digital archives give us perhaps the best examples of what electronic data should be preserved.

In a recent issue of *D-Lib Magazine*, Gail Hodge (2000) suggests that the question of selection is directly connected to the issue of *extent*, particularly when selecting complex websites. Noting that, in most countries, the major difference in collection policies between formal print and electronic publications is the question of whether digital materials are included under current deposit legislation, she suggests that guidelines to establish boundaries in such an unregulated situation are helpful. As examples she cites parts of the guidelines of the National Library of Canada (NLC) and the National Library of Australia (NLA), both leaders in establishing best practices.

The NLA, for example, archives only internal links of digital objects it chooses for archiving, while the NLC has chosen to archive the text of the linked object only if it is on the same server as the object that is being archived. In other words, the previous issue of the same periodical accessed through a hypertext link would be considered a part of the original publication, but another publication accessed through a hypertext link would not. Brewster Kahle's Internet Archive retains all links because the project aims to archive a snapshot of the entire internet. Another project Hodge cites as inclusive in its approach to archiving links of digital documents it is archiving is that of the American Astronomical Society. Like the Internet Archive it mainains all links to both documents and supporting materials in other formats, collaborating extensively with the various international astronomical societies, researchers, universities and government agencies in order to do so (Hodge, 2000).

In her conclusion, Hodge sums up the current approach to what to preserve with the observation that 'regardless of whether acquisition is done by human selection or automated gathering software, there is a growing body of guidelines to support questions of what to select, the extent of the digital work, the archiving of related links and refreshing the contents of sites' (Hodge, 2000).

Preservation Stakeholders

The stakeholders in the process of digital preservation include first the creators of the digital objects, who may be individuals, institutions or organizations. Other stakeholders may be publishers, distributors, systems administrators, libraries, archives and users. What unites all these stakeholders is their interest in adding to, or making use of, the value of digital information objects. The roles of the stakeholders in digital preservation, however, are yet to be clearly defined, although most likely digital information will be distributed across many sites, and responsibility for preserving access to that information will also be distributed. Existing collecting institutions, such as RLG libraries, will continue to be major players in archiving the objects they collect, at least over the short to medium term, since it makes sense to build on existing infrastructures. With stakeholders, as with the digital information objects themselves, a number of typologies of stakeholders have been suggested.

Libraries – both singly and in consortia – have so far been in the forefront of research into, and implementation of the beginnings of far-reaching preservation policies for digital resources. Although using national libraries as our primary archiving institutions for electronic data is an attractive option, there are barriers to overcome. First, depository legislation for electronic information varies widely among countries that have depository arrangements. Second, copyright is a problem even for publications originating in the library's country. Finally, there is the possibility that no national library can truly commit to acquiring by deposit all electronic publications that should be acquired or that such programs will be subject to the vagaries of budget appropriations.

In the realm of US federal government information, three separate systems work in concert to ensure current and future access to government records, documents and publications. Nonetheless, there is no comprehensive system or legal responsibility within the US federal government to identify, capture, retain and provide continuous public access to electronic files of government information.

Legal deposit is a statutory provision that obliges publishers to deposit copies of their publications in libraries in the country in which they are published. Legal deposit in most countries has traditionally applied to print publications. It is sometimes established through an act dedicated specifically and only to legal deposit, and other times is contained within copyright legislation. Exactly what is covered by legal deposit varies from country to country. The three issues that must be dealt with in order to accommodate electronic materials within legal deposit are: definition of the materials, acquisition of the materials and preservation of the materials. Legal deposit in the US covers all types of non-print publications. The Library of Congress receives CD-ROMs on a more or less comprehensive basis through legal deposit, but currently it lacks clear authority to collect online publications. In Europe, there are a number of initiatives involving legal deposit of electronic publications.

A British study funded in 1999 by the Library and Information commission, the Arts and Humanities Data Service (AHDS) and the Joint Information Systems Committee (JISC), and discussed in a paper at the *Preservation 2000* conference, found that 'the level of awareness of and interest in digital preservation is gradually increasing but is not keeping pace with the level of digital resource creation' (Jones, 2000). Institutions that were not involved in preserving traditional collections have not yet developed a strong sense of playing a role in preserving digital resources; individual researchers, however good their intentions, frequently lack clear guidance and institutional backing to enable them to feel confident of what they should be doing; digital resource creation is frequently a by-product of collaborative projects funded by yet another external agency, making allocation of responsibilities for preservation and maintenance difficult. Overall, the feeling is that 'there is still a need to raise the level of awareness of digital preservation, particularly among funding agencies and senior administrators with responsibility for the strategic direction of an institution' (Jones, 2000).

Methods of Preservation

Technological obsolescence comes about as the result of the evolution of technology. A separate issue is that of media deterioration. As of this writing, there is no one unambiguous answer to the problem of technological obsolescence, but there are several clear options being explored to deal with this cycle of obsolescence. The options fall into three main categories: refreshing, migration and emulation. Refreshing is copying digital files from one storage medium to another storage medium of the same type in order to prevent media obsolescence. Refreshing does not solve the problem of backward compatibility if the software changes, and so it cannot be viewed as a solution to digital preservation, at least not in itself. Migration – the periodic transfer of digital materials from one hardware/software configuration to another, or from one generation of computer technology to the next – is the current favorite strategy for preserving electronic data. Media refreshing is a part of migration, but migration involves the transfer of the entire digital environment, not just the physical storage medium. Migration is necessary every time the operating environment, including the hardware and the software, changes. Migration strategies vary with the type of digital data being migrated and are still in the process of development. The third digital preservation option being explored is emulation, or the development of software that performs the functions of obsolete hardware and other software. This strategy proposes that digital documents be stored in their original forms, along with the original software in which they were created, and that additional software be created to permit a more advanced computer at some future time to mimic the obsolete hardware.

In preserving digital objects it is access to the intellectual content (or visual content, if the digital object is an image or collection of images) we are preserving rather than the physical object or medium. In order to preserve access to the intellectual content, we must preserve the integrity of the intellectual content, even as we discard the original storage medium, software and hardware on which the digital object was created and accessed originally. Preserving the integrity of digital objects also involves developing techniques for verifying the authenticity of a digital object, that is, whether the digital object has undergone alteration of any kind for any reason since its creation.

There are a number of different strategies for converting the form of digital information as technology changes. They include transferring digital information from less stable to more stable media, from highly software-dependent formats to less software-intensive formats, and from a multiplicity of formats to a smaller number of common formats; developing and imposing standards; developing backward compatibility paths; and developing process centers for migration and reformatting.

Proponents of emulation as the preferred digital preservation strategy contend that digital preservation needs a solution that is extensible, since no one can predict what changes will occur, and that does not require labor-intensive examination and/or translation of individual documents. Migration does not supply these two essential conditions. Emulation, they state, does. Furthermore, running the original software under emulation on future computers is the only reliable way to recreate a digital document's original functionality, look, and feel. The digital tablet takes emulation one step further, offering an alternative strategy that would store not only the digital documents, the hardware and the software needed to run them, but also the power source needed to display the recorded information in some future era.

In discussing the 'how' of electronic archiving, there are additional issues, besides the method used to preserve the digital object, which must be taken into account both in choosing the preferred method and in implementing it effectively. They are *authenticity* of the digital object, that is, that it is unaltered from the original, that it is what it purports to be; and *copyright*, or levels of permitted access to the digital object.

Beagrie and Jones (2000), in the pre-publication draft of their preservation management workbook, state that at the end of 2000 two strategies dominate options for long-term preservation of digital resources – migration and emulation – and that both strategies have champions and detractors as well as acknowledged difficulties.

Emulation, however, has been the basis for several recent digital preservation projects that deserve attention. Hilary Berthon, Manager of National & International Preservation Activities in Australia, while conceding that 'there is no consensus yet on the "best" archiving model' and that 'we may never have a single archiving model' (Berthon, 2000), notes that, internationally, increasing attention is being given to the Reference Model for an Open Archival Information System (OAIS) being developed by the Consultative Committee for Space Data Systems as a new ISO standard. The OAIS model provides terms of reference, conceptual data models and functional models for interoperable open archives and defines the nature of 'information packages' in terms of both the content and what is necessary to understand, access and manage the content. Australia's PANDORA Project uses some of the OAIS concepts in its architecture; two projects – the NEDLIB project in the Netherlands and the CEDARS project in the UK – are full implementations of this model. NEDLIB has adopted the OAIS model as a framework on which to build its archiving model for deposit libraries and has added a Preservation Module that includes provision for both emulation approaches and digital migrations resulting from changed content, and CEDARS has implemented the OAIS model for a distributed digital archive of library resources (Berthon, 2000).

The concept of emulation, using physical or logical structures called 'containers' or 'wrappers' to provide a relationship between all information components, such as the digital object and its metadata, and software specifications, underlies the OAIS Reference Model, which utilizes the concepts of 'information packages' (IPs) composed of 'content information' and 'preservation description information' contained by 'packaging information'. The content information includes the digital object itself and the representation information needed to interpret it. The preservation description information includes information about provenance and context, reference information such as unique identifiers and a wrapper that protects the digital object against undocumented alteration (Berthon, 2000).

The NEDLIB project has been thoroughly documented in a study commissioned by the National Library of the Netherlands (the Koninklijke Bibliotheek) in 1999 and published online in April 2000 (Rothenburg, 2000). Rothenberg states that 'this study was intended to be the first phase of a longer-term effort by the KB to test and evaluate the feasibility of using emulation as a means of preserving digital publications in accessible, authentic, and usable form within a deposit library'.

The basic idea of the NEDLIB project was to test whether emulating obsolete computer hardware on future computer hardware can be used to confer longevity on digital publications by enabling their obsolete software to be run on future platforms. His report describes the first phase of the project, during which a prototype experimental environment for trying out emulation-based preservation using commercial emulation tools was developed. He describes the experimental conditions and environment, the results and the observations from the initial experiments. The results include proposed data, metadata and procedural models to support emulation-based preservation and recommendations for future experiments and experimental procedures. The analysis is presented in the context of the Open Archival Information System (OAIS) as well as the NEDLIB adaptation of the OAIS, the Deposit System for Electronic Publications (DSEP) (Rothenburg, 2000). Rothenberg states unequivocally that even using off-the-shelf emulation that was not specifically designed to be used for preservation, the experimental outcome was impressive:

> The appearance and behavior of digital publications under emulation was found to be virtually indistinguishable from their appearance and behavior on their original platforms. While this is far from conclusive (since many further questions remain to be answered) it is an indication that emulation-based preservation has significant potential and warrants further exploration.

In his discussion of authenticity criteria, Rothenberg admits that there is not yet an accepted definition of digital preservation that ensures saving all the aspects of a digital object, and that the choice of a particular digital preservation method or technology determines which aspects of a document will be preserved and which ones will be sacrificed. 'In the digital case,' he states, 'we must choose what to lose'(Rothenburg, 2000). The results of the NEDLIB study have convinced Rothenberg nonetheless that using software emulation to reproduce the behavior of obsolete computing platforms on newer platforms is the best way to run a digital document's original software in the far future and thereby recreate the content, behavior and 'look-and-feel' of the original document.

Developments in the issues of authenticity and intellectual property rights include a standard for version control developed at the National Library of Canada (NLC) and presented at *Preservation 2000*, and an intellectual property rights policy developed as another aspect of the CEDARS project.

Although the NLC by policy does not necessarily collect every version of all networked electronic publications, it does collect the first and subsequent editions of a publication. To determine whether a new version should be viewed as a new edition, it applies the following criteria:

- The version of the publication is announced as a new edition, that is, indicated in wording or by a number, date or code.
- The publisher regards the version as a new edition.
- The changes to the new version of the publication are significant. (Brodie, 2000)

In her report on NLC version control policy, Brodie makes an interesting statement on the implications of authentication (as opposed to authenticity) for preservation. 'Authentication,' she asserts, 'can be considered the enemy of preservation of authenticity' (Brodie, 2000). Tools of authentication, such as encryption, make preserving authentic documents very difficult because all the pieces of a public key infrastructure, encryption algorithms, encryption and decryption software, private keys, public keys, certificates, certificate authorities, etc, have to be preserved along with the encrypted document. As a result, the National

Archives of Canada has decided not preserve encrypted documents, but rather only to preserve the contents in unencrypted form.

Intellectual property rights lessons from the CEDARS project were presented at the CEDARS Conference held within the framework of *Preservation 2000* (Seville and Weinberger, 2000). The aim of the paper is to assist librarians and archivists in addressing the intellectual property rights issues arising during digital preservation activities.

General rights issues defined include:

- Copyright can cover many types of creative effort, including plays, paintings, sound recordings and the typographical format of certain published editions.
- Several copyrights may subsist simultaneously in a single item.
- The usual term of protection for copyright is 70 years from the end of the year of the death of the author.

Other rights issues discussed include:

- Rights in databases.
- Legal deposit.
- European Union Copyright Directive [the draft of which was then being negotiated and which was subsequently accepted by the European Union's Council of Ministers on 9 April 2001].
- Who owns the copyright for a given work?
- Has copyright been infringed?
- Is there an excuse for the copyright infringement?

A section on Rights Negotiation for Preservation includes instructions for preparing for negotiation and even a sample letter to send to the owner of the rights, and a final section on The Licensing Agreement defines the obligations of the archiving institution and suggests points for consideration (Seville and Weinberger, 2000).

Summing up the issues involved in intellectual property rights with regard to digital preservation, CEDARS' Intellectual Property Rights Adviser Catherine Seville warns that 'in order to ensure the preservation of digital objects, librarians and archivists . . . will have to assure the rights owners that the commercial value, and the integrity, of the preserved digital object will not be lost . . . By preserving digital objects, we ensure that future scholars will be able to build on today's research (Seville and Weinberger, 2000).

The Cost of Preservation

The costs involved in digital archiving can be divided into two main categories: the costs for converting information into digital form (or for acquiring data already in a digital format) and the costs for maintaining digital information. Estimating the costs of these processes is complex, and the cost of each element in the processes varies according a variety of factors. For example, if materials need to be digitized, cost is affected by whether the digitization is implemented on-site or through a vendor. In addition, the type of material, the degree of digitization, and the resolution of the digitization all affect the cost, as well as the general condition of the material being digitized. High-quality, 'preservation' projects cost more than access-oriented projects in which image quality is less important. Projects including both digital images of texts and machine-editable files converted from their paper originals through optical character recognition (OCR) technology or human keying, are even more expensive. A number of projects have shown that digital imaging itself only accounts for about one-third of the overall costs for imaging projects, with metadata creation often being as – or more – expensive than the physical conversion of materials into digital objects. Other studies have predicted that it will not be the conversion that will be the main cost of digital preservation, but rather the management of the project over the long term.

Digitization costs can be broken into 'basic costs' and 'technical costs'. Basic costs include project planning, quality control and document preparation activities. Technical costs include the cost of moving the original materials through the scanning process and the cost of writing an output file to the required resolution, bit depth and quality. It is much cheaper to scan individual sheets, if they can be run through a sheet feeder, than a bound volume or photographs, both of which must be scanned manually.

Several models for calculating costs have been developed. However, because costing studies are in themselves expensive and complex to carry out, there have really been only a few large-scale analyses of the costs of digital conversion and preservation. The most significant of these are Yale University Library's Project Open Book, Cornell University's Digital to Microfilm Conversion Project, and The Early Canadiana Online Project. There are also some comparative analyses from the UK. Most recently, Steven Puglia, from the National Archives and Records Administration (NARA), has provided an extensive analysis of digitization project costs at NARA and other institutions, in *RLG DigiNews*, and Kenney and Rieger (1999) report on recent cost figures from the University of Michigan, University of Virginia, and Cornell University digitization projects. Yale's Project Open Book explored and produced figures primarily on the costs of conversion. Anne Kenney, in her final report on the Cornell Project, also included estimates from various sources for archiving a digital book for 10 years. The costing study on the Early Canadiana Online Project, includes all costs associated with the production, cataloging, and sales of texts in microfiche or digital format.

One of the conclusions reached as a result of the Yale and Cornell studies was that, in spite of predictions that microfilm could be replaced by digital imaging, many people have come to feel that digitization may increase access to materials but does not guarantee their continued preservation (Chapman *et al.*, 1999). This attitude is reflected in the recent literature on the future of digital collections, for example in a report on a Mellon Foundation-funded study on the future of Oxford's digital collections: 'With reference to preservation, there was considerable unease within the library sector at the prospect of relying on a digital copy as a substitution for other formats; and most felt that film still provided the best preservation medium' (University of Oxford, 1999).

Therefore, the set of assumptions with which the Council on Library and Information Resources (CLIR) paper begins are as follows:

- Reformatting remains the only viable long-term strategy for preserving brittle paper.
- Until digital preservation capabilities can be widely implemented and be shown to be cost-effective, microfilm remains the primary reformatting strategy for brittle books. Although digital imaging can be used to increase access, preservation goals will not be considered met until a microfilm copy or computer output microfilm recording of digital image files has been produced, satisfying national standards for quality and permanence.
- Recommendations in this paper are limited to brittle monographs and serials containing monochrome text and simple graphics and microfilm created from the mid-1980s onward as part of a hybrid effort.
- Only strategies that are both quality-oriented and cost-effective are recommended, that is, high contrast microfilming and bitonal digital imaging.
- Options for both film-first and scan-first strategies are presented, providing guidance to institutions to determine the best course of action based on their collections, capabilities and needs. (Chapman *et al.*, 1999)
- The authors note that the two projects at Yale and Cornell revealed that the relationship of film to digital lies in aligning quality, cost and access, which in turn are affected by the characteristics of the source material being converted, the capabilities of the technology being used for the digital conversion and the purposes to which the digital end product will be put (Chapman *et al.*, 1999).

Therefore, the working paper is divided into the following four sections:

(1) Characteristics of microfilm as a source for digital conversion.
(2) Characteristics of microfilm as an end-product of digital conversion.
(3) Choice of a digital conversion path (film-first or scan-first).
(4) Development of metadata elements associated with digital image pages (Chapman *et al.*, 1999).

A table in the first section showing the impact of film characteristics on process time divides these characteristics into contrast/density variation, skewed pages, inconsistent gutter, internal splices, other film factors, reduction ratio, cleanliness and average density. Analyses of the data from the Yale project indicated, however, that the characteristics of the microfilm created had little or no impact on conversion costs. The conclusion reached with regard to this issue is that future developments in digital technology may offer greater promise to increase quality and reduce cost than any specific modifications in the creation of preservation microfilm.

The Cornell project showed that computer output microfilm created from 600 dpi 1-bit images scanned from brittle books meets or exceeds national microfilm standards for image quality and permanence. To achieve acceptable levels of image quality, a two-step process of converting original materials to Computer Output Microfilm (COM) is required:

- *Digitization*, or creating digital image files that adequately capture all the significant informational content of the original materials.
- *COM recording*, or utilizing a COM system capable of recording faithfully onto film all the information contained in the digital image files.
- Data from the Cornell project showed that the quality of the resulting COM will largely be determined by the quality of the initial scanning, not the film recording (Chapman *et al.*, 1999).

Data from both projects indicated that book characteristics, such as the presence of halftones, complex illustrations, darkened paper, faded inks or other factors associated with deterioration, can increase the costs of bitonal digital conversion from either the original book or the microfilm copy. Halftones added an additional $0.02/page (spread across an entire book and assuming that not all the pages will include halftones) because they required manual scanning rather than 'auto-mode' scanning, in which standard settings were used to capture all pages of the volume. The use of manual scanning increased scanning time per Cornell book by 40 minutes (from 86 minutes to 126 minutes) and per Yale book of 216 pages by 17 minutes (from 56 minutes to 73 minutes). The need to disbind the book and trim the binder's margin for scanning on the Xerox flatbed scanners (XDOD) increased preparation times, on average, by nearly 20 minutes per volume, representing an additional $0.023 per page cost (Chapman *et al.*, 1999).

Costs at the beginning of the projects for developing systems programming capabilities for handling, rotating and moving the image files and relevant targets, and for creating microfilm directory structures, tape generation scripts to automate the copying of files onto 8 mm tape, log files for quality control, and costs for other file management and tape creation activities averaged out to slightly over $0.01 an image (although the authors warn that programs developed for these projects may not all be transferable to other companies or other institutions). One other observation with regard to the costs associated with microfilm as a source for digital conversion is that there appear to be cost savings if the digitization and COM recording processes are combined into one effort (Chapman *et al.*, 1999).

The choice of a digital conversion path (film-first or scan-first) depends on which approach meets an institution's objectives for preservation (film) and access (digital images) at the lowest cost. Therefore, it is appropriate to compare the quality and costs of preservation microfilm to digital COM to determine whether the film-first or scan-first approach is more advantageous. The Cornell project established that digital COM can be of equal or superior quality to traditional 35 mm preservation microfilm and costs slightly less than $0.12 per page image. Both the Cornell and Yale reports point out, though, that the $0.12 per image for COM refers only to one generation of film, and that these costs also presume that bibliographic targets have already been created and are stored with the digital images. Based upon these findings, two preliminary conclusions are reached about the preservation component of the hybrid approach:

(1)   Film-first and scan-first offer comparable microfilm quality, but
(2)   COM production appears to be less expensive than microfilm production.

Other preliminary conclusions with respect to the digital images from the Yale and Cornell projects are that scanning from paper and scanning from film are comparable in cost, but the quality of scan-first digital image is better. Cost comparison tables for the two projects show that for 600 dpi 1-bit images, production scanning costs from $0.22 to $0.26 per image for paper scanning and $0.24 to $0.28 for film scanning (Chapman *et al.*, 1999).

The Hybrid Approach Decision Tree provides guidance for a number of situations.

(1)   When the goal is to produce digital preservation masters and preservation quality film when only brittle volumes are available, when both brittle volumes and microfilm are available and when only microfilm is available.
(2)   When the goal is to produce digital access masters and preservation quality film when only brittle volumes are available, when both brittle volumes and microfilm are available and when only microfilm is available (Chapman *et al.*, 1999).

Guidelines for the development of metadata elements, associated with the digital image project in the context of the hybrid approach, view preservation microfilm and the scanned images as the 'data' and all the collateral information related to these objects as metadata. Thus, the digital object will consist of:

(1)   digital masters (scanned page-images; each with a unique file name),
(2)   associated administrative metadata,
(3)   associated structural metadata (Chapman *et al.*, 1999).

Proposed administrative metadata elements are:

(1)   the technical target that documents the capabilities of the scanner that was used;
(2)   for digital preservation masters, bibliographic targets for COM output;
(3)   the name of the project;
(4)   the name of funding agency (ies);
(5)   the unique identifier for the object;
(6)   the designation of the object as 'digital preservation master' or 'digital access master';
(7)   the owning institution;
(8)   the copyright statement (including a note of any use restrictions);
(9)   the date the object was created (scanning date);
(10) the scanning resolution, bit depth, file format and version, and compression;
(11) the change history of the object: current version of object, with dates of migration and notation of which features in (10) were changed (Chapman *et al.*, 1999).

The minimum set of proposed structural metadata elements includes:

(1) correct page number associated with each digital image;
(2) internal navigation/structural points, sometimes referred to as features or feature codes, when present in the original (Chapman *et al.*, 1999).

The conclusions of the CLIR working paper generalize the results of the two studies on hybrid conversion in order to make them available to other institutions, stating at the same time that there are still several key issues to be resolved. The list of issues falls into four major categories.

(1) Decreasing the costs of converting microfilm to digital images.
(2) Improving the quality of the digital image project.
(3) Promoting COM as a preservation product.
(4) Furthering development of metadata for digital books and journals (Chapman *et al.*, 1999).

For each issue, various methods for achieving the stated goal are suggested, and a plea is made for greater and greater numbers of institutions to report on their allocation of resources in order to facilitate the development of ways to track and assess the real costs of conversion projects. Finally, the authors recommend that their paper serve as the starting point for further collaboration to find answers to these questions and enlighten the community in general about the critical investment they are being required to make into preservation and access (Chapman *et al.*, 1999).

Note

1   Based very heavily on the summaries of the first five chapters of my book, Lazinger, S.S. (2001), *Digital Preservation and Metadata: History, Theory, Practice* (Englewood, CO.: Libraries Unlimited).

References

Beagrie, N. and Jones, M. (2000) 'Preservation Management of Digital Materials Workbook: A Pre-publication Draft', October. Available: http://www.jisc.ac.uk/dner/preservation/ workbook.

Berthon, H. (2000) 'The Moving Frontier: Archiving, Preservation and Tomorrow's Digital Heritage', in: *VALA 2000–10th VALA Biennial Conference and Exhibition*, Melbourne, Victoria, 16–18 February [Online], available: http://www.nla.gov.au/nla/staffpaper/ hberthon2.html.

Brindley, L. (2000) 'Preservation 2000: Keynote Speech', in: *Preservation 2000: An International Conference on the Preservation and Long Term Accessibility of Digital Materials*. 7–8 December, York, UK. Conference Papers [Online], available: http:// www.rlg.org/events/pres-2000/brindley.html.

Brodie, N. (2000), 'Authenticity, Preservation and Access in Digital Collections', in:

Preservation 2000: An International Conference on the Preservation and Long Term Accessibility of Digital Materials, 7–8 December, York, UK. Conference Papers [Online], available: http://www.rlg.org/events/pres-2000/brodie.html.

Chapman, S., Conway, P. and Kenney, A.R. (1999), 'Digital Imaging and Preservation Microfilm: The Future of the Hybrid Approach for the Preservation of Brittle Books', *RLG DigiNews*, 3(1), February, 15, [Online], available: http://www.rlg.org/preserv/diginews/diginews3–1.html.

Hodge, G.M. (2000), 'Best Practices for Digital Archiving: An Information Life Cycle Approach', *D-Lib Magazine*, 6(1), January, [Online], available: http://www.dlib.org/dlib/january00/01hodge.html.

Jones, M. (2000), 'A Workbook for the Preservation Management of Digital Materials', in: *Preservation 2000: An International Conference on the Preservation and Long Term Accessibility of Digital Materials*. 7–8 December 2000, York, UK. Conference Papers [Online], available: http://www.rlg.org/events/pres-2000/jones.html.

Kenney, A.R. and Rieger, O.Y. (2000) *Moving Theory into Practice: Digital Imaging for Libraries and Archives* (Mountain View, CA: Research Libraries Group).

Lazinger, S.S. (2001), *Digital Preservation and Metadata: History, Theory, Practice* (Englewood, CO: Libraries Unlimited).

Rothenburg, J. (2000), 'An Experiment in Using Emulation to Preserve Digital Publications'. Revision 2000–05–11. Published by the Koninklijke Bibliotheek, Den Haag [Online], available: http://www.kb.nl/coop/nedlib/results/emulationpreservationreport.pdf.

Seville, C. and Weinberger, E. (2000), 'Intellectual Property Rights Lessons from the CEDARS Project for Digital Preservation', in: *Preservation 2000: An International Conference on the Preservation and Long Term Accessibility of Digital Materials*. 7–8 December 2000, York, UK. Conference Papers [Online], available: http://www.rlg.org/events/pres-2000/weinberger.html.

University of Oxford (1999), 'Scoping the Future of Oxford's Digital Collections. A Study Funded by the Andrew W. Mellon Foundation' [Online], available: http://www.bodley.ox.ac.uk/scoping/.

Chapter 8

Evaluating Electronic Information Services

Pete Dalton, Stella Thebridge and Rebecca Hartland-Fox

> The ultimate question for evaluation is: how are digital libraries transforming research, education, learning and living? (Saracevic, 2000, p. 368)

This chapter examines the role and value of evaluation in relation to the complex and rapidly changing world of Electronic Information Services (EIS) and highlights some of the key challenges to successful EIS evaluation in the context of UK academic institutions.

The Role of Digital Library Evaluation: Policy, Planning and Practice

It is important to understand the consequences of developing and interacting with digital libraries. Marchionini *et al.* summarize some of the key elements of digital library evaluation:

> Evaluation of a digital library may serve many purposes ranging from understanding basic phenomena (e.g., human information-seeking behavior) to assessing the effectiveness of a specific design to insuring sufficient return on investment. Human-centered evaluation serves many stakeholders ranging from specific users and librarians to various groups to society in general. Additionally, evaluation may target different goals ranging from increased learning and improved research to improved dissemination to bottom line profits. Each of the evaluation goals may also have a set of measures and data collection methods. Finally, the evaluation must have a temporal component that can range from very short terms to generations. (Marchionini *et al.*, 2001, p. 2)

It is important to clarify terminology in the context of digital libraries. Some use the term only to refer to a digital collection or to a separate group of such collections within a traditional library service. In this chapter, the term 'electronic information services' (EIS) is sometimes used in place of 'digital libraries' to encompass any electronically delivered services within the library or information function.

Evaluation is a fact-finding, evidence-based, value-measuring activity and, as such, should become an integral part of the management of all electronic information services. Specifically, evaluation relates to policy, planning and practice, for example:

- Policy: evaluation data can be used to assess the extent to which the outcomes of the EIS relate to the wider information service and institutional

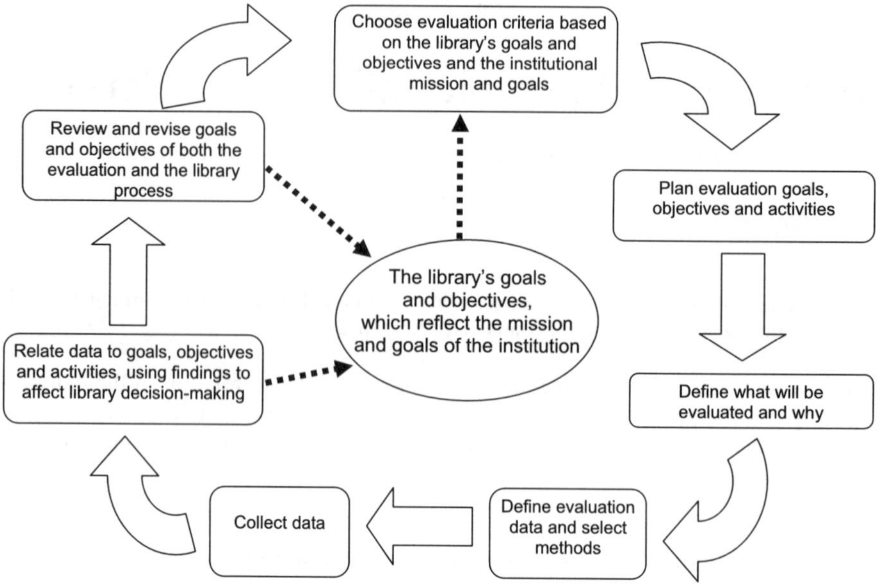

Figure 8.1 The evaluation planning cycle

outcomes. It can also be used to devise policies, for example, on electronic content and collection management
- Planning: evaluation data can inform the development of new electronic information services and technologies, validation or changes to existing services or discontinuation of services
- Practice: evaluation data can be used formatively to manage the day-to-day functioning of EIS or the usage of, and engagement with, specific electronic resources.

Evaluation is a process and, as such, requires the establishment of appropriate activities. These form a cycle, as Figure 8.1 demonstrates. (adapted, in part, from McClure, 2002).

The recognition of the importance of the evaluation planning cycle is intrinsic to an understanding of the importance of evaluation as a whole.

The Importance of Evaluation

Various authors have noted the benefits of evaluating digital libraries (Saracevic, 2000; Marchionini *et al.*, 2001). Shim *et al.* (2001a, p. 4) specifically describe the benefits of evaluation in relation to networked information services. They note that evaluation assists libraries to make a researched case for the development of their EIS. Furthermore, it aids competitive bidding for funding.

Financial

The increasing investment in digital libraries and EIS clearly demonstrates a need for evaluation. As Banwell and Gannon-Leary note:

> The issue of EIS performance is of growing concern today and interest in the topic is likely to increase as HE institutions commit more revenue to systems and services. Since considerable investment is being made, there is a need to find ways in which to assess the value of EIS. (Banwell and Gannon-Leary, 1999, p. 94)

Strategic Planning

Ongoing formative evaluation can contribute to ensuring that digital library resources, both technological and human, are effectively deployed and meet institutional strategic aims.

Users and Usage

Digital libraries are contributing to changes in the way in which academic institutions deliver services to users, the markets in which they operate and the collaborative partners with whom they work. Information professionals and researchers need to understand better the usage, effects and impacts of EIS on users, institutions and beyond. John Crawford articulates the need for evaluation in this respect:

> Evaluation will certainly be needed to understand the new challenges of electronic information and lifelong and distance learning, a world in which contact with the user will be irregular and perhaps infrequent. Evaluation will be needed to support the development of charters and expectation management for here the move to a customer-based model, disability rights legislation and the possibilities offered by the electronic information revolution will all need to be considered. (Crawford, 2000, p. 120)

Benchmarking

Evaluation data, particularly performance measurement statistics, can be used to provide benchmarking data for comparison against an institution's own past performance and against other members of a designated benchmarking group.

Stakeholder Interests

The focus and demand for evaluation can emerge from a variety of stakeholders: within the library service, within the host institution and outside the institution.

Many writers have written in detail about the parties with links to EIS. Saracevic (2000), Kelleher *et al.* (1996); Currier *et al.* (2001) and Winkworth (2001) have all compiled lists of these stakeholders, be they users, workers in the institution or bodies to whom the institution might be accountable. Winkworth's (2001, p. 722) list, which relates to stakeholders of EIS developments in the UK academic sector, is succinct in this respect:

- End-customers: students.
- Service purchasers: academic departments, institutions.
- Funders: funding councils, government, the taxpayer.
- Guardians of quality: QAA, professional bodies.
- Service managers.
- Staff.

Evaluators interact with stakeholders in a variety of ways, for example by: basic reporting to them, determining the effect/impact of EIS on stakeholders and assessing the stakeholders' satisfaction with EIS.

The involvement of stakeholders in the evaluation process can have benefits in serving to inform them of developments in the service and to gain their support in the development of the digital library. A fully rounded evaluation of EIS would seek to undertake evaluation in relation to a variety of the stakeholders. However, having a large number of stakeholders in digital libraries can make it difficult to provide a standard method of evaluation. As Kelleher *et al.* note:

> Different stakeholders are interested in different questions relevant to the kind of decisions they have to make. Often, they will have different or competing views about what is important, what constitutes success and how success might be measured. (Kelleher *et al.*, 1996, p. 6)

Identifying Evaluation Elements

Electronic information services (EIS) comprise a number of elements, such as users and collections, which can be evaluated in a variety of ways. These then need to be matched with evaluation criteria to establish appropriate measures and methods.

Digital libraries broadly consist of technical and social elements. Fuhr *et al.* (2001), Jones *et al.* (1999) and Saracevic (2000) have identified broad categories of EIS for evaluation purposes. These include varieties of user, collection and staff, as well as aspects of collections, such as selection, structure, access, interpretation, distribution and infrastructure. Other writers have applied further categorizations to aspects of digital libraries; for example, Chowdhury and Chowdhury (1999)

	Network evaluaton criteria						
Network component	Extensiveness	Efficiency	Effectiveness	Service quality	Impact	Usefulness	Adoption
Technical infra-structure							
Information content							
Information services							
Support							

Figure 8.2   Matching evaluation elements and criteria

specifically outline potential areas for evaluation in consideration of what to digitize within a library's collections.

Researchers have also developed criteria against which aspects of digital library development can be evaluated. Fuhr *et al.* (2001, p. 190), for example, outline the five criteria established by the European DELOS project:[1] 'extensiveness, effectiveness, efficiency, costing and quality'.

Having established the elements of EIS to be evaluated and the criteria to be used, it is important to match them together. Bertot and McClure (1998), in a study of public libraries in the United States, formulated a model to aid the process of evaluating networked information services (Figure 8.2): (From Bertot and McClure, 1998a)

This model breaks down networked information services into five component parts including, for example, technical infrastructure and information services. Against these elements are seven categories of measure, for example, 'extensiveness' and 'impact'. The model could serve as a template to enable practitioners to map their evaluation needs against the statistical data they will need to collect in each of the categories.

At present, the methods for evaluating digital libraries broadly parallel those used in traditional library evaluation, with the addition of evaluation processes developed for ICT. The path followed has, largely, been the traditional one of evaluating services in terms of inputs and outputs. Inputs are the raw materials that make up a library service or part of it – the budget, physical space, collections, equipment and staff – while outputs are measures of work undertaken, for example, in the context of electronic services, the number of log-ins to a particular page or service, or the number of online enquiries received and answered. Work has already been undertaken in this area with specific reference to EIS by:

- the Association of Research Libraries' e-metrics project (see note 7 later),
- the EQUINOX project (see note 6 later),
- the MIEL2 project (Brophy and Wynne, 1997).

Although some work has been done to investigate the possibilities of evaluating EIS in terms of outcomes and impacts, little of this has, so far, been transferred into practice. As digital libraries develop further, it is not inconceivable that there may be a need for entirely new ways of conceptualizing and conducting evaluations.

Challenges to Evaluation

Digital libraries are emergent complex systems. (Marchionini, 2000, p. 326)

It is this complexity that poses a considerable challenge for evaluators. In addition, the nature of EIS and institutional priorities for evaluation provide further challenges. The following section presents some areas where there can be difficulties in evaluating digital libraries in UK academic libraries:

- the merging of EIS and print-based services,
- statistical data,
- the rate of change in digital libraries,
- assessing outcomes,
- motivation to evaluate.

The Merging of EIS and Print-based Services

As libraries have moved from project-based development of digital libraries to seamless modes of service delivery, whereby EIS are often incorporated into the full information function, it is sometimes impossible, or at least impractical, to separate EIS from other library/information services and functions for evaluation purposes. This is particularly true of journal provision but is also true of survey methods, for example where general surveys on library impact are conducted across an institution.

One further difficulty with evaluating EIS is assessing which aspects are included in a particular organization's EIS and then determining which are going to be the subject of a particular evaluation exercise. This is not always straightforward. Users of UK higher education libraries might see no distinction between electronic information services created, provided and managed through the library and those purchased through vendors or provided elsewhere in the institution. They would also probably not be concerned with the fact that website links could take them to external sites. The library has no control over any of these latter information providers, yet effective evaluation would need users to be clear about which services they were required to judge.

Statistical Data

> Different journal hosts monitor different statistical information measures (searches performed, PDF documents downloaded, abstracts viewed, etc.) with little consistency between them. (Wolf, 2001, p. 252)

Electronic information services have the potential to generate a considerable amount of statistical data, more so than traditional library services. The potential for these statistics appears tremendous, particularly when one considers how problematic calculation of statistics for traditional library services can be, for example, the number of uses of a printed journal. Statistics also offer the opportunity to break down usage into article-based statistics or, occasionally, by user type or department (Ashcroft, 2000). However, the use of such statistics for evaluation purposes is not without problems. In the case of UK statistics on electronic journal and database usage, these are rarely produced in-house; rather, library services rely on the statistics from publishers/suppliers of EIS. However, the ease with which statistical information can be gathered about use of EIS is not always matched by consistency or reliability of data from those who supply and sell electronic information. Arrangements for the generation and delivery of statistical data also vary, as does the timeliness of any updates. These factors can impact on the analysis of statistical data (Eaton, 2002).

Several higher education institutions in the UK are tackling the problems and developing their own solutions in-house. This includes using questionnaires asking users about their patterns of usage for specific databases (Wolf, 2001) and the development of a systems infrastructure to capture links by users to each electronic information service (Eaton, 2002).

Even when libraries can use their own in-house data this approach is not without difficulties. Many libraries lack control over their own management information systems which do not allow accurate statistics of use to be identified. In non-converged library services for example, there can be a lack of collaboration between Information Technology and Library and Information functions in the effective development of in-house data. Meanwhile, staff in converged services can still feel constrained by technological systems and software.

Some practitioners calculate cost-benefit analysis as a method to evaluate electronic services. However, this is often a crude cost equated to use based on vendor statistics. Calculation of benefit in terms of use only provides a very basic level of value to users. Much has been documented on the meaning of 'value' or 'benefit', for example, the cognitive and affective reasons for using a service, the desired outcome of the interaction, the interaction itself and the subsequent nature of the results (Saracevic, 1997). This obviously goes much further than simple calculations of use.

As well as institutional solutions, the international Project COUNTER is an initiative that aims to ensure some standardization of vendor statistics.[2] In the first phase, the objective was to establish a code of practice to support librarians and publishers, while also identifying the needs of the various stakeholders. The Code of Practice was launched in January 2003 and further information is on the project website.

In the US, the Association of Research Libraries (ARL) through its e-metrics project (see note 7 later), has initiated testing of measures to describe electronic resources and services and has produced recommendations for improvements in reporting data and maintaining links between librarians and vendors (Shim and McClure, 2002).

The Rate of Change in Digital Libraries

It is acknowledged that digital libraries are constantly developing in terms of technologies and institutional or cross-institutional models of working. Evaluation must address these changes. Covey (2002, p. 3) quotes a survey respondent:

> How can libraries measure what they do, how much they do, or how well they do, when the boundaries keep changing?

Approaches to digital library evaluation must therefore be flexible, so developing standard evaluation approaches is problematic. In addition, the rate of change makes it difficult to undertake valuable longitudinal evaluation studies. For example, changes to collections and services or to student programmes mean that identical evaluation activities cannot be replicated year on year.

Assessing Outcomes

The ACRL Taskforce on outcomes assessment defined outcomes as 'the ways in which library users are changed as a result of their contact with the library's resources and programs' (ARCL, 1998).

There has been increased interest in the higher education sector in recent years, in the practice of outcomes assessment (in relation to teaching, learning and research), a process that reflects the changes resulting from a user's direct contact with the library's services, resources or instruction programmes, measured over a period of time (for example, a degree course). For libraries this is a formidable task. Challenges abound, for example, in gathering data about information-seeking behaviour while ensuring that it is unaffected by the users' knowledge that their behaviour is being monitored. Furthermore, in the area of student learning, outcomes assessment must involve longitudinal study in order to assess progress and the effects of resources and services over the time of a student's course. It must take into account the influence of teachers and library professionals in guiding students, as opposed to factors that constitute their self-taught learning.

Ford (2001) confirms that outcomes measures are the most under-represented of performance measures available. He analysed a range of existing measures (including those from the Effective Academic Library, 1995 and EQUINOX, note 4) against the categories in the model devised by Bertot and McClure (see Figure 8.2). He concluded that 'specific measures of quality, impact and usefulness are still largely awaiting definition' (Ford, 2001, p. 15).

Motivation to Evaluate

Numerous research and practical efforts and large resources are expended on digital library research and practice. Evaluation is not, by and large, a part of these efforts. (Saracevic, 2000, p. 362)

Librarians are not motivated to the same extent to carry out evaluation. A view prevails among some practitioners that evaluation is an add-on and not part of the main process of information delivery or development. McClure and Bertot (2001) suggest:

The burden still remains on researchers and practitioners who advocate the benefits from evaluation activities to convince organizations to participate willingly in, fund, and plan for assessments of their networked services and resources. (McClure and Bertot, 2001, p. xvii)

They further suggest that, rather than merely presenting findings of evaluation exercises, evaluators could also present recommendations and options for developing services. This would increase the acceptability of evaluation among sceptical managers.

Despite a general agreement that there is a need to evaluate services and the understanding that evaluation can provide useful evidence of the effectiveness, efficiency and value of electronic information services, many library managers do not evaluate to any great extent because of major challenges to their ability to take evaluation through from conception to service improvement. The eVALUEd project[3] found, in a survey of library and information services in UK higher education institutions, that time, money, lack of evaluation skills, lack of awareness of existing resources and research and inadequate statistical data were the major obstacles to these services' ability to carry out evaluation of their EIS, not forgetting the very real sense of 'survey fatigue' among all types of service user (eVALUEd Paper 1, 2002, pp. 17–20).

This is coupled with the fact that, despite the interest of a variety of stakeholders, there is no clear accountability in UK academic libraries to Government departments as there is in the public sector in the UK (because of the Best Value programme) or as there is in the academic sector in the United States.

In the US, there is a rigorous accreditation process for colleges. The eight federal accreditation agencies make specific demands in the area of outcomes assessment and this is well documented by Gratch-Lindauer (2002). It means that there are more developed processes in the US for collecting and analysing data to measure learning outcomes. More information about these is given in a later section on 'practical tools'.

There are several external organizations that could potentially require UK higher education libraries to evaluate their services, including their EIS, but they do not at present make substantial evaluation demands of libraries. These are documented by other writers (Ford, 1996, pp. 157–158 and Winkworth, 2001, pp. 720–723). The organizations include SCONUL (the Society of College, National and University Libraries), which has a library remit and already encourages UK higher education libraries to submit statistical data, the Quality Assurance Agency (QAA), which has an institution-wide remit, and professional bodies that accredit courses and may have minimum requirements for the library.

The Development of Performance Measurement

The substantial challenges to evaluation in the area of digital libraries have been addressed in various ways by a range of research projects and reports to establish performance measures across the library and information sector as well as in the newer and more fragmented area of EIS.

Theoretical frameworks for evaluating library services generally have been developed over the years and, in the UK, the HEFCE publication, *The Effective Academic Library* (1995) created a set of general performance indicators. However, the measures were deemed ineffective in the hybrid library context. This is documented by Barton and Blagden (1998), who themselves developed indicators for libraries based on SCONUL statistics. Although the report raises the need for awareness of indicators of performance in electronic information services, SCONUL data did not, at the time, support EIS, and therefore this aspect is lacking from the work:

> Although electronic information services have been a part of UK academic library services for some time now, the development of performance measures and electronic indicators for the electronic environment is still in its early stages. (Barton and Blagden, 1998, p. 37)

The MIEL 2 project formalized developments in the measurement of electronic library evaluation (Brophy and Wynne, 1997). It created measures for operational management, forward planning, evaluation and review, user satisfaction, delivery, efficiency and economy (Brophy and Wynne, 1997, p. 14). Further testing and development took place in the European Union-funded EQUINOX project (Library Performance Measurement and Quality Management System), which was completed in 2000. This developed a set of performance measures for electronic information services alongside those already developed for general library services (Barton and Blagden, 1998). Measures consist of 26 datasets which can be manipulated to provide 14 performance indicators.[4] These include: number of users and potential users; costs of electronic information services; usage of such services (broken down in various ways and including rejected sessions); number of workstations; staff numbers dedicated to electronic information services and data on training sessions.

The UK higher education sector's principal professional body in the information field, SCONUL, plays a crucial role in the collection of comparable data across all institutions and has both the will and the potential to develop this longitudinal database by linking raw data to appropriate performance indicators for libraries in general and EIS in particular.[5]

In the United States, the LibQUAL+ project[6] is a practical programme which is adapting to library contexts the quality aims of a customer service-based system for the commercial sector called SERVQUAL. In early 2003, the programme was piloted in a sixth of UK institutions via SCONUL (see note 5). Although this is a programme for general quality measurement in libraries, it should nevertheless provide useful information as to the transferability of the measures, particularly measures of EIS.

The ARL e-metrics project[7] attempts to examine data collection on the use and value of EIS. The project phases are:

- initial inventory of current practices at ARL libraries as to statistics, measures, processes and activities that relate to EIS;
- identification and field-testing of statistics and measures, recommendations of measures, and documentation for data collection;
- identification of links to educational outcomes and impacts, research, and technical infrastructure. (Blixrud, 2002, p. 3)

The developments outlined here have led to a small number of practical materials and these are outlined in the following section.

Practical Tools

While there is a large body of writing on evaluation of EIS, whether in relation to performance measurement, outcomes assessment or impact in general, there is little of direct practical help for the library manager. Tools can be devised to help users begin evaluation, particularly in new methods of evaluation that have emerged with electronically delivered services, for example, unobtrusive work through computer logging procedures (transaction log analysis) and online evaluation methods.

In the US, Bonnie Lindauer has developed a practical manual for outcomes assessment. There are forms to use and examples of use from other institutions, as well as key documents to help institutions conduct their own outcomes assessment programme (Lindauer, 2000).

Shim *et al.* (2001b) compiled a data collection manual for network statistics and performance measures. This has arisen from the e-metrics project of the ARL (see note 6) and is a useful collection of forms for standardized collection of data, together with information about designing an institutional set of performance measures.

Nelson and Fernekes (2002) have produced a practical workbook that focuses on outcomes assessment, offering, in 12 areas of library activity, selections from the ACRL College Standards on performance areas and measures that might be used to demonstrate compliance and sources to use for assessment data. Clearly this is of most use to practitioners in the US, but many of the tools could be adapted to the UK higher education situation.

In the UK, John Crawford (2000) compiled the Aslib guide to evaluating LIS. Although it covers all types of library, Chapter 6 is entitled 'Performance measurement for the electronic library' (Crawford, 2000, pp. 106–121). The following subject headings are included: what the electronic library does; users and usage;

identifying performance issues and performance indicators; EQUINOX indicators; use of electronic services in practice; survey methods; outcomes and consequences.

The need for evaluation is addressed in two new books to emerge from Facet Publishing for the information profession (Chowdhury and Chowdhury, 2003 and Gorman, 2002). Both have chapters on the evaluation of digital libraries, although Gorman's work focuses more closely on digital collections than on the whole infrastructure of EIS. There are few other published UK manuals, although the EQUINOX performance indicators and some SCONUL publications are of help in this area (Revill and Ford, 1996 and West, 2001).

Specific projects related to the evaluation of EIS have been noted. In summary, the following will contribute greatly to the need of practitioners in academic libraries in the UK for help with developing evaluation activity, skills to conduct evaluation and materials to use directly in their work:

- Project COUNTER (see note 2).
- EQUINOX performance indicators (see note 4).
- SCONUL activities (see note 5).
- The eVALUEd project toolkit (see note 3).

Conclusions

Evaluation has an integral role in the policy-making, planning and practice of digital libraries. It is likely that the requirement to provide evaluation data will increase as more electronic resources become available, the markets in which academic institutions operate continue to evolve and the many different stakeholders in digital libraries increasingly expect evidence of the value of EIS in supporting institutional goals.

There is no doubt that the evaluation of virtual services presents many challenges. Over time, it is hoped that some of these may be overcome through the work of a number of research projects and initiatives in the area. Of course, the rapid proliferation of EIS and the rate of change associated with this may bring further challenges to digital library evaluation in the future.

While it is not possible to predict accurately the future EIS landscape, it is incumbent on library and information services managers in higher education institutions to accept the value and importance of evaluation in order to:

- discover how these services are used,
- assess their impact (in order to secure further funding),
- manage EIS strategically,
- provide services tailored to users' needs.

In addition, the evaluation of EIS has a number of potential benefits which extend beyond the individual service and institution. These include:

- helping to develop a culture of evidence-based practice within academic libraries,

- raising the profile of EIS within the wider academic and library communities and beyond, for example, within government,
- providing evidence to support the work of professional bodies,
- contributing to the development of the library profession as a whole.

Digital library managers need to develop evaluation plans that can be routinely updated and improved in the light of new developments in research in the area. The prevailing view would appear to be that the best course of action is to make a start with an achievable evaluation of a contained aspect of a service. As Oakland writes in the business context:

> A good measurement system will start with the customer and measure the right things. . . . it is often better to start with simple measures and improve them. (Oakland, 2000, p. 122)

Indeed, it would seem that, with so many resources now invested in EIS, there is no longer in higher education libraries the option to do nothing about the evaluation of such services.

Notes

1 The DELOS project website is at: http://delos-noe.iei.pi.cnr.it/index.html.
2 The Project COUNTER website is at: http://www.projectcounter.org/index.html.
3 The eVALUEd project website is at: http://www.evalued.uce.ak.uk/.
4 The EQUINOX performance indicators are available at: http://equinox.dcu.ie/reports/pilist.html.
5 The SCONUL Advisory Committee on Performance Improvement (SCONUL ACPI) is at http://www.sconul.ac.uk/performance_ind/terms.htm.
6 LIBQUAL+ is at: http://www.arl.org/libqual/geninfo/faqgen.html.
7 The ARL e-metrics project website is at: http://www.arl.org/stats/newmeas/emetrics/index.html.

References

Ashcroft, L. (2000), 'Win-win-win: can the evaluation and promotion of electronic journals bring benefits to library suppliers, information professionals and users?', *Library Management*, 21(9), 466–471.

Association of College and Research Libraries (1998), *Task Force on Academic Library Outcomes Assessment Report* (Available at: http://www.ala.org/acrl/outcome.html).

Banwell, L. and Gannon-Leary, P. (1999), 'A review of the literature for the JUBILEE Project (JISC User Behaviour Information Seeking: Longitudinal Evaluation of Electronic information services)', *The New Review of Academic Librarianship*, 5, 81–114.

Barton, J. and Blagden, J. (1998) *Academic Library Effectiveness: A Comparative Approach*, British Library Research and Innovation Centre, British Library Research and Innovation Report 120.

Bertot, J.C. and McClure, C.R. (1998a), 'Measuring Electronic Services in Public Libraries: Issues and Recommendations', *Public Libraries*, 37(3): 176–180.

Bertot, J.C. and McClure, C.R. (1998b), *The 1998 National Survey of US Public Library*

Outlet Internet Connectivity: Final Report (Washington, DC: National Commission on Libraries and Information Science).

Blixrud, J.C. (2002), 'Measures for electronic use: the ARL e-metrics project', paper presented at the *Statistics in Practice: Measuring and Managing*, IFLA Satellite Conference, 13–25 August 2002, Loughborough, UK (available at: http://www.arl.org/stats/newmeas/emetrics/Blixrud_IFLA.pdf).

Brophy, P. and Wynne, P.M. (1997), *Management Information Systems and Performance Measurement for the Electronic Library: eLib Supporting Study* (MIEL2). Final report, JISC (available at: http://www.ukoln.ac.uk/dlis/models/studies/mis/mis.rtf).

Chowdhury, G.G. and Chowdhury, S. (1999), 'Digital Library Research: Major Issues and Trends', *Journal of Documentation*, 55(4), 409–448.

Chowdhury, G.G. and Chowdhury, S. (2003), *Introduction to Digital Libraries* (London: Facet).

Covey, D.T. (2002), *Usage and Usability Assessment: Library Practices and Concerns* (Washington, DC: Digital Library Federation; Council on Library and Information Resources) (available at: http://www.clir.org/pubs/reports/pub105/pub105.pdf).

Crawford, J. (2000), *Evaluation of Library and Information Services*, 2nd edn (London: Aslib) Aslib Know How Guide.

Currier, S., Brown, S. and Ekmekioglu, F.C. (2001) *INSPIRAL: Investigating Portals for Information Resources and Learning: Final Report* (available at: http://inspiral.cdlr.strath.ac.uk/documents/INSPfinrep.doc).

Eaton, J. (2002), 'Measuring user statistics', *Cilip Update*, 1(6), 44–45.

Effective Academic Library (1995), *The Effective Academic Library: a Framework for Evaluating the Performance of UK Academic Libraries*, A consultative report to the HEFCE, SHEFC, HEFCW and DENI by the Joint Funding Councils' Ad-Hoc Group on Performance Indicators for Libraries.

eVALUEd Paper 1 (2002), *Questionnaire to Higher Education Institutions in the UK: Analysis of Responses* (available at: http://www.cie.uce.ac.uk/evalued/Library/Paper1_Qu Analysis.pdf).

Ford, G. (1996), 'Performance assessment: the way forward', in: S. Morgan (ed.), *Performance Assessment in Academic Libraries* (London: Mansell), pp. 156–173.

Ford, G. (2001) 'Theory and practice in the networked environment: a European perspective', in: C.R. McClure, and J.C. Bertot, (eds), *Evaluating Networked Information Services: Techniques, Policy and Issues* (Melford, NJ: Information Today), ASIST Monograph Series, pp. 1–22.

Fuhr, N., Hansen, P., Mabe, M., Micsik, A. and Sølvberg, I. (2001), 'Digital libraries: a generic classification and evaluation scheme', in: P. Constantopoulos and I.T. Sølvberg, (eds), *Research and Advanced Technology for Digital Libraries*. Proceedings, of the *5th European Conference, ECDL 2001*, Darmstadt, Germany, 4–9 September. (Springer), pp. 187–199.

Gorman, G.E. (ed.) (2002), *The Digital Factor in Library and Information Services*. International Yearbook of Library and Information Management 2002–2003 (London: Facet).

Gratch-Lindauer, B. (2002), 'Comparing the regional accreditation standards: outcomes assessment and other trends', *Journal of Academic Librarianship*, 28(1–2), 14–25.

Jones, M.L.W., Gay, G.K. and Rieger, R.H. (1999), 'Project soup: comparing evaluations of digital collection efforts', *D-Lib magazine*, 5(11) (available at: http://www.dlib.org/dlib/november99/11jones.html).

Kelleher, J., Sommerlad, E. and Stern, E. (1996), *Evaluation of the Electronic Libraries Programme: Guidelines for Elib Project Evaluation* (London: Tavistock Institute) (available at: http://www.ukoln.ac.uk/services/elib/papers/tavistock/evaluation-guide/intro.html).

Lindauer, B.G. (2000), *Measuring what Matters: a Library/LRC Outcomes Assessment Manual* (Fairfield, CA: Learning Resources Association of California Community Colleges).

Marchionini, G. (2000), 'Evaluating Digital Libraries: A Longitudinal and Multifaceted View', *Library Trends*, 49(2), 304–333.

Marchionini, G., Plaisant, C. and Komlodi, A. (2001), 'The people in digital libraries: multifaceted approaches to assessing needs and impact', *Digital Library Use: Social Practice in Design and Evaluation* (available at: http://ils.unc.edu/'march/revision.pdf).

McClure, C.R. (2003), 'Evaluating Processes in an Academic Library Setting', unpublished working document, (Tallahassee, Florida: Information Use Management and Policy Institute).

McClure, C.R. and Bertot, J.C. (2001), *Evaluating Networked Information Services: Techniques, Policy and Issues* (Medford, New Jersey: Information Today) ASIST Monograph Series.

Nelson, W.N. and Fernekes, R.W. (2002), *Standards and Assessment for Academic Libraries: a Workbook* (Chicago: American Library Association).

Oakland, J.S. (2000), *Total Quality Management: Text with Cases* 2nd edn (Oxford: Butterworth-Heinemann).

Revill, D. and Ford, G. (1996), *User Satisfaction: Standard Survey Forms for Academic Libraries* (SCONUL Advisory Committee on Performance Indicators).

Saracevic, T. (1997), 'Studying the value of library and information services: I establishing a theoretical framework; II methodology and taxonomy', *Journal of the American Society for Information Science*, 48(6), 527–563.

Saracevic, T. (2000), 'Digital library evaluation: toward an evolution of concepts', *Library Trends*, 49(2), 350–369.

Shim, W. and McClure, C.R. (2002), 'Improving database vendors' usage statistics reporting through collaboration between libraries and vendors', *College and Research Libraries*, 63(6), 499–514.

Shim, W., McClure, C.R., Fraser, B. and Bertot, J.C. (2001a) *Measures and Statistics for Research Library Networked Services: Procedures and Issues*, ARL e-metrics phase II report (Washington, DC: Association of Research Libraries). [The authors refer to a former online version of this report. Pagination may have changed in the published report.]

Shim, W., McClure, C.R., Fraser, B.T. and Bertot, J.C. (2001b), *Data Collection Manual for Academic and Research Library Network Statistics and Performance Measures* (Washington, DC: Association of Research Libraries). (available at: www.arl.org/stats/newmeas/emetrics/phase3/ARL_Emetrics_Data_Collection_manual.pdf).

West, C. (2001), *Measuring User Satisfaction: a Practical Guide for Academic Libraries*, SCONUL briefing paper.

Winkworth, I. (2001), 'Innovative United Kingdom approaches to measuring service quality', *Library Trends*, 49(4), 718–731.

Wolf, M. (2001), 'Electronic journals: use, evaluation and policy', *Information Services and Use*, 21(3–4), 249–261.

PART 2
IMPLEMENTATION AND PRACTICE

Chapter 9

Building a Digital Library in 80 Days: The Glasgow Experience

Alan Dawson

Background

The Glasgow Digital Library (GDL)[1] is intended to be a regional, cooperative, distributed digital library, based in Glasgow, the largest city in Scotland. It attempts to combine theory with practice, research project with user service, and to balance the immediate needs of local partners and users with a global and long-term perspective on digital resources. It is not a typical digital library, but there is probably no such thing.

The GDL is based in the Centre for Digital Library Research (CDLR),[2] although it is operated as a cooperative venture. It was funded as one of several research projects under the theme of collaborative collection management.[3] Its long-term aim is to create a digital library to support teaching, learning, research and public information, but its initial requirement was to investigate and report on planning, implementing, operating and evaluating the library. This meant there was a need to create a library service in order to research its management and operation, although funding was provided only to carry out the research project, not to create a user service. Once the project was under way, this paradox was partially resolved by submitting additional funding bids for specific digitization projects, which allowed the library to create its own content. However, the time and work devoted to content creation and management meant that, by the end of the two-year research funding, there was little time for completion of some initial goals, such as evaluation, promotion and development of a sustainable financial model.

By early 2003, the GDL incorporated six main digital collections, with a total of around 5000 items.[4] Details of these collections are available via the GDL itself, along with documents recording its partners, policies and early development. Further information about the philosophy and development of the library is given by Nicholson and Macgregor (2002), while more information about its structure and collections is provided by Nicholson *et al.* (2003).

Issues, Problems and Solutions

In an extensive review of literature, databases and project websites concerning digital library research, Chowdhury and Chowdhury (1999) identified 16 headings and highlighted 'major research activities in each of these areas', aiming to give 'an indication of the research issues that need to be addressed and resolved in the near future in order to bring the digital library from the researcher's laboratory to the real life environment.'

Many of the issues identified are closely interconnected, so the headings are not entirely distinct topics, but they do offer a useful means of structuring the subject area. For each area, the issues, problems, solutions and lessons are identified. This is a value judgement (by the author), on a 1–5 scale, of the extent to which the issue is fundamental to the purpose and philosophy of the GDL. Some of this stems from the CDLR approach as a whole. For example, 'Standards' gets a 5 because standards matter – they are of fundamental importance to what the GDL is about, whereas 'Access and file management' is not an important issue and is rated 1, because at present the GDL is not concerned with user authentication or access control.

At the time of initial implementation, the main focus was on the collections and how to deal with their content, with little reference to research papers. The following evaluation of the relationship between theory and practice is therefore entirely retrospective.

Issue 1. Collection Development

Issues and Problems

In the early stages of the GDL, collection development was not a big issue because the focus was on establishing a collaborative framework for library operation, involving all project partners. Furthermore, there was little point worrying about collection development policy when there was no funding to carry out digitization anyway. It was necessary to deal with a preliminary issue of library purpose and philosophy, discussed in the next section, before taking a coherent view of collection development.

Solutions

Once the realities of what was feasible with available funding became clear, collection development could be addressed. Initially there were three main priorities.

- To make use of physical collections held by project partners, for both political and practical purposes (for example, the Red Clydeside collection[5]).
- To establish collections that illustrated the benefits of a collaborative project (for example, the GlasgowInfo collection[6]) by pooling resources that might otherwise result in duplication of effort.
- To create content that was not just *about* Glasgow, but also *for* Glasgow (for example, the Aspect collection[7]).

In practice, it was over a year before it was feasible to write a collection policy. Although the policy is terse and brief, it is important that it exists, has been agreed by project partners, and is publicly available.

Lessons

A coherent collection development policy is essential but cannot be created in a vacuum. It has to follow from a broad vision of library purpose and philosophy, and needs to balance ideals against practicalities, which may involve assigning development priorities. The policy is likely to require periodic updating and should be reviewed at least once a year.

Practical importance of this issue to GDL: 4
Time expended: 3 per cent

Issue 2. Development Methodology and Design Issues

Issues and Problems

A digital library system has been described as 'a number of servers, spread over the Internet, that interact with each other to meet user requests' (Chowdhury and Chowdhury, 1999). The organization and management of diverse collections of digital objects was a big issue for the GDL, but at a simpler level. The CDLR had already established a service meeting these criteria (CAIRNS[8]) but this was regarded as a distributed library catalogue rather than a digital library. The GDL was not initially concerned with interactions between distributed servers, but it did need a system for managing its content. This was less simple than it sounds, with multiple contributors, collections, file formats and access methods involved. The requirements of different elements of the GDL meant that, at one stage, similar (but not identical) information was being held and maintained in several different forms.

- Access databases containing titles and descriptions of digital objects.
- CDs containing folders of hundreds of images.
- Web pages offering prototype public access to images and documents.
- A library catalogue system holding MARC records of object metadata.

While there is nothing wrong with providing information in more than one form, there had to be mechanisms for integrating its management and ensuring that updating only took place in one location.

Solutions

A clear and consistent naming scheme was devised and adopted for all objects in all collections within the library. As Access databases were required as a condition of funding for three of the first six collections,[9] Access was chosen as the initial content and metadata repository for all six collections. Library content and metadata were then generated from Access in different forms for different purposes, for example web pages and MARC 21 records,[10] by including HTML mark-up and MARC tags in the database and using Visual Basic programs to automate the integration and exporting of content, mark-up and metadata.[11] In effect, this was a modular, flexible, low-cost content management system using common desktop software. The advantages of the modular approach for the GDL were that it facilitated flexible re-use of metadata, enabled content creation to be easily distributed amongst contributors, and allowed additional collections to be plugged in to the library relatively easily and cheaply.

Lessons

Managing diverse digital content from multiple sources does not necessarily require expensive content management software, but it can help. Most people, even librarians, are not as organized or systematic as they might be. Developing an efficient methodology for a heterogeneous distributed digital library requires a diligent and consistent approach from those involved, or rigorous control policies and mechanisms, or software tools that can compensate for lack of diligence and rigour. Basically, a library of any size and complexity has to be well-organized and managed whatever software is used.

Practical importance of this issue to GDL: 5
Time expended: 20 per cent

Issue 3. User Interfaces

Issues and Problems

There were five main requirements for the GDL web interface: consistency, flexibility, scalability, accessibility and feasibility. *Consistency* meant devising a design template that could provide visual coherence across all collections without imposing blanket uniformity. *Flexibility* meant enabling users to access library content in different ways – across as well as within collections. *Scalability* meant creating an interface that would look acceptable with only three or four collections yet be able to cope with dozens or hundreds. *Accessibility* meant meeting requirements of funding bodies and standard web accessibility guidelines.[12] *Feasibility* meant creating something quickly and inexpensively.

Solutions

As there was little time to spend creating and testing complicated designs, and no designers eager to show off their skills, the solution was to make a virtue out of necessity and seek simplicity. The content of the library was judged to be inherently interesting, with many striking images, so all that was needed was a clear set of labels and some example images to illustrate each collection, together with options for navigating the library as a whole – by place and by subjects – as an alternative to the collection-centred view.

Lessons

There are so many interface design options for a large and complex service that it is impossible to offer general guidelines in a short space.[13] The critical point is to understand the main priorities for the user interface, with an appropriate balance between simplicity and sophistication, complexity and accessibility, features and feasibility, style and substance. The use of templates and stylesheets (or similar mechanisms) to provide design consistency and flexibility is essential.

Practical importance of this issue to GDL: 4
Time expended: 7 per cent

Issue 4. Information Organization: Classification and Indexing

Issues and Problems

One of the aims of the library was to make it possible to search and browse across collections, so a broad but controlled method of information classification was required. The CDLR has substantial experience of using the Dewey Decimal Classification (DDC) scheme, in the long-established BUBL LINK catalogue of internet resources, so is familiar with the costs and benefits of this approach. BUBL also uses a complementary system of controlled browseable subject terms[14] which is popular with users, although lacking the depth of hierarchical structure offered by DDC. Both are desirable, but maintaining DDC classification and a controlled subject vocabulary is time-consuming and might not be sustainable for the GDL.

Solutions

The current approach is to use Library of Congress Subject Headings (LCSH) as the primary means of linking diverse collections into a coherent information structure. LCSH is far from perfect but it is large and widely used. One of its main problems is a cultural bias toward North America, which in some areas renders it amusingly inappropriate for a Scottish context.[15] LCSH is therefore supplemented by controlled local subject terms, agreed with project partners, where this is considered essential. The GDL subject terms are used in the web interface while the LCSH terms are included in the metadata and used in contexts where international compatibility is required.[16] In addition to subject terms, controlled authority files for place names and people names are used (where relevant) to provide library-wide consistency and an alternative to the collection-centred view.

Lessons

One of the beauties of a digital library is the flexibility it provides in allowing the same item to appear in more than one place, under different subject headings, or even as part of different collections. In order to make this feasible, a controlled information structure is required, such as LCSH or an alternative taxonomy. This can also serve to illustrate the scope and scale of collections, and influence topic chunking, as well as making searching more reliable. It is much easier to make changes to a controlled vocabulary than try to introduce retrospective consistency to an uncontrolled set of keywords.

Practical importance of this issue to GDL: 5
Time expended: 5 per cent

Issue 5. Resource Discovery: Metadata

Issues and Problems

Inevitably, there were numerous issues associated with metadata creation and management, some quite subtle and detailed. Only the most significant are mentioned here. One major question was whether to catalogue the original item or the digital copy, for example, was the author (MARC) or creator (Dublin Core) of a booklet the person who wrote it or the organization responsible for digitizing it? Perhaps the biggest issue was how to handle the whole metadata creation and management process, in order to ensure consistency when the same records appeared in multiple locations. There was even the prospect of both including metadata within data (DC records embedded in web pages) and data within metadata (item descriptions or even full text included in the 500 or 520 field of a MARC record). With a large collection of relatively small digital objects, the initially clear distinction between data and metadata began to crumble. Granularity was also a major issue – were individual metadata records required for every item in a themed collection, or could one use a few collection-level records? This problem of granularity appeared to require a mechanism for cascading metadata, analogous to cascading style sheets for web page formatting.

Solutions

Unsurprisingly, the solution adopted was to design a flexible database structure that was not tied to any particular metadata scheme, then to write content extraction routines (Visual Basic programs) that allowed metadata to be generated in different formats for different purposes. For example, separate forename and surname fields in the database for the Aspect collection were combined to produce standard name format for display via web pages, but a surname-first format for use in embedded Dublin Core metadata and in a separate file of MARC records. The use of default values in databases made consistent record creation relatively easy, but once the records had been detached from their nest and released into the world as independent items, each of them had to have the full metadata set included. No means for implementing cascading metadata[17] at a global level has yet been found.

Lessons

It is better to be accurate and consistent in creating metadata for a few key fields – for example, title, author, summary, date, subject terms – than to be so daunted by complexity that nothing gets done. The question of which metadata standard to use (Dublin Core, IMS, MARC etc) is not a lifelong commitment, as it is possible to translate between them (up to a point), if the metadata itself is in good shape. More difficult questions concern who should create the metadata, whether central editorial control is required, and how the process is managed. The ability to carry out repetitive but precise search-and-replace editing on specific metadata fields (or use an alternative control mechanism) is enormously useful, as it allows decisions to be taken early without worrying about future revisions. Controlled vocabularies or authority files are extremely useful for fields such as resource types, dates, people, organizations and places, as well as being essential for subject terms.

Practical importance of this issue to GDL: 5
Time expended: 10 per cent

Issue 6. Access and File Management

Comments

This topic may be better labelled as access control or authentication, as it is concerned with policies and procedures for controlling who can access different types of content. This is a big issue for commercial services and some digital libraries, but not for the Glasgow Digital Library, which is freely available to all.

Solutions

None required as yet.

Lessons

If access control is required then one needs a scaleable system capable of handling it and sound administrative procedures.

Practical importance of this issue to GDL: 1
Time expended: 0 per cent

Issue 7. User Studies

Comments

The CDLR has conducted user studies for other research projects, but these were not specified as part of the GDL project, although their potential benefit is accepted.

Solutions

None required as yet.

Lessons

Set priorities and accept that not everything can be done with limited resources.

> *Practical importance of this issue to GDL:* 1
> *Time expended:* 0 per cent

Issue 8. Information Retrieval

Issues and Problems

The GDL aims to offer users several search options – across the entire library, within a single collection, within a single field in a collection or the whole library, or cross-searching the GDL with other digital libraries and library catalogues. There are numerous software solutions available – on one occasion over 20 possible search tools were counted within the CDLR alone. In contrast to this richness and complexity there is the Google factor – web users have become used to the simplest possible search interface and very fast results. There are real difficulties in offering complex search options, and in summarizing the scope and meaning of these options, via a simple user interface.

Solutions

This is still an area under development. In the short term, priority was given to creating a flexible browseable interface to illustrate existing collections, as users need an overview of the content in order to carry out useful searches. Once this was in place, search options were added one collection at a time, using different software solutions for different collections.[18] This is not ideal from a user service perspective, as there is an inherent (although minor) inconsistency between search operations in different areas of the library. However, from a research perspective it is useful to investigate and understand different search solutions. In the longer term, the aim is to use intelligent scripting to provide cascading search facilities, that is, to search fields with the highest value first (such as titles and subject terms), then to search other metadata fields only if no matches are found, then continue with full-text searching or cross-searching only if no matches are found in any metadata fields. Although these options will be available explicitly via an advanced search interface, most users will probably use the simple search box. The cascading search[19] is intended to make a simple search as effective as possible and to transfer complexity from the interface to the information retrieval mechanism.

Lessons

Although conceptually simple, there are almost endless possibilities in providing complex search facilities for a digital library. Standard issues need to be resolved, such as indexing, relevance ranking, case sensitivity, phrase searching, stemming, pattern matching, Boolean searching and results paging. In the short term it is better to offer something currently feasible than nothing at all, but it is also advisable to have plans for better services and work towards them one step at a time.

Practical importance of this issue to GDL: 5
Time expended: 8 per cent

Issue 9. Legal Issues

Issues and Problems

Legal issues have not been a major headache for the GDL but still had to be addressed. As a short-term project and a partnership between several institutions, its legal status was unclear for matters such as intellectual property rights and liability. Where external funding was sought for digitization projects, the GDL had to secure rights to publish the materials created, as well as submitting them to the funding body.

Solutions

None. The question of legal status was left unresolved in the short term (there were many more pressing matters). The main legal requirement was to obtain written permission from copyright holders before digitizing any copyright material. The main implementation decision was whether to proceed in those few cases where the copyright holder could not be traced (initially no, later yes).

Lessons

Copyright is still a massive issue for most digital libraries, and service providers must be clear about their rights and responsibilities. It is important to understand the legal issues, take initial advice and follow legal requirements, but equally important not to be impeded by unnecessary legal detail or worried by improbable scenarios.

Practical importance of this issue to GDL: 2
Time expended: 1 per cent

Issue 10. Social Issues

Comments

This broad heading is used to refer to 'elements of the social world, including a sense of community, that we do not want to lose from our notions of "library".' (Chowdhury and Chowdhury, 1999). Researching these issues played a larger role in the initial plan for the GDL than in its subsequent development, but they were not ignored. There were three main areas where social interaction was considered: between project partners, between the library and its users, and amongst users themselves.

Solutions

None really, other than the usual mantra that good communication is very important. For project partners, the GDL relied on the trusty mailing list, which has some advantages over more active or intrusive methods. This will also be the preferred solution for user communication until there is evidence of demand for something more sophisticated.

Lessons

Communications and meetings may appear to contribute little of tangible benefit, but are valuable in keeping partners informed of developments and enthusiastic about outcomes. An active and committed user community cannot be enforced but has to be earned, for example by providing compelling content, by making it easy for users to contact the service (and each other) and by responding promptly to feedback.

> *Practical importance of this issue to GDL:* 2
> *Time expended:* 2 per cent

Issue 11. Evaluation of Digital Information

Issues and Problems

There are two main issues here – ensuring users accept the authenticity of library content and preventing others copying and misrepresenting it. As a non-commercial venture, the GDL is more concerned with open access and flexibility than with protecting content from being copied. However, it has had to consider the question of whether digitally to enhance materials in order to improve their presentation, even though the aim of digitization was to create an accurate copy of the original source material.

Solutions

Most attention has been paid to image manipulation, but similar principles apply to text, audio, video and other content types. In practice, images are routinely manipulated after creation; they are converted from TIFF to JPEG format, reduced in size, and thumbnail images may be created. Sometimes borders are trimmed, edges sharpened, and gamma correction adjusted to lighten dark areas. None of this affects the authenticity of the material – it is common practice and does not involve misrepresentation. In a few cases, image editing has been carried out. For example, some leaflets from the Aspect collection had been delivered to individual contributors and so included their names and addresses. Rather than risk damaging the original by tearing off a sticky label, the personal details were edited out after digitization – a sensible procedure that does not affect authenticity. A small step further involved digitally enhancing a few images from the Red Clydeside collection, where the original was worn or damaged, for example.

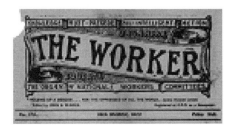 

For the GDL, this has been the limit of digital manipulation; the aim is to preserve and accurately portray the original material, not misrepresent it. Yet these examples show the issue is less clear-cut than might be imagined. It is a big step from completing a background colour to adding missing words to a document or missing faces to a photograph, yet any manipulation at all could raise questions about authenticity.

Lessons

If measures are needed to protect online content then technical solutions are available, such as digital watermarking. Proving the authenticity of objects is a different matter, where solutions are more social then technical. Digitization involves making value judgements, so it is advisable, in a policy document, to define limits for any digital manipulation, ensure those involved understand and adhere to them, and inform users of this policy. Such a policy could also cover general editorial conventions such as wording, spelling and use of value judgements in item descriptions. As well as being inherently useful, consistent use of explicit guidelines helps ensure the value of digital information and the reputation of the library.

Practical importance of this issue to GDL: 3
Time expended: 3 per cent

Issue 12. Evaluation of Digital Libraries

Comments

As a research project, the GDL could claim to have fulfilled its obligations by submitting a final report to its primary funding body, with any practical value to library users being a bonus. This argument is simplistic and disingenuous, but could be used to justify the absence of any formal evaluation process.

Solutions

None as yet. Ideally there would be qualitative evaluation, via user studies, and quantitative evaluation, by analysing usage logs of web pages and search terms to determine the scale and nature of library usage (for example, see Dawson, 1999). In practice such formal evaluation is unlikely until the library has been further developed and promoted.

Lessons

As no practical guidance can be given based on implementation, a theoretical perspective is offered. Usability assessment based primarily on interface design is 'too narrow a basis for evaluating something as complex as a DL . . . evaluation of a DL's effectiveness has to be in terms of its impact on users' work' (Chowdhury and Chowdhury, 1999). In other words, there is little point in having a beautifully designed interface to a collection that no one is interested in, or a superb collection that is too hard to get at.

> *Practical importance of this issue to GDL:* 2
> *Time expended:* 0 per cent

Issue 13. Standards

Issues and Problems

More than any other topic, the question of standards permeates other issues, especially resource discovery, information organization, and preservation. The GDL is committed to compatibility with international standards. Easily said, but meaningless in itself, when there are so many standards to choose from. The challenge for the GDL was not just to specify the standards it will use but to create a coherent information environment and set of procedures that enable content contributors to adhere to the standards in a practicable and straightforward manner.

Solutions

Choice of standards for the GDL was determined by its global outlook and concerns for long-term interoperability. Key standards are Dublin Core and MARC

21 for metadata, LCSH for subject vocabulary, AACR2[20] for resource descriptions, SQL for information retrieval, XHTML and W3C web accessibility guidelines for web pages, TIFF and JPEG for image format, and Z39.50 for cross-searching with other catalogues (OAI may also become important in future). These standards are supplemented by editorial guidelines and authority files for place names and resource types. Although local in scope, these are equally important in providing consistency of resource description across collections and assisting information retrieval.

Lessons

The standards listed above are quite different from each other in purpose and implementation. In order to make sensible decisions about which standards to use in a digital library it is essential to be aware of their scope and purpose (and the primary purpose of the library), but not necessary to understand the technical details of each one. Compliance with standards for service providers (as opposed to software providers) is rarely technically difficult but does require clear policies and disciplined work practices. Adherence to chosen standards should not be seen as an additional burden to be imposed after content creation but as an inherent part of the digital library development environment.

Practical importance of this issue to GDL: 5
Time expended: 7 per cent

Issue 14. Preservation

Issues and Problems

Another aspect to the principle of 'think globally, act locally' is 'think long-term, act short-term'. The GDL aims to create, describe and manage content with an indefinite life-span, including historical material that may still be of interest in hundreds of years' time. There are three main categories of concern: physical storage media (disks, CDs, tapes and so on), content format (relational databases, Word documents, web pages, image files and so on) and information structures (MARC, DC, LCSH and so on).

Solutions

For content and metadata, the solutions lie in structures and standards. Textual content held in a consistent manner in a structured database can always be exported to another format – even to plain text. International standards such as MARC21 will not disappear overnight, even if by 2203 it has become MARC41. Storage media may be more of a problem, as there is no reliable way of predicting future technical developments, so a good policy is to keep master copies of data in two formats and be prepared to migrate should either become outdated. Retaining a paper copy of every printable object in a digital library might also guarantee preservation, but would rather miss the point. Another possibility worth considering, if material is deleted or edited as well as added, is to take a complete snapshot of library content at fixed intervals, say annually.

Lessons

Only store content in a software package if you are sure you know how to get it out again. Be prepared to store material in a different format to that used for public access. Make sure you can always match metadata to content (for example, a well-preserved old photograph might be quite interesting, but it has far greater value if it is known who or what it was and when and where it was taken). Think long-term.

Practical importance of this issue to GDL: 4
Time expended: 2 per cent

Issue 15. Implications for Library Managers

Comments

There are two complementary issues here – implications for existing managers of physical libraries and implications for those who have responsibility for digital libraries but may not think of themselves as librarians. Some management issues are similar, such as dealing with user enquiries, others rather different, such as content maintenance and preservation. One major difference between the GDL and most physical libraries is that it creates and commissions content as well as collecting and managing it.

Solutions

None as yet. The GDL is still grappling with possible transition from research project to user service. Ongoing library management is a key issue to be addressed before this transition can occur.

Lessons

In a cooperative enterprise it is important for all partners to feel part of the library and be committed to its development, but cooperative management can be slow and inefficient. Someone needs to be in charge on a daily basis who can understand technical issues but not be subservient to them, and can take responsibility for maintenance matters such as collection updating, software upgrading, feature development and user enquiries.

Practical importance of this issue to GDL: 3
Time expended: 1 per cent

Issue 16. Future Directions

Under this heading, Chowdhury and Chowdhury (1999) summarized initiatives and projects that were beginning or ongoing in 1999. Four years is a long time in digital library research, so it is worth considering a more recent view of the field (Soergel, 2002), which presented 'a broad-based digital library research and development framework . . . to evaluate and integrate existing research and practice and to provide a structured vision for what digital libraries can be'. Soergel's framework consists of three guiding principles and 11 specific themes for digital library research. The principles relate to ideological and social issues and will be discussed later, whereas the themes relate to future directions and are briefly assessed below, again by relating theory to practice.

Soergel's Themes for DL Research and Development

Theme 1. DLs Must Integrate Access to Materials with Access to Tools to Process these Materials

Comment No real problem in practice if most user access is via web browsers with a plug-in for handling PDF. Where special software tools are needed, libraries need to decide how far to adjust the user interface to accommodate repetitive messages about access to supporting software.

Theme 2. DLs Should Support Individual and Community Information Spaces

Comment This is a value judgement that depends on the vision and purpose of the library (see issue 17 below). It may not be feasible or appropriate for all digital libraries. For the GDL it is regarded as a long-term priority in the collection development and management policy. In the short term it is far from practicable with current resources.

Theme 3. Digital Libraries Need Semantic Structure

Comment Absolutely. This theme covers similar ground to issues 4 and 5 above and is indeed, as Soergel argues 'of prime importance'. Without semantic structure then, a digital library is barely a library at all, more the digital equivalent of a charity shop with content piled into unsorted heaps.

Theme 4. DLs Need Linked Data Structures for Powerful Navigation and Search

Comment Soergel considers this a special case of theme 3, but with added value for users by providing 'links across disciplines and across digital libraries'. It is hard to question this principle, but putting it into practice requires subject expertise as well as effective software tools. For a library such as the GDL in an early stage of development it remains an aspiration rather than a practicable proposition.

Theme 5. DLs Should Support Powerful Search that Combines Information across Databases

Comment   Cross-searching is an important principle for the GDL, partly because it can draw on experience available locally from implementing the Z39.50-based CAIRNS service. Even so, the facilities offered by current CAIRNS technology fall some way short of the sophisticated retrieval and presentation from 'distributed access to heterogeneous systems' envisaged by Soergel. This is a major research and development area for the CDLR, yet it is still a pilot rather than an operational service for the GDL. For digital libraries without similar infrastructure and expertise, this will be a difficult theme to pursue.

Theme 6. DL Interfaces Should Guide Users through Complex Tasks

Comment   This is fine if you know what the complex tasks are likely to be, which may be true in subject-specific digital libraries with well-established user communities, but is not the case in a newly-created regional library such as the GDL. This theme is related to that of creating learning materials, which is considered under heading 19 below.

Theme 7. The DL Field Should Provide Ready-made Tools for Building and Using Semantically Rich Digital Libraries

Comment   This theme lies at the heart of the traditional divide between research and practice. The ultimate aim of much research is to deliver useful guidance and solutions for practitioners, yet the specific requirements of the GDL illustrate how difficult it is to provide generally-applicable software tools. For example, the GDL was *required* by funding bodies to submit content in Access databases, it was *required* to create websites to offer public access to content, *required* to offer cross-searching via Z39.50, and *required* to create MARC records for uploading to local and remote databases, and to do all this for a heterogeneous set of collections. There was little chance of any existing toolkit incorporating this functionality, so the GDL had to work out its own development methodology, enabling content and metadata for all collections to be integrated and re-used for different purposes from a single source. Other large libraries will have different, but perhaps similarly complex, requirements. Simpler digital libraries can perhaps be created with existing tools such as Greenstone software.[21] As ever, the main difficulties are not in information technology but in information description and management.

Theme 8. Innovative DL Design Should be Informed by Studies of User Requirements and User Behaviour

Comment   Undoubtedly true, but does the design have to be innovative, if the content is of inherent value? The digital library field has had no period of stability to allow user familiarity. Perhaps some web-based services (again Google springs to mind) are extremely popular owing to their simplicity and predictability – in fact their lack of innovation. They provide simple interfaces to large collections, so perhaps digital libraries can learn from them too.

Theme 9. DL Evaluation Needs to Consider New Functionality

Comment   Soergel's main point here is the same as in issue 12 above, that evaluation of effectiveness has to be in terms of the purpose of the library and its impact on users' work, not just its interface.

Theme 10. Legal/Organizational Issues of Information Access and Rights Management Need to be Addressed Using New Technology

Comment   Yes, but the benefits must outweigh the costs, which may be legal as well as technical and organizational, so the inclination of many digital libraries will be to remain open-access and non-commercial if possible.

Theme 11. DLs Need Sustainable Business Models

Comment   Indeed, but easier said than done, especially in a field largely funded by short-term projects. This theme has the potential to undermine the other ten, as they are all potentially expensive. It may be difficult to justify expenditure on themes where the benefits are unclear or immeasurable. Soergel's point is valid, but the solution elusive. The GDL operates at the low-cost end of the field, where funding for digitization projects amounts to hundreds or a few thousand pounds, not millions. It might be possible to have a sustainable business model with a small budget, but one has to be realistic about the extent to which research issues and themes can be incorporated into a user service.

Additional Digital Library Issues

Some significant issues that arose in implementing the Glasgow Digital Library do not easily fit into the above 16 issues and will be briefly considered.

Issue 17. Library Purpose and Philosophy

Comment

The way a digital library addresses the issues described above ought to reflect its underlying principles of operation, such as who the library is for, what is its vision, and who is paying for it. Soergel (2002) partially addresses this issue by proposing three 'overarching guiding principles'.

- some see the DL field focused on serving research, scholarship, and education, but in order to achieve their full benefit for society and a concomitant viable business model, DLs must also support practice.

- Some see DLs primarily as a means for accessing information, but in order to reach their full potential, DLs must go beyond that and support new ways of intellectual work.
- Some see DLs as providing services primarily to individual users, but DLs must also support collaboration and communities of practice.

These principles are neither right nor wrong, they are value judgements that may not apply to all libraries. Their relevance for the GDL varies according to whether its status is one of research project or user service. An example of an alternative principle for a digital library would be to promote social inclusion by providing simple, low-cost solutions to enable as many people as possible to contribute digital content within a coherent library framework. Different principles are not necessarily mutually exclusive, but they should be explicit so they can help determine the priorities of the library manager, the content of the collection development policy and the nature of implementation.

Solutions

As a regional initiative, the GDL has been something of a cross between a public library and a higher education library. Its content is not geared to particular courses, nor limited to groups such as students, children or even Glaswegians. The involvement of public libraries at steering group level has ensured it aims to provide public information as well as material suitable for teaching, learning and research.

Lessons

Any digital library needs a clear sense of direction. Implementation will be difficult if the goalposts keep shifting. Decisions should take account of underlying principles as well as short-term priorities and technical possibilities.

> *Practical importance of this issue to GDL:* 5
> *Time expended:* 2 per cent

Issue 18. Content Creation

Issues and Problems

Objects do not digitize themselves. Although implicit in other issues, the question of how to carry out digitization and what file types and content formats to use is not explicitly addressed by Chowdhury and Chowdhury (1999), yet is of fundamental importance to any digital library. Equipment, such as scanners, cameras, microphones and portable hard disks, is needed, or funding to pay service providers. Nor do items line themselves up in a queue next to the scanner or camera. Research has to be carried out, items selected for quality and relevance, captions written and edited, even titles may need inventing. Decisions have to be made about image resolution, file sizes, file formats, workflow processes. Even with a basic formula of text and web pages, options include XML, HTML, PDF, Word, RTF, plain text, and decisions have to be made about symbols and characters sets. For image format there are yet more choices. JPEG is common, PNG becoming more widespread, and TIFF possibly recommended for printing or preservation, there are compression options to choose, and a balance required between image quality/size and speed of access. Large images, such as maps, require special software solutions at client or server end, or both. Another major issue is whether to carry out optical character recognition (OCR) on text files held as images. This is time-consuming if results are properly edited, yet offers the substantial added value of fully-searchable text. For sound and video files, MP3 and MPEG are common but by no means universal, and there is a range of proprietary formats.

Solutions

For digitization itself, a mixture of solutions was used. Some were carried out internally on a simple desktop scanner, some by project partners, some by a specialist service (including all large images and glass slides). Using different methods was not a problem in itself but did require careful administration. Similarly, some research and content selection were carried out by the GDL research assistant, some by project partners, and some by external contractors with specialist knowledge. The choice of formats was sometimes determined by the funding body for a collection – TIFF at 300 dpi was the common image file specification. For public access, the GDL offers lower-quality higher-speed JPEG files for screen display, with high-quality images available if requested by users for printing. XHTML is preferred for text, with PDF only used if essential for retaining complex layouts. OCR is carried out if feasible and is carefully checked before publication. MP3 will be used for audio files once these become available.

Lessons

Digitization itself can be very quick – images can be captured in seconds – but the prerequisite selections and decisions, and the subsequent manipulation and management processes, are not trivial. They are crucial, regardless of where the digitization itself occurs. File formats that are standard and predictable, as above, might still be the best choices in the circumstances. It is important to be aware of options and to make choices that suit the library's priorities.

Practical importance of this issue to GDL: 5
Time expended: 20 per cent

Issue 19. Learning Materials

Issues

An organized collection of objects can constitute a valid and valuable digital library, yet many libraries will wish to add value to these objects by creating educational resources based on them, drawing out themes and timelines and emphasizing interrelationships. This task requires subject expertise, it may require tailoring content for a particular target audience, with appropriate design features and additional metadata, and may entail introducing personal judgements. It is usually expensive and time-consuming, yet it can also bring the library to life.

Solutions

In the absence of time or funding to produce learning materials, the GDL approach has been to semi-automate the process where possible, drawing on the values of controlled metadata fields for people, organizations and dates to auto-generate illustrated indexes and timelines linking related items together. Better results could certainly be obtained by additional research and hand-crafting of materials, but this simply is not always possible. The automated process is feasible and the added value is judged to be worth the extra work involved. It is also satisfying to see metadata being used to worthwhile effect.

Lessons

Terminology is important but imprecise. The more educational value added to a digital library, the more it becomes reasonable to describe it as a virtual learning environment. The trick is to do this while preserving the library contents as independent items that can still be re-used and assembled in different ways for different purposes.

Practical importance of this issue to GDL: 3
Time expended: 3 per cent

Issue 20. Promotion and Publicity

Issues

Digital libraries need a promotional strategy that reflects their purpose and philosophy. One difficulty is in deciding when to promote a library if it is under constant development. Premature hype can be damaging and breed cynicism, yet funders and partners may require early promotional activities. Effective publicity may generate user demands on a library which cannot be met, so needs careful planning and timing.

Solutions

None really for offline publicity, although an early awareness day did generate a flurry of interest. For online promotion, the GDL approach was to release a prototype at an early stage of development, as a taster of things to come and evidence of progress. This was also useful in raising awareness, and ensured prominence of GDL content in web search engine results, but it also entailed subsequent design and URL changes.

Lessons

Unless a library has a captive audience, a combination of methods is advisable. Xie and Wolfram (2002) found that 'The majority of respondents reported they were informed about the state digital library service (Wisconsin) through physical libraries', suggesting that printed notices and leaflets are a worthwhile complement to online publicity. For task-oriented users and researchers, the ease of discovering individual library items via web search engines should not be underestimated. Accurate and differentiated titles and metadata within static web pages is invaluable for this purpose.

Practical importance of this issue to GDL: 2
Time expended: 2 per cent

Overview

Many professions note a gap between research and practice. The digital library field is not like that, but there are parallels. Practitioners may have good ideas and be aware of possibilities but simply have neither time nor funds to do much about them, so they prioritize and compromise. This does not mean that such digital library research is irrelevant or misguided, but it means not all of it can be applied. Practitioners must focus on the art of the possible. For some large programmes and institutions the possibilities are very wide, for others very limited. Many of the issues and problems described will be encountered, and all practitioners need to understand them, but the solutions adopted will vary. The decisions on which these solutions are based will be easier to make if the library has a clear purpose and set of policies, and if the implementers understand the broader issues as well as immediate priorities. Few of the solutions adopted for the GDL were technologically innovative, but they were achievable, they suited its particular requirements, and they sustained its potential for long-term scalability and interoperability with other digital libraries.

If any lessons learned from the Glasgow Digital Library experience can be of value elsewhere, then that adds to the GDL's success as a digital library research project. Whether it can ultimately be successful as a digital library service remains to be seen.

Notes

1 The Glasgow Digital Library is available at http://gdl.cdlr.strath.ac.uk/. The 80 days of the title refers refers to the time available to the author to carry out implementation.

2 The Centre for Digital Library Research was formed in August 1999, bringing together long-standing research interests in the digital information area at the University of

Strathclyde. Key aims are to combine theory with practice in innovative ways and to be a centre of excellence on digital libraries issues. As well as a practical focus, its research and development has a holistic approach, aiming to encompass all areas of digital library research, including social and human issues as well as technical and structural matters.

3   Initial two-year funding was from the Research Support Libraries Programme, an initiative with a vision to 'facilitate the best possible arrangements for research support in UK libraries' (http://www.rslp.ac.uk/).

4   The word 'item' is beautifully vague. The quoted figure includes every document, web page and image stored centrally. There are fewer than 5000 catalogue records, as some records describe multi-image objects, such as leaflets. On the other hand, hundreds of catalogue records describe distributed items, which may be considered part of the library. These items were recorded by the GDL and integrated into it (up to a point) but not created by it.

5   Red Clydeside: a history of the labour movement in Glasgow 1910–1932 (http://gdl.cdlr.strath.ac.uk/redclyde/).

6   GlasgowInfo: directory of links to current information concerning the city of Glasgow (http://gdl.cdlr.strath.ac.uk/glasgowinfo/).

7   Aspect: a digital collection of materials from elections to the first Scottish parliament for almost 300 years (http://gdl.cdlr.strath.ac.uk/aspect/).

8   CAIRNS allows the simultaneous searching of multiple library collections of print and electronic resources held by Scottish libraries and information services (http://cairns.lib.strath.ac.uk/).

9   Funding for two collections was from SCRAN (http://www.scran.ac.uk/) and for two collections from the Resources for Learning in Scotland consortium (http://www.rls.org.uk/). Captions and metadata for both were required to be submitted in Access databases, with similar but not identical table structures.

10 MARC records were created in text format and subsequently converted to machine-readable MARC format by using the free MarcEdit software (http://www.onid.orst.edu/'reeset/marcedit/).

11 The process of creating fixed web pages from an underlying database, as opposed to dynamic creation in response to user request, is known as static rendering by some systems.

12 W3C Web Content Accessibility Guidelines (http://www.w3.org/TR/WAI-WEBCON-TENT/).

13 Jakob Neilsen's guidance is still useful and relevant, many years after it was first offered (http://www.useit.com/).

14 Access to BUBL LINK via controlled subject terms is from http://bubl.ac.uk/link/. The DDC view of the same content is available via http://bubl.ac.uk/link/ddc.html.

15 For example, to use LCSH terms 'soccer' and 'bars (drinking establishments)' rather than 'football' and 'pubs', both cornerstones of Glasgow culture, is to invite ridicule for a Glasgow-based service. The CDLR, the National Library of Scotland and other partners are involved in a long-term initiative to extend and internationalize LCSH, working with SACO for subject terms and NACO for place names (http://www.loc.gov/catdir/pcc/).

16 The CDLR subscribes to the OCLC Connexion service (formerly CORC) and is evaluating its use for collaborative cataloguing and other purposes. In this context the use of LCSH and other established authority files is essential (http://www.oclc.org/connexion/).

17 Cascading metadata may be referred to as inherited metadata in other contexts.

18 The ease of importing Access databases into the SQL Server made this the simplest

solution to implement, with ASP or Cold Fusion scripts controlling the interface and search requests.
19 Cascading search may be referred to as automatic search broadening in other contexts.
20 *Anglo-American Cataloguing Rules*, Second Edition.
21 The Greenstone suite of software for building and distributing digital library collections was produced by the New Zealand Digital Library Project (http://www.greenstone.org/).

References

Chowdhury, G.G. and Chowdhury, S. (1999), 'Digital Library Research: Major Issues and Trends', *Journal of Documentation*, 55(4), 409–448, http://www.aslib.co.uk/jdoc/1999/sep/05.html.

Dawson, A. (1999), 'Inferring User Behaviour from Journal Access Figures', *Serials Librarian* 35(3), http://bubl.ac.uk/archive/journals/serlib/v35n0399/dawson.htm.

Nicholson, D. and Macgregor, G. (2002), 'Learning lessons holistically in the Glasgow Digital Library', *D-Lib Magazine*, July/August, http://dlib.org/dlib/july02/nicholson/07nicholson.html.

Nicholson, D., Dawson, A. and Macgregor, G. (2003), 'GDL: Model infrastructure for a regional digital library?', *Widwisawn*, 1, January, http://widwisawn.cdlr.strath.ac.uk/Issues/issue1.htm.

Soergel, D. (2002), 'A Framework for Digital Library Research: Broadening the Vision', *D-Lib Magazine*, December, http://dlib.org/dlib/december02/soergel/12soergel.html.

Xie, H. and Wolfram, D. (2002), 'State Digital Library Usability: Contributing Organizational Factors', *Journal of the American Society for Information Science and Technology*, 53(13), http://www.asis.org/Publications/JASIS/vol53n13.html.

Chapter 10

The Development of UCEEL: A Digital Library for the University of Central England

Chris Dodd and Judith Andrews

Introduction

The University of Central England (UCE) is a large university based in Birmingham, UK with a student population of 23,000. The student body is a complex mix of full-time, part-time, post-graduate, post-experience and distance learners. There are nine academic faculties offering a broad range of courses, many leading to professional qualifications but with an emphasis on vocational education rather than the humanities. In common with library services in many new universities, the UCE Library Service is responsible for multiple campus service points spread across the city.

During the late 1990s, UCE Library Services worked hard to enhance the quality of its services and to move forward with the electronic delivery of information. However, it was aware that there was an ongoing demand for increased flexibility in the way it supported the needs of its users. The concept of a digital library that could provide round the clock access to a wide range of information was recognized as a way of addressing this need for flexibility. However, the path from the adoption of an idea to its actual realization is never simple and this chapter aims to provide an overview of the challenges and the solutions adopted by UCE.

Background

The proposal for the development of a digital library was introduced officially in a Library Development Plan in March 1999. The proposal was discussed in various university groups but was still very much at a theoretical level. To gain a view on the best way to proceed, the Director of Library Services attended the ACM Digital Libraries Conference in San Francisco in August 1999. What became clear from the conference was that UCE did not have the staff resources or the time to build a system from scratch. It was agreed that the most appropriate strategy for UCE would be to procure an off-the-shelf system that could be customized to the University's specific needs.

Definition

There are many definitions of what a digital library is or could be. As UCE's needs were discussed it became clear that its digital library would be a very broad application rather than a single purpose service. The definition of what UCE is creating is:

> A digital library system that provides a means of integrating digitised text, image, audio and video resources. These resources can then be delivered across a network to authorised users wherever they are located, whenever they need them.

Potential Benefits to UCE

It was intended that the digital library would bring a wide range of benefits. These include:

- UCE, in common with many other institutions, has a large number of students who are studying at a distance. A second important element within the student body is part-time students who are working on a full-time basis. These students have to plan their visits to the campus and the Library very carefully as they have little time to waste. An important benefit is that UCEEL (UCE Electronic Library) will allow students to access key material remotely, off-campus. They can also choose to access it at a time that is convenient to their lifestyle and preferred study pattern.
- Academic libraries have always been under pressure to provide appropriate access to key course texts. In recent years, this pressure has grown, as students are less able to purchase essential texts due to increasing financial pressures. A second major benefit of UCEEL is that it will allow chapters of key texts to be made available to all students studying a particular module.
- UCE is committed to widening participation in Higher Education. This means that a percentage of students come from non-traditional backgrounds. UCEEL brings potential benefits in this context in that it allows students to work at their own pace, providing the opportunity for them to return and review a specific resource as many times as they wish without the same pressures of time and access as they would experience if they needed to borrow a physical item from the Library.

Funding

It was soon apparent that the estimated funding required to establish a digital library and meet the wide remit of UCE needs and challenges would be substantial. The internal discussions on the way forward coincided with the announcement of a new methodology of allocating capital funding to UK Higher Education institutions. The UK's Higher Education Funding Council for England (HEFCE) indicated that it had made a notional allocation to each Higher Education institution and that, before releasing this funding, it required each institution to submit detailed bids to indicate how the money would be spent.

After high level discussions within UCE it was agreed that the entire HEFCE capital funding for the university for 2000–2002 (just over £1 million) would be invested in a digital library. This funding has been used for a number of digital library purposes.

How we Delivered UCEEL

The Development Plan

The birth of the digital library commenced with the obvious need for a name or brand for the new entity. UCEEL (UCE Electronic Library) was selected after a competition for suggestions.

A plan, based on the bid submitted to HEFCE, was implemented in July 2000. This included timescales to purchase and customize the digital library system, build the infrastructure, the team, the web interface, the standards and, of course, develop the content. Many of the PRINCE project management principles were applied, including establishing timescales with GANTT charts. At the end of the plan an exit strategy was required as there were a number of outcomes promised to HEFCE with targets running until 2011.

At the senior level, a steering group oversaw the roll-out of the plan, with a management group and project control board to turn the plan into a practical reality and tackle the many challenges that would inevitably arise.

Purchasing the System

In early 2000, a call was issued for expressions of interest from system suppliers. In July of that year, after going through a full tendering process, the contract was awarded to the LSC Group (LSC). The system they supplied was the FORMTEK ORION system, developed in the US by Lockheed Martin. It is a sophisticated document management system with a well-established customer base in a large number of large-scale companies, such as Volvo and Boeing. Behind the system lies an Oracle database installed on a Windows 2000 platform. The system includes a full text retrieval module based on the Verity search engine and a special licence was negotiated with Verity. The inevitable cost of licences and maintenance would obviously become an ongoing commitment but one that was carefully negotiated with the system supplier at the start. For example, all future upgrades and new versions are included in the annual maintenance and licence agreement. In addition, UCEEL is covered by the University's Oracle site licence.

The UCEEL Team

The UCEEL team is based within Library Services and has grown since 2000. It now consists of six posts, the Digital Library (DL) Manager, two DL Officers, Principal DL Assistant and two Digital Library Assistants with substantial ongoing input from key IT Services colleagues. Other input into the team's decisions comes from the Director of Library Services, the Director of IT Services, and members of the Library Management Group.

Recruiting for UCEEL was not going to be easy, particularly as new technical skills, especially around metadata and operating digitization equipment and software, would not be readily available. This was made clear in the recruitment process, but all posts received a good response from potential candidates. Training and experience has been gained over time from a variety of sources, including in-house training, external courses provided by organizations such as BUFVC (British University Film & Video Council) and customized training from the Higher Education Digitization Service (HEDS). This has shown that staff with a library background can successfully adapt to the digital environment and its challenges through a bespoke approach to developing knowledge and skills. The team will be receiving further training in JavaScript and other web-based development tools to help them work even more closely with IT colleagues in ongoing system development.

In the early stages of system development, the LSC Group provided consultancy services and carried out most of the actual system development. After the UCEEL team received detailed training in the FORMTEK ORION system, the balance shifted with a view to much of the system development being carried out in-house. The team maintains a close dialogue with their LSC Group project manager and this ensures that issues and questions are addressed appropriately.

Network Infrastructure and Hardware

The development of UCEEL has been facilitated by the University's infrastructure. It has an IBM ATM network which can supply 25 MB per second to the desktop with guaranteed bandwidth for video and audio streaming. Work is about to begin on replacing this with a new Ethernet network.

IBM Netfinity servers were purchased to run the central UCEEL system – with separate servers for the live or 'production' system (with web gateway software), a test and a development system. A separate server for video and audio streaming was also purchased in anticipation of this future development.

End User Hardware, Software and Digitization Suites

Money was allocated for the purchase of hardware and software, to upgrade and increase the numbers of Library public access PCs and to build a sophisticated digitization suite to create the content. In addition, colour laser printers and additional screen reading and text enhancement software for users with visual impairments were purchased for campus libraries.

Each of the nine academic faculties received an allocation of £50,000 from the £1 million. This was intended to facilitate their use of the system. To receive their allocation each faculty was required to produce a bid document outlining how they would use the digital library, how this use would allow the university to meet the outputs required by HEFCE and what equipment they proposed to buy to meet their objectives. They were encouraged not just to purchase PCs but digital scanners, cameras and other equipment of their own to help create content that would then be hosted on UCEEL.

Finally, a central digitization suite was required for the UCEEL team. HEDS provided consultancy advice on our needs in terms of scanning equipment, software and facilities. This also led to the procurement of two large format (A1 plus) specialist book scanners (made by Zeutschel from Germany). The new colour Zeutschel model is the only one, at the time of writing, operational anywhere in the UK and Northern Europe.

Separate HEDS recommendations for digital audio and video capture, conversion, editing and production led to the purchase for the UCEEL team of both Mac and PC-based digital video and audio suites along with broadcast quality camera equipment and editing software.

It was agreed that the digitization suite would be primarily used internally within the university to create content for UCEEL. However, the suites would also be available to help meet HEFCE targets by offering digitization services to internal and external customers.

Storage

A major problem for any digital library is electronic storage. Again HEDS provided advice based on UCE's potential growth over the next 10 years. Estimates were made of storage requirements for electronic texts, special collections, digital audio and video. The totals were terrifying! Total storage space required by 2010, excluding audio and video, was estimated at 5 terabytes. Total storage space, inclusive of 20,000 hours of audio and 18,000 hours of video, would total 88.5 terabytes.

Some of the HEFCE funding would clearly be required to help meet these estimated storage requirements. This funding contributed to the university's procurement of a new Storage Area Network (SAN) storage solution for the whole university. Without going into any technical details the digital library servers are now connected to the SAN with a current storage capacity of over 6 terabytes. A large (automated) data linear tape silo, amongst other storage hardware, was procured to allow for 'near line' storage and archiving in the future when UCEEL content reaches some kind of 'critical mass'.

System Development and Issues

It was agreed that the most appropriate way of starting the UCEEL system development was a small, very clearly defined project. It was very important that this was an application of the system that addressed a real need, not just something that did not have a long-term value. After due consideration it was decided that the ideal pilot project would be the transfer of a standalone electronic exam paper system. As the team moved forward with the pilot it became clear that the decisions that were made would be crucial to the development of the whole system, including web interface design, metadata, file formats, authentication, copyright and IPR, and evaluation.

Authentication

This was one of the most difficult issues that the team had to address. FORMTEK ORION itself was not the problem; it supported the creation of any number of user groups, sets of privileges and access restrictions. However, the team was aware that copyright clearance would dictate that UCEEL users would have to be authenticated to ensure that only UCE staff and students could access copyright cleared material. They also knew that the sheer size of the university and its complexity required a sensible, simple approach for the benefit of users.

After a great deal of discussion it was decided that the system would use Library Borrower and Personal Identification Number (PIN) as the required identifiers. To transfer borrower information into UCEEL, a flat file is used containing a basic set of information about each user from the Library's TALIS library management system. In turn, TALIS receives updates from the student records system – data such as name, course, academic department, course end date. To gain access to UCEEL a user is prompted to enter their borrower and PIN number. In the future, this may in turn be replaced by a student number that will effectively act as a single sign-on to many UCE electronic services.

Management Information

The development of Management Information (MIS) data has taken longer than first envisaged. User records imported from TALIS were originally very basic. Additional data about each user, such as course and department, now adds more detail to the information produced. The MIS data are produced in report form every month and are of value to system administrators, budget holders (those paying for content to be available on UCEEL – mostly faculty librarians and tutors), Library Management Group and end users. The system can provide specific data on users and items; for example, how often a particular item has been retrieved, opened, downloaded, printed or saved to floppy. This may influence whether the item is worth retaining on UCEEL when copyright clearance is due for renewal. Data can also be gained on how users are searching UCEEL. Web Trends (Intelligence Suite) is used to evaluate web layer activity.

Metadata

The team was very much aware of the need for interoperability with other systems and that a great deal of care would be needed as they created the metadata for the system. It was decided that using the Dublin Core International Standard would be the most effective method of addressing this need. However, as the team delved further they soon realized that although Dublin Core is an international standard it is not applied in a standard way. In the end, the team sought advice from HEDS and their help was invaluable. After a huge amount of work by the UCEEL team and cataloguing colleagues, the team arrived at an agreed set of metadata.

Metadata standards were customized for each UCEEL collection. Needless to say, although some of these elements are automatically populated, much of the metadata still requires considerable manual input. It was agreed there would be two metadata sets assigned to each file or groups of files – works level and object level. Works level data describe the actual content of the digital file. Object level provides data on the digital file itself – including information for digital preservation purposes (for example, file modification history). Dublin Core elements lie at the heart of both metadata sets. However, there are variations on elements added to the basic Dublin Core set dependent upon the nature of the collection. These include Dublin Core Qualifiers, Learning Object Metadata and other elements recommended by, for example, the Research Libraries Group and the CEDARS project over the last few years.

Document Formats

The format of the documents within the system was a very important decision. The team knew that ORION would support a wide range of formats. However, there were two important requirements that had to be met, that is, to ensure the integrity of each document and to comply with copyright clearance conditions. As a result of these considerations, it was decided that the PDF format would be adopted. In the future UCEEL's full text retrieval module will be implemented in most collections. This means that most collections would require hidden text files underneath the PDF – additional work for the UCEEL team but improved searching for the end user. In addition, as the team moves forward with audio and video, new decisions will be required about the most appropriate formats to use.

Interface

UCEEL's user interface was crucial to the success of the project. It needed to be clear, easy to use and it had to cater for users with visual impairments. The team worked with LSC to create three trial interfaces and then worked with UCE's Centre for Information Research to evaluate them. Three groups were used to gain feedback; they were Information Studies students, Faculty of Education staff and students and Library Services staff. They were asked to give their opinions on all interfaces on a range of issues. A substantial amount of feedback was received and it led the team to return to LSC and to the drawing board. The current interface is an amended version of version number four. The team also successfully tested this version on the Bobby website (http://bobby.watchfire.com/bobby/html/en/index. jsp). This website establishes whether the site is suitable for users with visual impairments.

Within a relatively short period of time it became clear that the user interface was dating faster than had been anticipated. As the interface influences how the overall system is perceived by its users, it was decided that it needed to be redesigned. The team worked with the University's Institute of Art and Design to redesign the UCEEL interface and logo. Part of the work included an assessment by the Institute's User Lab to ensure ease of use and accessibility. The new interface was implemented in October 2003.

Content Development and Issues

At UCE, the content of the digital library is influenced from three main directions.

- The first strand of development is dictated by the needs of the faculties, that is, to support their specific learning and teaching objectives. The earliest project planning included the provision of key chapters and journal articles to support course delivery. The faculty bidding process described above identified a much wider range of applications for UCEEL within the faculties and these proposals will form the basis of the UCEEL Team's core work over the coming years.
- The Library Service will influence the second development strand. The Library holds a number of special collections that are not readily accessible due to their value and condition. Examples of these are to be found in the Art and Design collections and the Conservatoire. It is the intention that these collections will be digitized where copyright clearance can be obtained to make them more widely available.
- The third strand is being developed in response to central University requirements. This is illustrated by the decision that abstracts of MPhil and PhD theses will be hosted on UCEEL. In addition, the University's central document library has been transferred into a new collection that has been established using the FORMTEK ORION software and hosted within the UCEEL system.

Copyright

As described above, copyright influenced a number of the decisions on how the system should develop, particularly in relation to authentication and document format. One fundamental decision that was made from the outset was that there would not be any risks taken when it came to copyright issues. Therefore, here again the team sought the advice of the experts and joined HERON (Higher Education Resources On Demand). All copyright clearance requests are sent to HERON. On the issue of student projects, the team seeks the student's permission to digitize via a copyright waiver form. Copyright material used within the project is blocked out.

The team have found HERON to be a good intermediary for gaining permissions rather than chasing publishers and rights holders directly. However, there have been a number of problems. Budget holders, mostly faculty librarians, have encouraged tutors to request material. This is encouraging but many requests have proved too expensive for current budgets and have been declined. The preparation work in processing requests means some wasted effort. However, it is a relatively new service and the UCEEL team do not want to discourage requests. To aid future decision making, the team are developing a database to track experiences and build knowledge of publishers, their rates and processing time.

Another change in thinking is that, in the early days, there was much talk about obtaining commercial copyright clearance so that UCEEL could host video. As we move forward it is likely that the majority of the video and audio material hosted by UCEEL will be created and produced by students and staff in-house. One reason for this is that, in addition to potential copyright costs, commercial producers are changing their delivery methods and using CDs that offer networking options as well as videos. This is encouraging and no doubt it may prove more sensible to use the commercial product than to reinvent very expensive wheels.

Evaluation

The team knew that evaluation had to play an important part in their work to ensure that what was developed could be refined on an ongoing basis to meet the needs of UCEEL users. The initial evaluation related to the interface development as described above. A valuable opportunity arose when the UCEEL team was asked to participate in a testbed site in the eVALUEd project funded under the HEFCE Good Management Practice initiative. The project relates to the evaluation of electronic information services and will develop a transferable model for e-library evaluation in higher education as well as dissemination and training in e-library evaluation, especially digital libraries. More information is available at http://www.cie.uce.ac.uk/evalued/.

Communication

Communication within the University is very important to the team. As described above, the funding for the initial set-up represented all the University's capital money for a three-year period; therefore, it is important that colleagues know how their money is being used. Communication is important to ensure that academic colleagues engage with UCEEL so that they consider how they could use it in their work – the team needs their knowledge and imagination. It is also important that Library staff are informed and involved. This is a major development and there is a certain amount of anxiety as they are aware that over time it could change the Library Service. In addition, they are at the sharp end when it comes to demonstrating UCEEL, answering questions about it and promoting its use within the faculties and the library. The routes the team are using include meetings with key faculty staff, a regular bulletin e-mailed to all UCE staff, and demonstrations of the system wherever possible. The team has worked hard to try to ensure that UCEEL is seen as the University's system not the library's. They are encouraging faculties to tell them how they want to use the system. It is recognized that there is a price to pay for this, as it is likely that this will mean that each faculty could use the system in a different way. However, it is felt that this is an important way of ensuring that UCEEL becomes embedded within normal learning and teaching practice and thereby ensuring its future development.

Current Position

Chronology of Current Content

The chronology of developments to date are as follows: the exam paper system went live March 2001; the three other core collections (journal extracts, books, and student dissertations and projects up to Masters level) went live November 2001; MIS System went live May 2003; Contemporary Jewellery Collection went live April 2003 (this collection from Birmingham Institute of Art and Design contains over 27,000 images of jewellery designs created by a wide range of international jewellery designers).

Ongoing Growth

UCEEL has developed differently to the team's original expectations. They had envisaged they would work with two faculties at a time and that once something had been developed for them they would then move on to work with the next two. The reality has been different. Once the team established these initial collections and shared information about them they found that most faculties wished to use their functionality. Therefore, the system development has taken place on a wider front than had been expected. In practice, this has been a more effective process allowing the involvement of all faculties earlier than would have been possible under the initial model.

Future Tasks and Challenges

New Collections

Most recently work was carried out on two new collections which were released in early 2004; they are a Higher Level Theses collection and an images collection.

The UCEEL team has a complex balancing act to achieve. This is due to the current position of UCEEL in its development cycle. The team needs to manage the tension between an operational system that brings the daily demands of processing requests, obtaining copyright, scanning and checking-in cleared material with the ongoing need to develop new collections and functionality. In addition, the team is working within an environment of rapid change that inevitably affects the team's planning. An example of this has occurred recently. One of UCEEL's projected developments was a module information collection requested by several faculties. Within the last few months, UCE has decided that it wishes to procure an institutional VLE (Virtual Learning Environment) and the UCEEL team has now decided that this requirement would be better addressed within the VLE development.

Integration with other Electronic Services

A further important challenge is the need to achieve a closer integration of UCEEL with a range of other electronic systems within UCE. Close integration is vital as artificial barriers to use will be a major turn-off to students seeking the easiest route to satisfying their information needs. The team needs to achieve integration with two main systems, the Library's TALIS management system and the new University VLE. It is hoped that new TALIS developments in relation to their catalogue will facilitate some of these links.

Video and Audio Development

One of the next main development areas for the Team to investigate is adding audio and video capture, storage and delivery to UCEEL. Many of the requirements identified by the faculties relate to audio and video applications. This content will require considerable editing and 're-packaging' to become genuine learning resources of benefit to other students. Ideas include recording law student advocacy and debating sessions (Moots) and mock courtroom sessions. Students filmed during teaching practice, with the permission of the local education authority and schools involved, is a popular idea with the Education Faculty. Both faculties purchased some equipment from their HEFCE allocations to undertake such work.

Functionality and Searching

Currently, each collection has its own search options depending on the type of collection it is; for example, journal articles can be searched by volume and series. Faculty and School are used as search terms within the exam paper collection. The team needs to develop cross-collection searching drawing on the common metadata found in all collections, for example, keyword, title and date. Developing indexes (for example, an A–Z of authors and timelines) will also be important to improve searching and navigation. These will be challenges perhaps helped by new JSP (Java Server Page) web development tools for use with a new version (v.5) of FORMTEK: ORION, due for release Summer 2004.

Digitization Services

UCEEL is now offering digitization services to internal and external customers to help optimize the use of digitization suites as well as meet HEFCE income generation targets ongoing to 2011. This forms an essential element in UCEEL's exit strategy. The specialist large format scanners offer unique opportunities to assist the 'heritage sector', in particular, to digitize any size bound volumes, including fragile bindings, maps, manuscripts and illustrations, in full colour as well as grey-scale and bitonal (black and white). Images and photographs are another area of specialization.

The ongoing commitment of the university to UCEEL is also borne out by the fact all UCEEL team members are now on permanent contracts. Nevertheless, the exit strategy is extremely important and has led to the development of a business plan to sustain UCEEL and hopefully provide a potentially valuable source of income and publicity for Library Services in the future.

Conclusions

UCEEL is starting to develop rapidly and is making a real impact in helping to support teaching, learning and research across the university.

Like all digital libraries, UCEEL has required a fair degree of customization.

The need to integrate UCEEL with other e-services and catalogues, both local and remote, is a continuing challenge. Good impartial advice has been essential; HEDS certainly provided this throughout the initial HEFCE development and has helped with the exit strategy. Ultimately, building content that is relevant, timely and supports all the teaching, learning and research activities of the institution is what it is about. This process never ends. Growth areas of content development include delivering digital video and audio, such as copyright-cleared TV/radio broadcasts and film/clips.

To have any chance of success, cooperation at all levels must be serious and the total commitment of the university goes without saying. Sustaining enthusiasm and energy from library staff and the need for a dedicated UCEEL team have been essential. IT colleagues with the technical skills base to provide in-house support, advice and to continue with system developments have also proved invaluable.

Those thinking of developing their own multimedia or even a text-based-only digital library will probably benefit from a similar bespoke approach, which works best regardless of funding and the resources available to establish the system. After all, only the host institution knows what it really wants to do with its digital library.

Chapter 11

Networked Digital Library of Theses and Dissertations (NDLTD)

Edward A. Fox, Gail McMillan, Hussein Suleman,
Marcos A. Gonçalves and Ming Luo

Introduction

This chapter describes the Networked Digital Library of Theses and Dissertations (NDLTD, see www.ndltd.org), as an example of digital library practice. It builds upon discussion in earlier chapters on policy – touching on content, preservation, evaluation, and economics. In the remainder of this section we explain the rationale, give a library perspective, and explain our very broad perspective regarding evaluation. In the next section we describe the community served and involved. The third section discusses the content, especially at the level of collection, considering its management, size, and access. The fourth section relates this work to the world of scholarly publishing, including perspectives of authors and publishers, also considering intellectual property rights and preservation. The last section points toward future growth in membership, organization, and services.

Purpose, Goals and Objectives

NDLTD was launched in 1996 to enhance graduate education through the deployment of digital library technology. Its goals include: to ensure that graduate students are prepared to function in the Information Age, to enhance the expressiveness of theses and dissertations, to expand the infrastructure in universities to support institutional repositories, and to broaden access to student research worldwide. Its objectives include: to increase graduate student understanding of electronic publishing and digital library concepts and technologies, to allow integration of multimedia and hypermedia content and methods when appropriate in theses and dissertations, to make it easy for universities to host a digital library of their own (student) works, and to allow students worldwide much freer access to much larger amounts of scholarly research undertaken at universities.

Library Perspective

Theses and dissertations document the academic heritage of a university and serve as prototypes of scholarly communications from budding researchers and the future professoriate. These documents typically contain a survey of current awareness of published literature, the latest research methodologies, and new findings in research and scholarship.

For decades, libraries have stored and circulated this final product of graduate students' educational efforts. The expansion of the internet has brought dramatic changes in the whole enterprise of research and education including electronic theses and dissertations (ETDs) that now reach outside the realm of the university (that is, beyond students, faculty and libraries) into the research community and the world of digital libraries. Theses and dissertations always have been a means of sharing knowledge and culture; doing so electronically expands the methods and approaches available for learning at distant locations, particularly internationally, and gives students the opportunity to learn about electronic publishing and digital libraries. Educational initiatives such as ETDs, which target graduate students, have the potential to help train future generations of scholars, researchers and professors. ETDs are one genre, within the larger world of electronic publications, which represents major changes and challenges to established ways of thinking and operating within the academic and research communities.

ETDs provide libraries with the opportunity to improve services and increase accessibility to information for current as well as future users. Libraries can save both time and money by reducing or eliminating many manual processes. Even without benefiting from procedures for deriving the cataloging record from the digital document, because ETDs do not have to be bound, labeled, security stripped, bar-coded, checked out, checked in, shelved, and re-shelved, libraries can save about 73 per cent of the cost of processing paper theses and dissertations (McMillan, 2001b).

A problem avoided by ETDs is the one title/one user limitation of works on paper and microfilm; an ETD is simultaneously accessible to multiple users. ETDs are more frequently accessed than their paper counterparts, but increased use does not require additional library staff time. Computer programs 'move' submitted works through the approval process to availability, with security/backup copies and archiving at a variety of locations. Since there clearly are so many benefits that derive from ETD programs, we will lead into later discussion through the following brief introduction to evaluation.

Evaluation

Digital library evaluation is recognizably an extremely complex and difficult task (Saracevic, 2000; Fuhr *et al.*, 2001). The complexity is mainly due to the inherently inter-disciplinary nature of the field (Fox and Marchionini, 1998; Gonçalves *et al.*, 2003) as well as the competing visions of the different communities involved in the area (for example, research versus practice, information science versus computer science) (Borgman, 1999).

We have adopted a broad and integrated vision of digital libraries in which to consider a number of elements for evaluation of NDLTD, including numerous human, system and society-centered criteria. Those include membership and collection growth, including considerations about international interest and support, access (information seeking activities, physical distribution); student learning and skills development; worldwide availability of ETDs; and qualitative and economic aspects (for example, usability and economic impact). Our evaluation instruments include logging accesses, collecting surveys, holding focus groups, and undertaking usability studies of digital libraries. Details of each of these instruments, the metrics they use, and results of the analyses, are presented below, after we consider key aspects of community and content.

Community

According to our '5S' theory of digital libraries, we should consider five key aspects of such advanced information systems: Societies, Scenarios, Spaces, Structure and Streams (Gonçalves *et al.*, 2003). The first of these concerns users, teams, collaboration, target audience groups, social concerns, and community issues. In the case of NDLTD, we are interested in students, faculty (advisors, mentors, examiners), librarians, graduate administrators, researchers, universities, and other institutions supporting ETD activities. The latter two groups directly relate to NDLTD since they make up its members.

Membership

Tables 11.1–11.3 show NDLTD membership as of March 2003. In less than four years, NDLTD has tripled the number of registered members (from 59 members in May 1999). There are currently 176 members: 67 US universities (Table 11.1), 86 non-US universities (Table 11.2), and 23 institutions/regional centers/organizations such as UNESCO (Table 11.3). These numbers demonstrate the growth of global interest in ETDs as international participation, represented as a fraction of the total membership, grew from less than one third in 1999 to one half in 2003. In addition, by early 2002, at least 11 of the registered NDLTD members had already started requiring mandatory submission of electronic theses and dissertations, indicating a very strong commitment to the initiative. (In Tables 11.1–11.2, universities currently requiring ETDs are marked with an asterisk.)

National Projects

NDLTD is a worldwide initiative. It has worked to expand awareness of the benefits of ETD initiatives at universities around the globe. In the following, we give a brief description of five international projects, which have been influenced by, or collaborated with, NDLTD. Others are evolving, for example, in Spain and China, but due to lack of room we cannot describe them here.

USA. Work on ETDs began with a meeting in Ann Arbor, Michigan, USA in November 1987 when UMI invited a number of universities and companies to consider how SGML (Standard Generalized Markup Language, an ISO international standard and parent of both HTML and XML) might support a move towards electronic versions of dissertations. Over the next several years, Virginia Tech, working with SoftQuad, developed an SGML Document Type Definition and a small number of SGML representations of dissertations. However, it did not seem feasible to spread this methodology to other institutions until Adobe devel-

Table 11.1   NDLTD membership – US universities

USA Universities (67)

Air University (Alabama)	University of Central Florida
Baylor University	University of Colorado
Boston College	University of Florida
Brigham Young University	University of Georgia
California Institute of Technology	University of Hawaii at Manoa
Clemson University	University of Illinois, Urbana-Champaign
College of William and Mary	University of Iowa
Concordia University (Illinois)	University of Kentucky
Drexel University	University of Maine*
Duquesne University	University of Missouri-Columbia
East Carolina University	University of Nevada, Las Vegas
East Tennessee State University*	University of New Orleans
Florida Institute of Technology	University of North Texas*
Florida International University	University of Oklahoma
Florida State University	University of Pittsburgh
Georgetown University	University of Rochester
George Washington University	University of South Florida
Johns Hopkins University	University of Central Florida
Louisiana State University*	University of Tennessee, Knoxville
Marshal University	University of Tennessee, Memphis
Massachusetts Institute of Technology	University of Texas at Austin*
Miami University of Ohio	University of Virginia
Michigan Tech	University of West Florida
Mississippi State University	University of Wisconsin, Madison
Montana State University	Vanderbilt University
Naval Postgraduate School	Virginia Commonwealth University
New Jersey Institute of Technology	Virginia Tech*
New Mexico Tech	Wake Forest University
North Carolina State University*	West Virginia University*
NorthWestern University	Western Kentucky University
Pennsylvania State University	Western Michigan University
Regis University	Worcester Polytechnic Institute
Rochester Institute of Technology	Yale University
Texas A&M University	

oped the Portable Document Format, PDF, and the Acrobat family of supporting tools. Once that occurred, Virginia Tech began working with UMI, the Council of Graduate Schools, and the Coalition for Networked Information to support ETD efforts. A series of meetings, each involving roughly ten universities, allowed key concepts to develop and interest to expand. In 1995, the Southeastern Universities Research Association awarded a grant to Virginia Tech to develop and disseminate the concept in the region. In 1996, the US Department of Education awarded a grant to Virginia Tech to expand the effort nationwide. Thus, the NDLTD was born, and a base of interest grew in the USA. While this has typically been done at the level of individual universities, in Ohio a program developed, supported by

Table 11.2   NDLTD membership – international universities

International Universities (86)

Aristotle University of Thessaloniki (Greece)
Assumption University of Thailand (Thailand)
Australian National University (Australia)
Biblioteca de Catalunya (Spain)
Centro University La Salle-UNILASALLE
  (Brazil)
Chinese University of Hong Kong (Hong Kong)
Chung Yuan Christian University (Taiwan)
Chungnam National U., Dept of CS (S. Korea)
City University, London (UK)
Curtin University of Technology (Australia)
Darmstadt University of Technology (Germany)
Freie Universitat Berlin (Germany)
Gerhard Mercator Universitat Duisburg
  (Germany)
Griffith University (Australia)
Gyeongsang National University, Chinju
  (Korea)
Helsinki University of Technology (Finland)
Humboldt-Universität zu Berlin (Germany)
Indian Institute of Technology, Bombay (India)
Lund University (Sweden)
McGill University (Canada)
Nanyang Technological University (Singapore)
Naresuan University (Thailand)
National Sun Yat-Sen University (Taiwan)
National Taiwan Normal University (Taiwan)
National University of Singapore (Singapore)
Pontificia Universidade Católica de Minas Gerais
  (Brazil)
Pontificia Universidade Católica do Rio de
  Janeiro (Brazil)
Pontificia University Católica de Campinas-PUC/
  CAMPINAS (Brazil)
Pontificia University Católica do Parana-PUC/PR
  (Brazil)
Pontificia University Católica do Rio Grande do
  Sul-PUC/RS (Brazil)
Rand Afrikaans University (South Africa)
Rhodes University (South Africa)*
Shanghai Jiao Tong University (China)
St. Petersburg State Technical U. (Russia)
State University of Campinas (Brazil)
Universidade Estadual Paulista (Brazil)
Universidad de Chile (Chile)
Universidad de las Amèricas Puebla (Mèxico)
Universidad Politecnica De Cartagena (Spain)
Universidade Federal Fluminense (Brazil)
Universitat Autonoma de Barcelona (Spain)*

Universitat d'Alacant (Spain)
Universitat de Barcelona (Spain)
Universitat de Girona (Spain)
Universitat de Lleida (Spain)
Universitat Oberta de Catalunya (Spain)
Universitat Politecnica de Catalunya (Spain)
Universitat Politecnica de Valencia (Spain)
Universitat Pompeu Fabra (Spain)
Universitat Rovira i Virgili (Spain)
Universitat Bibliothek Munchen (Germany)
Universitè Laval (Quèbec, Canada)
Universitè Lyon 2 (France)
University Católica de Brasilia-UCB (Brazil)
University Católica de Pernambuco-UNICAP
  (Brazil)
University Católica de Salvador-UCSAL (Brazil)
University Católica de Santos-UNISANTOS
  (Brazil)
University Católica Dom Bosco-UCDB (Brazil)
University do Vale do Rio dos Sinos-UNISINOS
  (Brazil)
University of Antioquia (Medellin, Colombia)
University of Bergen (Norway)
University of British Columbia (Canada)
University of Edinburgh (UK)
University of Glasgow (UK)
University of Guelph (Ontario, Canada)
University of Hong Kong* (Hong Kong)
University of Hyderabad (India)
University of Melbourne (Australia)
University of Mysore (India)
University of New Brunswick (Canada)
University of New South Wales (Australia)
University of Novi Sad (Yugoslavia)
University of Pisa (Italy)
University of Pretoria (S. Africa))
University of Queensland (Australia)
University of São Paulo (Brazil)
University of Sydney (Australia)
University of Tampere (Finland)
University of the Free State (South Africa)
University of Utrecht (Netherlands)
University of Waterloo (Canada)
University of Western Ontario (Canada)
Uppsala University (Sweden)
Wilfrid Laurier University (Canada)
Xiamen University Library (China)
Yupei University of Science and Technology
  (Taiwan)

Table 11.3   NDLTD membership – institutions

Institutions (23)

British Library	Instituto Brasileiro de Informação em Ciência
Cinemedia	e Tecnologia (IBICT)
Coalition for Networked Information	MathDISS International
Committee on Institutional Cooperation	National Documentation Centre (NDC,
Comunidate Virtual de Aprendizagem Da	Greece)
Rede de institucoes Catolicas de Ensino	National Library Of Canada
Superior	National Library of Portugal
Consorci de Biblioteques Univ. Catalunya	Office of Scientific and Technical Information
Diplomica.com	(Department of Energy)
Dissertationene Online	OhioLINK
Dissertation.com	OCLC
ETDweb	Organization of American States (OAS)
Ibero-American Sci. & Tech. Ed. Cons.	SOLINET
(ISTEC)	Sudanese National Electronic Library (Sudan)
	UNESCO

OhioLink, to allow engagement by all public and private colleges and universities. Growth of NDLTD in USA was further encouraged by a series of annual conferences. Although international in scope and attendance, it is only with the sixth (May 2003) in the series, that the conference has been held outside the USA – in Berlin, Germany.

Germany   After the US, the first serious financial support for ETD activities was by the German government, reflecting the keen interest in dissertations in that country. The project 'Theses Online', sponsored by the German Research Foundation (DFG), and initiated by a subgroup within the Initiative of the German Learned Societies for the Advancement of Digital Information and Collaboration, started in spring 1998. It was completed in March 1999, with a conference held in Jena, Germany. DFG funded a second research and development project, from March 1999 to March 2000, at a level of €300,000, placing heavy emphasis on collaboration with libraries and university computing centers. Among the learned societies involved in these projects were those in chemistry, computer science, education, mathematics and physics. Participants in the second proposal also included five German universities, computing centers, libraries and the German National Library (DDB). Please see http://www.educat.hu-berlin.de/diss_online/englisch/index1e.html.

Australia.   Seven institutions in Australia, led by the library at the University of New South Wales, began collaborating in 1998/99 to accept electronic theses from postgraduate students. This 'Australian Digital Theses Project' (ADTP) (http://adt.caul.edu.au/) has standardized on SGML and PDF as document formats. The collection's oldest work dates back to 1968. The ADTP has led to a national program under the auspices of the Australian National Library. It is expected that

Australia will be the first nation with comprehensive support for ETD efforts at all universities.

India.   The Vidyanidhi project (Urs and Raghavan, 2001), based at the University of Mysore and sponsored by India's National Information System for Science and Technology (NISSAT), is a national effort to create, maintain, and provide network access to a digital library of Indian theses. It is a direct consequence of the initiatives identified in India's Information Technology Action Plan. The impetus has come primarily from a policy initiative that makes it mandatory for all universities in the country to host 'every dissertation/thesis on a designated Web site.' Vidyanidhi is intended to demonstrate the utility of digital library technologies in maintaining as well as enhancing both access to, and visibility of, Indian academic research. Vidyanidhi will eventually emerge as a distributed input and database environment for the ETDs digital library. It has begun, however, as a centralized repository facilitating network access. This is necessary and important for the purpose of evolving a national consensus and agreement on all relevant issues and standards. However, the goal – to assist the end-user community in obtaining access to one of the most neglected and under-utilized of all resources – remains irrespective of the structure and technology that ultimately emerges.

Brazil.   The Brazilian Digital Library in Science and Technology Project (BDL), developed by the Brazilian Institute for Scientific and Technical Information (IBICT), stresses the impact of the web on publishing and communication in science and technology and also on information systems and libraries. The two main objectives of the BDL project are: (1) promoting electronic publishing of different full text materials (for example, theses, journal articles, conference papers, 'grey' literature) by the Brazilian scientific community to amplify their national and international visibility; and (2) achieving interoperability among those heterogeneous electronic information resources available on the web. The project also provides consulting services to help institutions implement their own ETD programs, as well as the Open Archives Initiative protocol to help institutions become data providers (see the section below concerning Management). In addition to supporting the Dublin Core, the BDL uses a specific metadata format to meet the requirements of Brazilian institutions and funding agencies. The ETD portion of the BDL intends to collect ETD metadata from all Brazilian institutions of higher education into a Union Catalog and to run services on top of the catalog. Interest in BDL is growing, as is involvement in NDLTD; in March 2003 all ten of the Catholic universities in Brazil joined. This should help expand content, which is the topic of the next section.

Content

At the heart of NDLTD is an electronic thesis or dissertation (ETD). These works typically are described using a metadata standard, such as MARC21 or ETD-MS (Atkins *et al.*, 2001). The latter is based on the Dublin Core standard, and was developed by the NDLTD Standards Committee after several years of international discussion. Thus, NDLTD has encouraged improved management of ETD content worldwide.

Management

The ETD collections managed by NDLTD members have traditionally been independent of one another. Thus, in most cases, an ETD can be located by an end-user only if the archive containing the ETD is consulted directly. This is far from the ideal case of an end-user searching through all available ETDs through a unified interface.

To get closer to this objective, NDLTD has adopted the Open Archives Initiative's Protocol for Metadata Harvesting (OAI-PMH) (Lagoze *et al.*, 2002) as a means of accumulating metadata from all member sites into a merged collection. The OAI-PMH is an application-layer network protocol to transfer XML-encoded metadata records from one machine to another. Core features of the protocol exploited by NDLTD include the ability to obtain only recently updated records on a periodic basis and the support for multiple metadata formats. The latter has enabled the use of MARC21 and/or ETD-MS for theses and dissertations, in addition to the required Dublin Core format.

All NDLTD members are encouraged to support the OAI protocol, thereby enabling access to their ETD metadata using a simple and open standard. NDLTD maintains a Union Catalog (i.e. an OAI archive) that harvests this metadata from each collection on a periodic basis and republishes it as a single merged collection. This merged collection is then used by service providers such as VTLS (VTLS, 2002) and the ODL-based ETD Union Catalog (Suleman, 2002) in order to supply global discovery services, such as a cross-collection search engine, to users.

Size

The number of ETDs across the NDLTD universities/institutions has grown at a rapid pace: from a few dozen at Virginia Tech in 1996, to 4328 ETDs at 21 institutions in March 2000, to 7268 ETDs at 25 institutions in July 2001, and 13724 at 35 member institutions in November 2002. Table 11.4 shows a breakdown of the numbers of ETDs as of November 2002, organized by member institution. The statistics were collected from three sources: (1) a count of the number of ETD metadata records in the NDLTD official Union Catalog as of November 2002, harvested from member institutions that already implement an OAI interface (represented by the code UA in the table column 'source of information'); (2) an online survey conducted by Gail McMillan in July 2001, which represents only those institutions that responded to the survey by that time (code SV); and (3) an independent experiment, performed in May 2002, on web-crawling and extracting metadata from ETD websites (Calado *et al.*, 2003) (code CW). For overlapping institutions (that is, those that appear in more than one source of information), we chose the maximum number (which in most of the cases accounts for the most recent numbers).

These statistics do not take into account scanned theses and dissertations, which

Table 11.4 NDLTD collection size

University/Institution	ETD Collection size	Source of Information (maximum)
ADT: Australian Digital Thesis Program (Australia)	238	SV
University of Bergen (Norway)	45	SV
California Institute of Technology	364	UA
Concordia University	3	CW
Consorci de Biblioteques Univ. de Catalunya (Spain)	151	SV
East Tennessee State University	106	SV
Humboldt-University (Germany)	439	CW
Louisiana State University	352	UA
Mississippi State University	33	SV
MIT	62	SV
National Sun Yat-Sen University (Taiwan)	1786	CW
North Carolina State University	301	SV
Ohio Link	932	CW
Pennsylvania State University	83	SV
Pontifical Catholic University (PUC-Rio) (Brazil)	90	SV
Gerhard Mercator Universitat Duisburg (Germany)	412	UA
Rhodes University (South Africa)	134	CW
Technische Universität Dresden	18	UA
Universitat Politecnica de Valencia (Spain)	189	SV
University of British Columbia	2	UA
University of Florida	174	SV
University of Georgia	121	SV
University of Iowa	6	SV
University of Kentucky	30	CW
University of Maine	27	SV
University of North Texas	337	SV
University of South Florida	40	UA
University of Tennessee	12	SV
University of Tennessee, Knoxville	28	SV
University of Virginia	619	CW
University of Waterloo	105	CW
Uppsala University (Sweden)	1711	UA
Virginia Tech	3646	UA
West Virginia University	1006	SV
Worcester Polytechnic Institute	122	CW
Total	13724	

make up a substantial portion of the total NDLTD collection. There are roughly 26 ETDs from scanned works at the New Jersey Institute of Technology, 150 at the University of South Florida, 5581 at MIT, and 12,000 at the National Documentation Center in Greece. This sample gives a total of 17,751 scanned theses and dissertations; which are in addition to the 13,724 'born digital' ETDs. Thus, we know of over 30,000 ETDs and are sure that there are thousands of

Table 11.5   Access statistics for two services built atop NDLTD Union Catalog

	NDLTD – VTLS Virtua (6/02 – 12/6/02)	ODL-based Prototype Service (10/00 – 12/6/02)
Successful requests	241,473	883,151
Average successful requests per day	1,323	1,121
Distinct hosts served	12,820	15,782
Data transferred (Gb)	4.21	10.74
Average data transferred per day (Mb)	23.61	13.96

unreported ones at other institutions, including institutions not in the Union catalog or covered by the web-crawling experiment. Furthermore, we note (as per the discussion in the Levels of Access section below) that the numbers given represent only the 'world-accessible' works at universities, and ignore the thousands of others in controlled collections (for example, hundreds of thousands at companies like UMI/ProQuest, or at universities in cases where patent issues are temporarily of concern).

Access

Figures 11.1–11.4 highlight the quantitative and qualitative aspects of access to ETDs. Figures 11.1 and 11.4 deal with the Union Catalog described above, and so only reflect about a dozen sites. In Figure 11.1 we compare access by the two main service providers, VTLS running its Virtua software, and Virginia Tech running its Open Digital Library prototype software (ODL). Table 11.5 gives more details.

Figure 11.4 considers only the ODL service. In contrast, Figures 11.2 and 11.3 deal only with the Virginia Tech collection, since we have the access logs available.

Figure 11.1 demonstrates that use of the Virtua system keeps increasing. As with all systems serving primarily a university community, access counts vary widely from month to month, depending on academic calendars. We also note that the ODL service, which came along much later than the Virtua service, is quite popular, with access counts also increasing rapidly.

Figure 11.2 provides details of access to the Virginia Tech collection, over the prior 3 years, indicating relative counts for countries. It is clear that the access counts have consistently increased from year to year. It appears that countries with significant internet infrastructure have among the highest counts, but that there is a considerable spread in interest worldwide. Figure 11.3 presents the same type of result, focusing on internet domains as opposed to countries. As expected, the 'edu' domain is most popular, but there also is interest from 'com' and 'net'.

Finally, Figure 11.4 gives a more functional view of accesses, comparing counts for the various functions. Most accesses involve a request for a metadata record for some ETD. Next in popularity is search, followed by the system harvesting to support the Union Catalog. Other functions include showing all available metadata forms, indexing, and browsing.

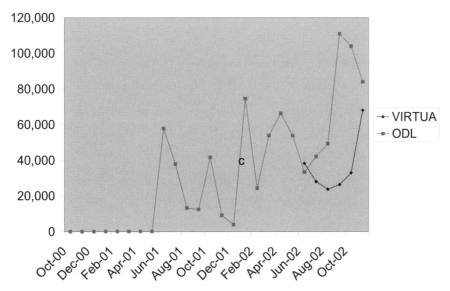

Figure 11.1   Monthly access to NDLTD Union Catalog (searching and browsing 10/00–11/02)

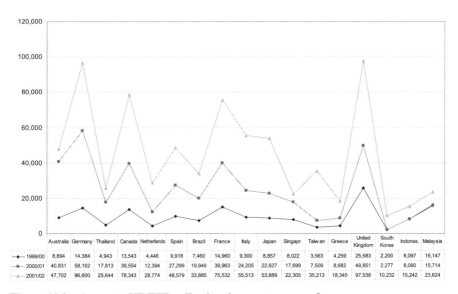

Figure 11.2   Access to VT ETD collection, by country, over 3 years

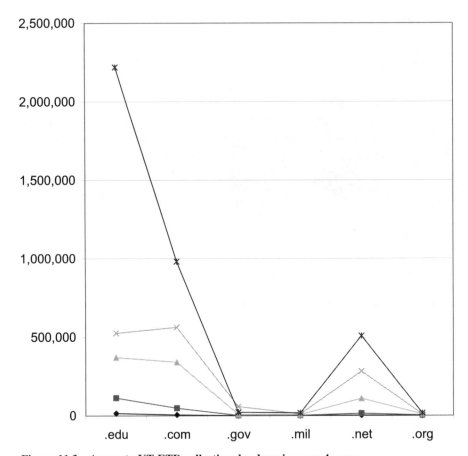

Figure 11.3 Access to VT ETD collection, by domain, over 4 years

Scholarly Publishing Perspectives

In this section we look at ETD issues more from a policy perspective, considering the views of key stakeholders. We also consider author controls on access, handling of intellectual property rights, and preservation in the long term.

Most universities allow their students to make choices concerning who will have access to their ETDs. With a paper-based approach, interest and accesses were low, so libraries did not generally have to restrict access to their collections. When the Graduate School withheld access it was primarily to protect patent applications, which were small in number. Today, with ETDs, in part because of the intense interest in ETDs, authors may select from various levels of accessibility (see the next subsection), ranging from completely available to entirely restricted/hidden.

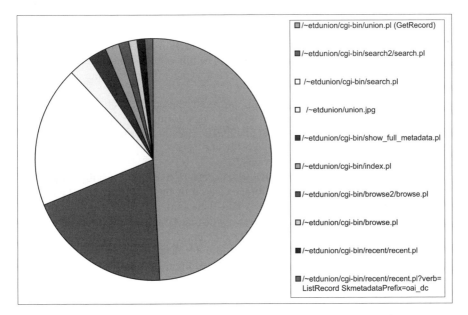

Figure 11.4   Most accessed operations, by number of requests (ODL – Union Archive site)

NDLTD encourages that restrictions should exist for specific and limited periods of time, so that works become accessible as soon as appropriate.

Levels of Access

Unrestricted access means that readers do not encounter any constraints on internet access. Libraries providing ETDs with unlimited access include bibliographic data in their online catalogs with links to the digital documents. Many also provide a variety of other access points. The majority of authors at NDLTD member institutions select unrestricted access for their ETDs, tacitly supporting a timely, easy, and inexpensive means of sharing information.

The option to *partially restrict access* creates the comfortable environment that many feel most closely parallels having bound theses and dissertations in the library. Similar to the situation for various online article databases that libraries license for their university communities, in this case ETD readers can be limited to the author's university and to on-campus library users. Many consider this to be the easiest way to transition from library-only to worldwide access. This level of access is often selected to comply with publishers who threaten to reject journal submissions related to an ETD because of considering any work published online.

An advantage of restricting access to campus is that everyone associated with the originating university can have access from a variety of locations both inside and outside the library at all hours, and when someone else is also looking at the same ETD. Members of the author's university are recognized by their computers' IP addresses or their university-assigned user IDs, like a closed-stacks library where users must show university identification to gain access. Inter Library Loan will receive requests for restricted access ETDs; this option should only be allowed if authors allow these files to be shared through typical library lending and delivery services beyond the author's university.

Prolonging restricted access to their university-based research and scholarship should be the responsibility of the authors. Monitoring restricted access can be accomplished programmatically. The challenge arises in determining when to move the document from restricted to worldwide access, for example, after some maximum time period, of say 1–5 years.

Fully restricted access denies all users access to the ETD. Usually there is no information about the ETD in the library catalog or the ETD database. Generally, only the authors and their committees and their family members will know that this document has been completed, along with the Graduate School or approving unit of the university.

Whether completed in paper or electronic formats, there are conditions that require theses and dissertations to be entirely withheld from public access, particularly during US patent applications. This protection is easily provided in the online environment, but when this option is too readily available, many authors will choose it out of fear of the unknown rather than as a result of need. We know from survey data collected from Virginia Tech's authors that many faculty advisors recommend restricting or withholding access to reduce problems for the future generation of faculty in getting published. They fear that traditional scholarly or commercial publishers will not accept a manuscript derived from the whole or part (for example, chapter, data, appendix, etc) of an internet-accessible work. Perhaps they should reconsider this matter; constraining ETD access to their university communities may serve the transition from library-only to worldwide access.

Author's Surveys

Comparing the survey responses from the first half of fiscal year 2002/03 and all of fiscal year 1999/2000 reveals some changing attitudes and practices among graduate students submitting ETDs at Virginia Tech.

Answers to questions that arise while preparing one's ETD are generally provided by the same people/groups, over time. We see little difference in the numbers for 2002/03 as opposed to 1999/00. The largest number still consult their friends (17.7 per cent and 20.2 per cent) while relatively few (although increasing slightly from 1999/00) consult their committee members (6.1 per cent and 4.8 per cent), or the New Media Center (NMC) staff (6.5 per cent and 4.6 per cent). Students found the NMC staff more helpful in 2002/03 (24 per cent) than in 1999/00 (19.8 per cent) and fewer found them not helpful, 1.8 per cent against 3 per cent. The VT ETD web continues to be a useful source of information, used by 88 per cent in 1999/00 and 90.6 per cent in 2002/03.

Far fewer students attend ETD workshops to learn about the initiative and to secure basic training regarding ETD preparation – 5.8 per cent against 11.6 per cent – but those who do, continue to find them useful. The 2002/03 survey respondents found the workshops 3.5 times more useful, while in 1999/00 they found the workshops to be more than 5 times more useful.

According to survey respondents, they found it less difficult than they expected to create a PDF file, down 7.6 per cent to 17.5 per cent of the 2002/03 respondents. Students' expectations that submitting at ETD would be difficult dropped over 5 per cent between 2002/03 and 1999/00, while there was a 6.5 per cent increase in the number that found online submission 'much less difficult'.

ETDs can be submitted from anywhere. There was more than a 13 per cent increase in the number of students submitting from their off-campus workplaces between 2002/03 and 1999/00. Slight increases in remote submissions were also noted from Virginia Tech's Northern Virginia Center (2.1 per cent) as well as from other universities (3.4 per cent).

Graduate students consult Virginia Tech ETDs, although slightly fewer in 02/03 (74.4 per cent) than in 99/00 (77.9 per cent). In 2002/03, 26.8 per cent consulted 3–5 ETDs, while in 1999/00 only 18.7 per cent consulted this many.

After completing their studies and successfully defending their ETDs, authorship is an expectation of most if not all graduates who earned doctorates. (The survey respondents are not separated, and included both masters and doctoral candidates.) More than 80 per cent plan to publish among the 2002/03 group; conference proceedings will be the venue for 20.74 per cent while 2.36 per cent plan to publish books. About the same percentage each year plan to publish journal articles, 50 per cent. There was a dramatic increase in the percentage that are uncertain about publishing anything, 15.35 per cent in 2002/03 compared with 0.1 per cent of the 1999/00 respondents.

When asked why they restricted access, the surveys reveal that slightly fewer faculty as well as many fewer publishers are giving this advice. In 2002/03 44.6 per cent of students said the faculty advised them to restrict access to their ETDs, while in 1999/00 47.6 per cent said they did. However, there was a 5.3 per cent drop in the number of publishers giving this advice, down to 2.9 per cent from 8.2 per cent of the survey respondents.

Intellectual Property Rights

At the same time that authors select the level of access, they should give the library and the university explicit permission to store and provide access to their works. Working with ETDs provides an opportunity for all participants in this initiative to become familiar with copyright laws. For example, libraries can take the opportunity to document their standard practices and to adapt them for their digital libraries, asking authors formally to permit their libraries to preserve, store, and provide access – just what libraries have done without permission with traditional theses and dissertations. As an aid to universities, we offer the following example statement that is in use at Virginia Tech.

Sample ETD Copyright Statement

  I [the author] hereby grant to [the institution] and its agents the non-exclusive license to archive and make accessible under [specified conditions] my thesis, dissertation, or project report in whole or in part in all forms of media, now or hereafter known. I [the author] retain all other ownership rights to the copyright of the thesis, dissertation, or project report. I also retain the right to use in future works (such as articles or books) all or part of this thesis or dissertation.

In addition, I hereby certify that, if appropriate, I have obtained written permission from the owner(s) of third party copyrighted matter to be included in my thesis, dissertation, or project report, allowing distribution [as specified].

Rights of Authors

Whether authors are creating electronic or paper theses or dissertations, it does not change their moral or legal rights and obligations. While university policies vary, it is frequently the custom that the person who creates a work is the owner of the copyright. Therefore, the (student) authors of electronic theses or dissertations are the copyright holders and own the intellectual property of their ETD. It surprises some faculty that, although advisors may have provided the research dollars (for example, through grants) that funded the research and although they may have provided the laboratory and equipment that graduate students used to conduct the research, the author of the ETD is the copyright holder. Within the United States, this means that authors decide how their works will be reproduced, modified, distributed, performed and displayed in public. Out of courtesy, however, students are encouraged to discuss the matter of access level with their advisor and mentors, so as to promote goodwill and to expand understanding of copyright matters.

Publishers

Publishers, who in some cases early in the life of the ETD initiative threatened the future publications of ETD authors (for example, the American Chemical Society discouraged making ETDs world-accessible), have generally modified their policies. Three independent surveys of publishers showed their willingness to consider articles from ETDs on par with articles from paper theses and dissertations. A large and growing number of publishers readily acknowledge that articles from ETDs are derivative works that can be published in academic scholarly journals. Publishers such as Elsevier Science have openly supported the ETD initiative from its earliest days.

The three surveys of scholarly journal publishers were conducted in 1999, 2000 and 2002. They revealed that the overwhelming majority of publishers are not deterred from considering articles from ETDs for their publications. These surveys collected data using Virginia Tech's Digital Library and Archives online survey database to gather and report responses. See the survey data at http://lumiere.lib.vt.edu/surveys/results/.

Joan Dalton (librarian, University of Windsor) surveyed publishers and editors of scientific journals about their policies and attitudes towards ETDs; Dalton reported her findings at the annual ETD conference in 2000 held at the University of South Florida's Tampa campus. Dr Nancy H. Seamans (librarian as well as graduate student in Instructional Technology at Virginia Tech) surveyed social science and science-and-technology studies journal editors and publishers in late

2000. Bobby Holt (a graduate student in History at Virginia Tech) surveyed humanities book and journal publishers in early 2002. The majority of Seamans' and Holt's respondents were not-for-profit publishers.

In 1999, Dalton found that 86 per cent would publish works derived from ETDs (Dalton and Seamans, 2003). Seamans reported that 82 per cent of her survey respondents in early 2001 answered that they were willing to accept articles from ETDs (Dalton and Seamans, 2003). Both Dalton and Seamans reported that there was more a perception, than actual evidence, of a problem (McMillan, 2001a).

Respondents to Holt's early 2002 survey gave conflicting information, although 87 per cent responded that their policies do not specifically refer to works electronically accessible on the web and 44 per cent responded that editorial policies had not yet been set on this issue. Twenty-three per cent said that editorial policy included ETDs 'widely available through a Web-based archive' as prior publication while they commented '. . . this publication would not rule out consideration of the manuscript' and 'a dissertation should be revised before it is submitted to a publisher for consideration'. Fifty per cent of his respondents also answered, 'manuscripts derived from Web-based dissertations are considered on an individual basis'. Only 3 per cent said 'Under no circumstances. Manuscripts derived from research made widely available via the Web are considered previously published'.

Among all the surveys, this response describes the overwhelming opinion:

> . . . the issue is not whether the material was previously accessible in the print or electronic form of a dissertation. What we look for are works that if they began as dissertations have been significantly revised in such a way that they now represent legitimate book manuscripts derived from mature research and writing.

John Eaton, Dean at Virginia Tech's Graduate School, surveyed graduate student alumni in 1998 and 1999 and asked about publishing articles derived from their ETDs. All of those who had successfully published reported that they did not have any problems getting articles accepted due to their theses or dissertations being online and readily available on the internet.

Keith Jones from Elsevier stated publicly and emphatically at the ETD conference in 2001 that his company encourages its authors to link their articles in Elsevier journals to their personal websites and also authorizes their academic departments to provide such links. Jones reported that Elsevier understands the importance of getting new authors such as graduate students to publish in his company's journals early in their careers because then they are likely to continue to publish there. The fact is, for many, publishing in an Elsevier journal is an important source of academic validation, and the subsequent availability of those articles from other non-profit and educational sources is not a threat. Several publishers have similarly attested that ETDs are not published works, in a variety of sites, such as http://www.ndltd.org/publshrs/index.html.

Preservation

Academic departments determine the quality of the work of their students, while the individual thesis/dissertation committees approve the student's work on its own merits. Often, the Graduate School oversees mechanical considerations, the purpose of which is to provide a degree of uniformity, to ensure that each thesis or dissertation is in a form suitable for reading and/or viewing online, and that it can be preserved. The University Archives at Virginia Tech ensures long-term preservation and access to these records of graduate students' research.

The best way to preserve electronic information is to keep it alive and continuously used in multiple locations. As soon as it is taken offline and not used (that is, forgotten), it will be difficult to retrieve the media that produced it and made it accessible. With digital materials, libraries give access and simultaneously prolong the life of the work, ensuring the durability of the present through stable media. Prior to ETDs joining the library's collection of traditional theses and dissertations, it is appropriate to announce a commitment to maintain these online information resources for long-term access. A library's Special Collections Department and/or its University Archives are often responsible for storing and preserving theses and dissertations. Typically, they will create and document parallel standards, policies, and procedures for electronic theses and dissertations.

Formats

The library must strive to ensure that particularly its unique electronic resources, such as ETDs, will be available indefinitely. To keep ETDs reader-friendly and to retain full access will mean migrating current formats to new standard formats not yet known. This is why standard formats should be the only files accepted. Migration may be done through the collaborative efforts of the various computing resources of a university, although the library maintains the submission software, the database of ETDs, and the secure archive.

The life of an online dissertation in PDF format is said to be at least 100 years, according to OCLC research scientists. In addition, the Acrobat Reader is an open source program; systems programmers could potentially create their own PDF readers if the need arose. Still, many feel very uncomfortable about preserving and archiving ETDs because they do not have the historical evidence that paper and – to a certain extent – microfilm have. Nothing can change this but the passage of time.

Other multimedia found in ETDs such as video (for example, .qt, .mov) and sound files (for example, .aif, .wav) have shorter life expectancies. It is better to use international standards, such as MPEG and JPEG. Further, when these and other file formats (as well as HTML links) accompany PDF files there are fewer worries. The body of work found in the PDF file is the substance of the dissertation or thesis, and the inaccessibility of the supplemental supporting media files is unfortunate but may not be detrimental to the main work itself.

Replication

The Internet2 Distributed Storage Initiative (Beck and Moore, 1998) and LOCKSS (Lots Of Copies Keeps Stuff Safe – see Reich and Rosenthal, 2001) are projects that NDLTD is working with in order transparently to mirror ETDs and their metadata for faster and more reliable access. It is hoped that such efforts will have multiple benefits. First, there should be faster access if copies of collections are available in all regions of the world, since network delays should be less. Second, loss due to a university having problems with its collection or servers should be minimized. Finally, loss due to deliberate attempts to corrupt an ETD should be minimized, since it will be much harder to make unauthorized changes to an unknown number of widely distributed copies.

Future Plans

NDLTD Growth and Organization

NDLTD membership continues to expand, and as time progresses, more and more of the members shift from pilot to production activities. Since ETD 2003 was held in Berlin, Germany, there should be growth over the next few years, in Eastern Europe in particular. Thanks to support by UNESCO, the 'ETD Guide' has been prepared in English, French, and Spanish (Moxley *et al.*, 2002). UNESCO also is supporting training efforts in Latin America (along with ISTEC and OAS) and Africa. It is expected that expansion of NDLTD in these regions will lead to much greater interest in the research in these parts of the world than has occurred in the past.

As NDLTD expands, it is important that its organization evolves. In 2003, it will incorporate in USA as a non-profit (501 c 3) institution with worldwide scope. An international board will complement the existing steering committee to ensure that activities represent the needs of all the regions of the world. Initially, Virginia Tech will serve as the secretariat for NDTLD, providing core services, free of charge.

Enhanced Services

As NDLTD grows, interested parties will continue to contribute to the overall success. Virginia Tech will continue to provide various services, and will continue to seek sponsored funding to expand those services further. In addition, other key partners are providing core services.

First, VTLS runs a computer to support access to the Union Catalog. Its Virtua software supports multilingual searching and browsing, as well as other standard digital library functionality.

Second, OCLC will expand the Union Catalog. OCLC will work closely with individual universities, consortia, and other bodies to expand the list of sites from which they can harvest metadata. In addition, they are extracting from WorldCat all the metadata for theses and dissertations, which number roughly 4.5 million. From among those, they will identify the subset that has a URL or other indicator that an ETD is present. Both the 'TD' and the 'ETD' collections will be available using the Open Archives Initiative Protocol for Metadata Harvesting.

In addition to the work of these partners, Virginia Tech and others will work to improve and expand services. Based on a study of what might be most helpful, the following list has been developed:

- The ETD-MS metadata format has support for authority control information and, if these fields are populated by ETD archives, they can be used to attribute works correctly to unique individuals and organizations.
- Citations can be extracted from the source ETDs, or from XML representations where such exist, to cross-link the documents in a manner similar to ResearchIndex/CiteSeer (Giles *et al.*, 1998).
- Recommendations can be generated for individual users or user communities to suggest relevant documents based on the use of the system by other users. Profile-based filtering is an alternative that stores research interests of individual users and then uses these to check for relevance among newly submitted ETDs.
- Currently, the ETD-db software (Atkins, 2002) manages the workflow of ETD submission but it does not handle the process of review and acceptance by the school. This software can be extended or supplemented to automate the process fully.
- Full-text searching can be supported in addition to current access to the Union Catalog, which only considers metadata.
- Search facilities can be further enhanced by adding support for cross-lingual searching, where the search terms are provided in one language but the documents are written in another.

In conclusion, we note that with very little funding, a large international digital library has emerged, grown, and improved. This may represent the first of many efforts wherein moving toward digital library technology leads to so many benefits and savings that the digital library is self-sustaining, and expands to provide valuable services worldwide.

Acknowledgements

The work described herein was funded in part by Adobe, CNI, IBM, Microsoft, OCLC, SOLINET, SURA, UNESCO, and VTLS; by NSF through grants IIS-9986089, IIS-0080748, IIS-0086227; and by US Department of Education through FIPSE Program P116B61190.

References

Atkins, A. (2002), *Resources for Developers of ETD databases*. Website http:// scholar.lib.vt.edu/ETD-db/developer/.

Atkins, A., Fox, E.A., France, K.R., and Suleman, H. (2001), *ETD-ms: an Interoperability Metadata Standard for Electronic Theses and Dissertations version 1.00*, NDLTD. Available at http://www.ndltd.org/standards/metadata/.

Beck, M. and Moore, T. (1998), 'The I-2 DSI Project: An Architecture for Internet Content Channels', *Computer Networking and ISDN Systems*, 30(22–23), 2141–2148.

Borgman, C.L. (1999), 'What are digital libraries? Competing visions', *Information Processing and Management*, 35(3), 227–243.

Calado, P., da Silva, A.S., Ribeiro-Neto, B., Laender, A.H.F., Lage, J.P., Reis, D.C., Roberto, P.A., Vieira, M.V., Gonçalves, M.A., and Fox E.A. (2002) 'From the web to a

Digital Library: The Web-DL Architecture', JCDL '2003, *Third Joint ACM/IEEE-CS Joint Conference on Digital Libraries*, 27–31 May, Houston.

Dalton, J. and Seamans, N.H. (2004), 'Electronic Theses and Dissertations: Two Surveys of Editors and Publishers', in Fox, E.A., Feizbadi, S., Moxley, J.M. and Weisser, C.R. (eds), *The ETD Sourcebook: Theses and Dissertations in the Electronic Age* (New York: Marcel Dekker), in press.

ETD (2002), *The ETD Guide*. www.etdguide.org.

Fox, E.A. and Marchionini, G. (1998), 'Toward a Worldwide Digital Library', Guest Editors' Introduction to special section (pp. 28–98) in *Digital Libraries: Global Scope, Unlimited Access. Communications of the ACM*, 41(4), 28–32. http://purl.lib.vt.edu/dlib/pubs/CACM199804.

Fuhr, N., Hansen, P., Mabe, M., Micsik, A. and Solvberg, I. (2001) 'Digital Libraries: A Generic Classification and Evaluation Scheme', in *Proceedings at the European Conference on Digital Libraries*, 2001 (Berlin: Springer).

Giles, C.L., Bollacker, K.D. and Lawrence, S., (1998) 'CiteSeer: An Automatic Citation Indexing System', in *Proceedings of the Third ACM Conference on Digital Libraries*, Pittsburgh, pp. 89–98, PA, USA, 23–26 June.

Gonçalves, M.A., Fox, E.A., Watson, L.T. and Kipp, N.A. (2003), 'Streams, Structures, Spaces, Scenarios, Societies (5S): A Formal Model for Digital Libraries', Technical Report TR-03–04, Computer Science, Virginia Tech, http://eprints.cs.vt.edu:8000/archive/00000646/.

Lagoze, C., Van de Sompel H., Nelson, M. and Simeon W. (2002), *The Open Archives Initiative Protocol for Metadata Harvesting – Version 2.0*, Open Archives Initiative, June 2002. Available at http://www.openarchives.org/OAI/2.0/openarchivesprotocol.htm.

McMillan, G. (2001a). 'Do ETDs Deter Publishers? Coverage from the Fourth International Symposium on ETDs', *College and Research Libraries News*, 62(6), 620–621.

McMillan, G. (2001b) 'What to Expect from ETDs: Library Issues and Responsibilities,' *Fourth International Conference on ETDs*, 24 March, Cal Tech.

Reich, V. and Rosenthal D.S.H. (2001), 'LOCKSS: A Permanent Web Publishing and Access System', *D-Lib Magazine*, 7(6), available at http://www.dlib.org/dlib/june01/reich/06reich.html.

Saracevic, T. (2000) 'Digital Library Evaluation: Toward Evolution of Concepts', *Library Trends*, 49(2), 350–369.

Suleman, H. (2002), *ODL-based ETD Union Catalog*, Website http://purl.org/net/etdunion.

Urs, S.R. and Raghavan, K.S. (2001), 'Vidyanidhi: Indian digital library of electronic theses', *Communications of the ACM*, 44(5), 88–89.

VTLS (2002) *VTLS*, website http://www.vtls.com

Chapter 12

The Variations and Variations2 Digital Music Library Projects at Indiana University

Jon W. Dunn, Mary Wallace Davidson, Jan R. Holloway
and Gerald Bernbom

'Variation' in music is:

> A form founded on repetition, and as such an outgrowth of a fundamental musical and rhetorical principle, in which a discrete theme is repeated several or many times with various modifications . . . The roots of the word *variatio* in the adjective *varius* originally referred, in non-specialized antique usage, to an impression of mixed coloration in plants and animals . . . Thus from the very beginning we see foreshadowed the twofold musical meanings of variation as technique and as form. (Sisman, 2003)

Variations, a digital library system for music in use at Indiana University (IU), provides near-CD-quality access to more than 8000 sound recordings for students and faculty. Developed at IU in the mid-1990s, in part to serve as an alternative to 'hard-copy' course reserves in the Library of the Indiana University School of Music, Variations is now heavily used for access to digitized versions of printed and recorded music whether for reserves, classroom, studio or private study use. In February 2003, some 75 classes in the School of Music had placed materials on reserve in Variations, which received an average of 1000 accesses per day.

Variations2 is a research and development project that is currently building a digital music repository linked to a set of applications for the use of music in research and instruction. Its searchable digital database of sound, musical score images, and symbolic score notation may help students, instructors, and researchers analyse music in new ways, forge new relationships with the data, and create new pedagogical approaches. The component-based architecture of the Variations2 system is designed to survive inevitable evolutionary changes in technology. The Variations2 system also serves as a platform for research in related areas, including metadata development, usability/human–computer interaction, networking, and intellectual property.

Context: Indiana University and the School of Music

Founded in 1820 at Bloomington, IU is a major public research university and among the oldest state universities in the Midwestern US. Its campuses include the main residential campus at Bloomington and the large urban campus in Indiana's capital, Indianapolis, along with six other campuses across the State.

IU has embraced information technology (IT) as an important tool in teaching and research. All students, faculty, and staff have access to current computing hardware, software, printers, and networks that support work in their areas. Beyond the university, IU manages the network operations center for the Abilene Internet2 network, and has helped build network connectivity to research and education institutions in the Asia Pacific. This IT-rich setting provides a climate hospitable to research in the application of IT to teaching and research.

The Indiana University School of Music, located in Bloomington, is among the nation's largest, with some 1500 degree candidates and 150 full-time faculty. The School offers graduate and undergraduate degrees in 22 musical instruments, early music, church music, musicology, theory, voice, jazz, music education, conducting, composition, ballet, audio recording, and stage direction (Indiana University, 2001). The William and Gayle Cook Music Library serves the School's faculty, staff and students as its primary clientele, and is also one of the nation's largest (IU, 2002c).

In the School of Music, IT gained an early foothold. A graduate elective in computer programming for music research was offered in 1967 and, in 1968, a computer music studio was built, housing a mini computer. In the mid-1970s, professors developed instructional programs for aural skills and established a music learning laboratory. By 1989, the School had created the position of director of computing for the School of Music.

With the growing importance of digital information, the Music Library turned to digital means for distributing that information. In 1987, the installation of a Novell network made it possible to distribute text, computer-assisted instruction programs, and music notation sources over a network, rather than to stand-alone workstations. This digital traffic accounted for only a portion of library circulation. Music students routinely requested more than 5500 sound recordings per month, many requesting the same materials at any given time. To preserve fragile originals and provide multiple copies for circulation, librarians dubbed copies onto cassette tapes, with some loss of audio quality. A system that could offer multiple patrons simultaneous, high-quality access to sound over a network was seen as an immediate solution to a host of issues (Burroughs and Fenske, 1990).

Variations: Beginnings

The sound component was the first phase of Variations to be developed. The convergence of various technologies in the early 1990s – high-fidelity PC audio hardware, streaming multimedia servers, hierarchical storage management systems, and the web – enabled the development of the first Variations prototypes. In addition, the construction of the new Cook Music Library facility provided an opportunity for funding and large-scale implementation of such a multimedia delivery system. Built using a combination of internal funding from the School of Music, the Libraries, and University Information Technology Services, and in-kind donations of equipment and software from IBM, Variations was first tested in the spring of 1996 as a reserves system for sound recordings in a large undergraduate music theory class. Later that year, Variations provided the platform for all course audio reserves in the Cook Music Library. It could stream high-fidelity recordings to library workstations, seminar rooms, and staff workstations and so quickly became a key part of the Library's support of teaching in the School of Music.

The technical development of Variations involved more systems integration than straight software development. Commercial hardware and software products were combined with components developed at IU to create a client–server environment based on an ATM network and IBM streaming media and storage technologies.

In its current configuration, the Variations system consists of an archive server (IBM RS/6000 with attached IBM 3494 tape library and three IBM 3590 high-speed tape drives) which stores the primary copies of sound files, and a playback server (another IBM RS/6000 running IBM VideoCharger software) which caches recently used files on a hard disk array for streaming to clients. This two-level storage hierarchy reflects the typical usage pattern of an academic library, and particularly of course reserve use, in which at any given time only a small portion of the collection is actually in use. Locally written software ties the two servers together and provides a web user interface. The current configuration is very similar to the original one deployed in 1996, but with additional storage capacity and updated software. In addition, the ATM network has been replaced with less expensive switched Ethernet technology.

Content is captured for the system by technicians in the Music Library working at digital audio workstations. They create CD-quality sound files from analog or digital media in Microsoft's WAV format at an audio sampling rate of 44.1 kHz and sample size of 16 bits with two channels – the parameters used by audio CDs and supported by common PC audio playback hardware. These WAV files are transferred each night to the archive server, where they are converted into MPEG-1 layer II format at a compression ratio of 3.6:1, reducing storage requirements while keeping sound quality high. The WAV files are stored offline on tape, while the MPEG files are kept available in 'nearline' storage on tape in the archive server.

Metadata for recordings in Variations consist of the existing USMARC (MARC, 1999) bibliographic records in IU's online public access catalog (OPAC), plus ASCII text metadata files in a locally defined format. These metadata files contain additional technical and structural metadata used in navigation and management of the digital sound files.[1]

Variations sound recordings are delivered to some 100 Windows computer workstations, scattered throughout the Music Library and equipped with sound cards and headphones. Many are also equipped with MIDI synthesizers/keyboards. These workstations also deliver basic computing functions including e-mail and word processing, library-specific functions (such as access to CD-ROM databases and the OPAC), and music computing functions, including software for ear training, music notation editing, and composition.

To use Variations, a student launches a web browser to the Music Library Home Page, clicks the 'Course reserves' link, selects a course number, and chooses the recording from a list organized by composer and title. Access to Variations recordings is also possible through links from records in the OPAC and from faculty-created course home pages. The locally written Variations Player applica-

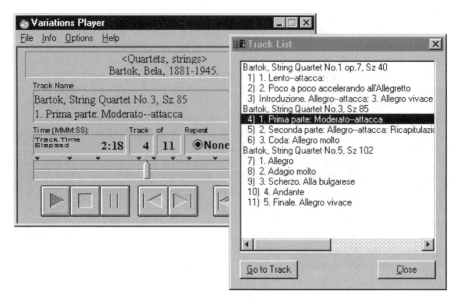

Figure 12.1   Variations sound player application

tion (see Figure 12.1) is used to control playback, allowing the user to navigate easily to particular tracks or time offsets. A single user can open multiple files at once to study comparisons between performances, and any number of users can listen to the same file at any given time, yet have independent control over playback. On an experimental basis, scanned versions of some printed musical scores have been made available to supplement the recordings in Variations, but the system is not as fully developed for scores as it is for recordings.

The term 'Variations' was chosen for its resonance with the musical form, 'theme and variations', and also as it alluded to the musician's need for material in a variety of formats, including text, sound, video, music notation, and images, in an integrated setting. This system provided a variation on the traditional means of delivering sound, and an alternative to the standard method of checking out hard-copy library materials placed on reserve. Developers also assumed the system would continue to be refined to handle the multiple formats in which scholars study music: score, sound, text, video, and so on. The plural form of the name captures the nature of Variations as a work in progress.

Variations was unique at the time in creating a digital music library, not merely an audio reserve system. Since then, several major projects have digitized discrete collections of music in their entirety, and academic music libraries have developed digital audio reserve systems of various sorts.[2] Moreover, Variations launched a cycle of development that enabled new relationships between researchers and their data, and allowed for new ways of teaching and conducting research. Variations and its subsequent iterations promise to open the doors to new ways of studying music. As happens when technology is applied to the study of any academic field, new landscapes of inquiry invariably suggest themselves. These, in turn, suggest new ways of applying technology to deepen and enrich the study of the field. The next generation of the system, Variations2, illustrates this point: it not only extends the technical capabilities of Variations, but also serves to support research in related areas, including metadata development, usability/human–computer interaction, networking, and intellectual property.

Variations2: The Next Evolution

The Variations2 project became one of the first modules in IU's Digital Library Program (IU, 1997–2002), which was established in 1997, and is a collaborative effort of the Libraries, the Office of the Vice President for Information Technology, the School of Library and Information Science, and the School of Informatics. Its broad program of collections and activities promotes the scholarly use of digital content and networked information. Associated research and development projects extend the state of the art in digital libraries and help develop understanding of the organizational, technological, and human factors involving the use of digital libraries.

In support of Variations2, in September 2000, IU was awarded $3 million by the Digital Libraries Initiative, Phase 2 (DLI2), a multi-agency US federal program with funding from the National Science Foundation and the National Endowment for the Humanities, in response to a proposal entitled, 'Creating the Digital Music Library'. Seventeen faculty and staff investigators from two campuses (Bloomington and Indianapolis) were assembled from University Information Technology Services, the Libraries, the School of Music (on both campuses), the School of Law (Indianapolis), and the School of Library and Information Science, under the direction of Michael McRobbie, IU's Vice President for Information Technology and Chief Information Officer. In addition, seven other institutions (three in the United States, three in the United Kingdom, and one in Japan) had agreed to participate as satellite sites.[3] Variations2 intends to 'move digital music libraries into a new phase – beyond creating, organizing, and dissemination of digital objects – to the seamless immersion of digital content into the education and research process' (IU, 1999, p. 4).

The Variations2 system under development moves far beyond the first iteration of the Variations project in that it provides a far more complex layered array of repositories, access and user interface components, and applications. While the only searching mechanisms in Variations were the university's OPAC and/or web-based reserve lists, the Variations2 project is developing its own descriptive, structural, and administrative metadata. While in Variations the digitized file formats were limited to audio and graphic images of musical notation, Variations2 adds digital music notation and video. The project will also seek to integrate content-based music information retrieval technologies developed by other researchers.[4] That is, by encoding musical incipits (themes), or even a complete musical work in a digital music notation format, we intend to provide the ability to search by means of the music itself (themes or phrases or entire works) as well as by the 'name' of the music, or some other attribute such as the composer or performer.

The system also provides multiple interfaces, not only to take advantage of new kinds of files, but also to present them in different ways to teachers, learners or researchers, and system administrators. While Variations presented simply an audio player or page image viewing screen, Variations2 offers possibilities for greater interaction with the music itself. Further, Variations2 has its own search and administrative (cataloging) interfaces so no longer depends on other systems for those functions. Using 'bookmarks', the user can capture and save references to small portions of a musical work, however they are represented, for close comparison with iterations of similar phrases elsewhere in the same work or in other works. Facilities for synchronizing graphic representations (musical scores) with audio representations (recordings) are being developed, so that one may see and hear and bookmark the representations simultaneously, allowing freer concentration on musical cognition.[5] An interface is also being developed that permits the student to analyze the melodic and harmonic content of a work through bubble diagrams, and to present the work as an assignment to be corrected by the instructor.[6]

Using Variations2

The search process in Variations2 has been designed specifically for those who are knowledgeable about music repertory. Metadata are stored so as to maintain the rich relationships among people (composers, performers, and the like), works (conceptually defined), versions (performances, notational representations), and containers (specific albums or editions) in order to provide musicians with a more intuitive and meaningful searching and browsing experience. When users initiate basic or advanced searches, they progress through a series of screens that allow them to specify the components of their searches (see Figure 12.2 for an example).

For example, some contributors have multiple roles as agents with respect to a given piece of music. Leonard Bernstein was a composer, arranger, and pianist; he also conducted his own works and those of others. Users of the advanced search can immediately narrow their searches beyond composer and title by using fields for other contributors (performer, editor, arranger), format, key and mode (major, minor). These enhancements make search results far more specific and reduce the number of times users must comb through the unsorted sets of results often generated by online catalog searches.

Once a user chooses a version of a work, a player or viewer opens, depending on whether the user has chosen a musical score, an audio piece, or a video recording. Navigation in Variations2 will be considerably more sophisticated, thanks to a hierarchical, nested display of whole works, parts of works, analyzable sections within a part and, in some cases, granularity to the exact measure of the work (see Figure 12. 3).

Variations2 has moved far beyond the original concept of a digital library to take its place in the interactive classroom. We have integrated Variations2 content into a music appreciation course for the non-major studying at a distance via

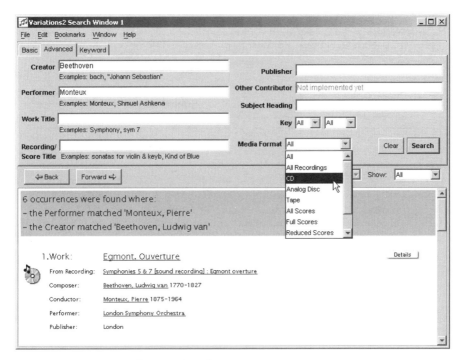

Figure 12.2   Variations2 search interface

'Oncourse', IU's online course management system.[7] Assessments will compare the effectiveness of a lecture-based class supplemented with digital content to one presented fully online, including threaded discussions. An instructional authoring environment, designed for faculty teaching music theory and other courses for music majors, will support the creation of classroom presentations and lessons in musical melodic and harmonic analysis. These lessons will integrate and synchronize the digital library's holdings, a music notation editor, form diagrams and other music visualization techniques, and provide the ability to pose questions and accept and evaluate answers.[8]

Variations2 System Architecture

Successful digital library systems must offer persistent access to their content despite the inevitable technological progress that will occur over their lifetimes. There is great risk of building systems with excellent functionality that will disappear when file formats, storage media, hardware, software, or other technologies become obsolete. In addition, to be truly useful, digital library systems can no longer be stand-alone monolithic systems. They must be able to be integrated into

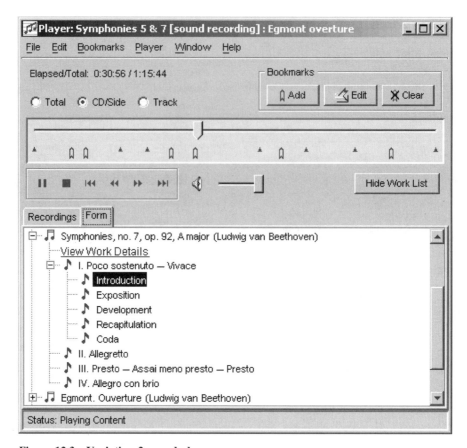

Figure 12.3   Variations2 sound player

the larger digital information environment, including course management systems, the OPAC, and licensed, externally served information resources.

The system architecture of Variations2 has been conceived from the start as modular, open, and extensible, and is being built with the assumption that there will be multiple pathways through which users discover and access its contents, along with multiple user interfaces for various tasks. Variations2 is viewed not just as a self-contained digital library system, but also as a platform for the development of additional domain-specific applications that use the contents and services of the digital music library.

Conceptually, the Variations2 system architecture has been envisioned as a series of abstraction layers that separate the functions of the library and define the interactions between these functions (see Figure 12.4). At the base of the architecture are repositories of content (audio, score images, score notation, video) and

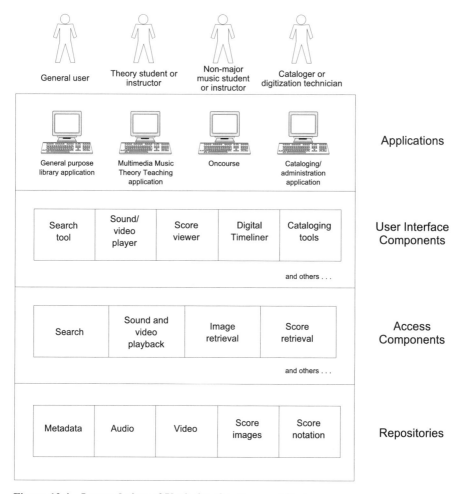

Figure 12.4   Layered view of Variations2 system architecture

metadata. Above these repositories sits a layer of system services or application program interfaces (APIs) for searching and retrieving data from the repositories. Above the system services are user interface (UI) 'components' that expose these services in a form that users can use. Some of these UI components are relatively straightforward, such as a metadata search tool, a sound player, and a score image viewer. However, others offer a greater degree of interactivity and specialized features that go beyond search, display and playback. Examples of the latter include a synchronized score viewer and sound player and the Timeliner tool for creating diagrams of musical form using content from the library. Finally, at the top lie the actual software applications through which users interact with the library. These software applications integrate the underlying UI components with additional interfaces to create a fully functional environment in which the user can accomplish various categories of tasks.

Variations2 is being developed primarily using the Java programming language. In addition, many class libraries are available as open-source or freely licensable commercial products to help with such issues as XML processing and streaming media playback. For ease of implementation, since both client and server are being written in Java, we have used Java's RMI (Remote Method Invocation) as the communications mechanism between client and server. Ultimately, a more language-neutral solution may be preferable.

Repositories

The underlying metadata repository has been implemented using IBM's DB2 relational database software running on IBM's AIX operating system. However, Java classes sit on top of DB2 to shield access components and applications from the implementation detail of the repository. These classes also serve to translate metadata records to and from an XML-based representation for purposes of data import and export. This should allow us to substitute other relational databases or data storage mechanisms (for example, a native XML database such as Software AG's Tamino) with relative ease. The audio content repository is implemented using Apple's Darwin Streaming Server open-source, RTP/RTSP-based media server running on Linux. The score image repository uses a simple Apache web server, also running on Linux. Audio content is currently stored using Apple's QuickTime file format, which can accommodate a number of different content encodings, including MP3 and MPEG-4 AAC, and is controlled at the client via Apple's QuickTime for Java API. Image content is stored in the DjVu format, originally developed by AT&T Labs, which we have found offers much better onscreen display for scores than other formats such as PDF. Again, for both image and audio access, components at the services layer isolate the UI components and applications from the implementation detail and allow other multimedia formats and delivery technologies to be substituted in the future. Master copies of both image and audio content are also stored offline in TIFF and WAV formats, respectively.

Because we are dealing with copyrighted content, we must provide the ability to control access based on the properties of both the content and the user. Initially, we are securing access by requiring users to authenticate with a personal username and password. For IU users, this is accomplished using IU's existing Kerberos authentication infrastructure. For satellite site users, we are initially handling user management ourselves by running our own Kerberos server, but we hope to be able to integrate with such emerging technologies for cross-institution authentication and authorization as the Internet2 project's Shibboleth architecture (Internet2, 2003). As intellectual property requirements are further defined, additional access controls will be designed.

In any system involving streaming media delivery, network performance is a key concern. We had originally intended to identify various network quality of service

(QoS) methodologies that might be appropriate for the streaming delivery of inter-active multimedia and to engage in implementing and testing these methodologies in a local laboratory as well as via our network connections to satellite sites. How-ever, the fact that all of our satellite sites are now connected to high performance research and education networks that generally have bandwidth to spare, combined with some fundamental viewpoint changes within the QoS research community (principally a shift in responsibility for dealing with QoS issues from hardware to applications) has led us to take a slightly different focus. We are studying the performance of our application through user feedback and data supplied by network instrumentation and are using this information to determine network requirements for scaling up Variations2 use and to make recommendations for tuning application parameters, particularly QuickTime Streaming parameters.

User Interface Components

The primary user interface components include the following.

Search Tool

The search tool is the primary interface though which users locate content in the system by searching or browsing descriptive metadata. Unlike traditional library OPAC interfaces, ours is specifically designed for music content, with search fields labeled using musical terms (for example, composer) and the concept of the musical 'work' as embodied in our data model prominently exposed to bring the various instantiations (recordings and scores) of a given work together in the interface. Basic, Advanced, and Keyword searches are available. In the Basic and Advanced options, rather than being taken directly to a result set of recordings and scores, the user is walked through a series of 'disambiguation' steps in order to clarify the composer, performer, and work entered, and is ultimately brought to a list of instantiations (recordings and scores representing individual works) rather than a list of containers. The selection and arrangement of search options were informed by looking at user needs through inspection of logs of inquiries at the Music Library reference desk and discussions with library users. For example, because most music searches are for some form of 'known item' (for example, the user has a composer, performer, and/or work title in mind), these are the fields present in the Basic search option.

Sound Player

The function of the sound player is to play back sound recordings from the library's collection. In addition to the standard CD-player-like controls found in all sound players (for example, play, stop, pause, and so forth), the interface also provides navigation within a given sound recording through the use of structural metadata stored in the system. Two means of navigation are available: users may view a list of the 'tracks' or 'bands' from the original recording and move forward/backward between tracks, or click on a track title to jump to a specific track. In addition, users may navigate based on the structure of the musical work using an outline of the work structure that is consistent across all instantiations of that work in various recordings and scores. For example, all recordings of Beethoven's fifth symphony would be accessible by movement. This is accomplished through the work structure/structural binding facility of Variations2 metadata, discussed below. In future versions, we will extend the capabilities of the sound player to video.

Score Viewer

The score viewer provides similar navigation functionality for digitized images of printed musical scores, offering standard image viewer controls (forward/backward page, zoom, and so on) along with structural navigation based on the underlying metadata. The ability to print a score (depending on access controls) is also available.

Bookmarks

Both score viewer and sound player provide access to a bookmarking function that allows users to mark time points or page offsets in recordings and scores for future use. Variations2 bookmarks may be relabeled and arranged into folders, similar to web browser bookmarks or favorites.

Sound-Score Sync Tool

The sound-score synchronization tool will allow a user to open a score and sound recording of the same musical work and seamlessly navigate through the two together. The most basic manifestation of this is 'automatic page turning,' for example, while the sound is playing, the score will turn pages to follow the performance. Perhaps the more useful capability is being able to turn to a specific page in the score or enter a specific measure number and have the sound recording move to that same point. Sound–score synchronization is initially being implemented using a single window that combines sound player and score viewer controls. This simplifies the user interface over the alternative of having multiple sound player and score viewer windows synchronized to each other, but has the limitation of allowing for only one sound recording and one score to be in use at any time. Synchronization would also be useful for multiple recordings (for example, comparing performances) or multiple scores (comparing editions).

Timeliner

The Timeliner tool can be used to create musical form diagrams using a simple 'bubble' visualization. A horizontal line represents a section of sound from a recording in the system. A nested series of bubbles may be created above this timeline to indicate sections and subsections of the work, and these bubbles may be color-coded and labeled to illustrate repeating elements of the music. These diagrams may be saved to disk or printed for presentation.

Score Notation Viewer/Editor

This tool, which has not yet been designed or developed, will be used to display digital music notation content from the library, in a similar fashion to the score image viewer. However, the use of music notation stored in a logical representation potentially allows for much greater capability than exists with score images, including the ability to zero in on particular parts or to play back the score to a MIDI instrument. There is also a possibility for providing some basic editing functions, which may be particularly useful in classroom teaching situations, although we will have to be careful to define the boundary between our tool and full-blown music editing software packages such as Finale and Sibelius, to which we should be able to export our content for cases when advanced editing is necessary. One major issue with score notation is choice of file format. Many music representation formats are available, both proprietary and open, but no true standard or clear best choice exists. We are evaluating a number of different options (Byrd and Isaacson, 2002).

Applications

We are currently focusing on a core digital library access application that provides search, retrieval, and viewing capabilities using the components identified above. However, we plan to work on other applications, including an authoring environment to support instructional developers in the creation of online educational materials that make use of digital library content. This application will allow users to create multimedia documents by assembling a set of Variations2 content and UI components (for example, sound player, score viewer, Timeliner), supplemented by additional components for text display, question-drilling, and other tasks, into classroom presentations and independent exercises for students. Such capabilities will allow instructors to play music selections, view scores, illustrate musical concepts through the use of music notation and form diagrams, and assess students' abilities to hear, understand, and categorize music.

We have created prototypes typical of the sort of lessons and presentations that could be created using such a tool in order to help evaluate usefulness and to guide our design of this authoring and delivery environment (see Figure 12.5).

Metadata

The metadata research in Variations2 is ambitious in that it attempts to develop a data model that permits searching, retrieving, displaying, navigating and documenting musical works while preserving their musical relationships. Current local OPAC systems based on USMARC do not adequately support these activities, chiefly because of the particular characteristics of musical works; that is, high incidence of multiple authorship (Papakhian, 1985); works known under various titles in the same or different languages; and the presence of multiple works in one publication,

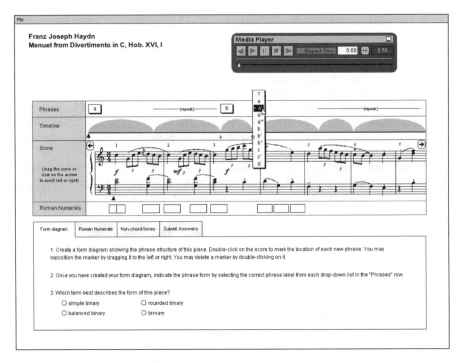

Figure 12.5   Music theory lesson prototype

particularly recordings, so that it is difficult to associate attributes (composers, performers, descriptors, duration) with individual works. Musical works are manifested and digitized in various formats other than text; that is, printed music ('scores') digitized as graphic images and notation files, audio recordings, and video. Some characteristics are shared among different instantiations of the same work, and some differ. Each music search query is uniquely constructed from various types of attributes, and individual users want to navigate search results differently.

Thus, we have defined descriptive, structural, and administrative schemas. The descriptive metadata build on the USMARC format for transmission of bibliographic information. But we have defined four levels of entities in order to preserve the relationships among them (works, instantiations, containers and media objects), and a fifth (contributors) to establish the agents of their creation at any one of those levels (see Figure 12.6).[9]

The first level is conceptual, representing the ideal 'Work' (individual or collective) and what we know about it (link to a creator, statement of form or genre, instrumentation, key if applicable, named divisions, date and place of composition and first performance if known), accompanied by source documentation.

The 'Instantiation' record represents each individual performance or graphic

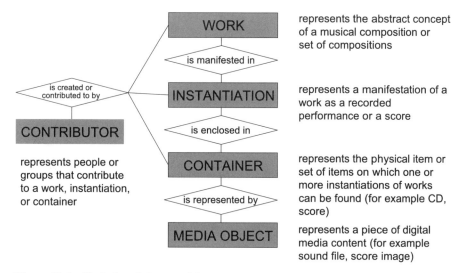

Figure 12.6   Variations2 data model

version found in a 'Container'. Contributors associated with instantiations are performers, directors (of videos) and the like. Some of the descriptive information associated with an instantiation varies from that of the associated work (for example, date of performance), and information about the extent of the work is added (duration, pages). 'Container' records are minimal, combining information about a published recording or score (for example, titles, publication or release dates) with links to the instantiations for all of the works present.

Three principal types of structural metadata have been defined in Variations2: 'container structure', 'work structure', and 'work bindings'. Container structure serves to identify the physical items (for example, CDs, LPs, score volumes) that make up a container, as well as the subsections within these items (for example, sides, tracks, pages), to facilitate navigation of a digitized recording or score as if the physical item were in hand. Work structure is used to identify and describe the discrete hierarchical elements of a given work. The discrete elements may be labeled with titles appropriate for their internal compositional sections (for example, arias or movements). These sections may be further subdivided by labels indicating such formal components as exposition, development, recapitulation, *da capo*, and so on. The finest granularity may be marked by labeling measure numbers. Work bindings are associated with each instantiation and serve to tie particular time or page ranges within the media objects of a given instantiation to the abstract structure of the corresponding work.

The administrative metadata comprise data that allow us to track various kinds of information about the metadata creation (sources of information and vocabulary), as well as the status of record creation or update, digitized media information (file

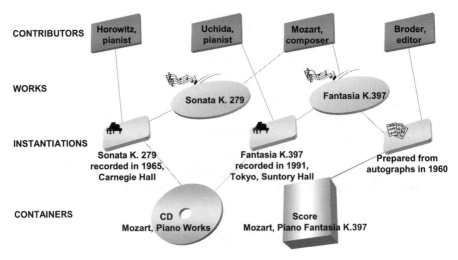

CONTRIBUTORS

WORKS

INSTANTIATIONS

CONTAINERS

Figure 12.7   Variations2 data model example

format, compression, bit and sampling rates, resolution, hardware and software used), copyright declarations, access control and, for containers, any external standard numbers and statement of condition (for preservation purposes). Our intention is to record any information needed to migrate or preserve this development in future technology, and we plan to make use of emerging standards in this area, particularly for technical metadata, for example, the MIX standard for images (Library of Congress, 2002c) and the work being done by the Library of Congress on audio and video technical metadata (Library of Congress, 2002a). An illustration of the data model with examples may be seen in Figure 12.7.

We are importing existing score and sound objects from Variations and mapping some data from USMARC records for the original containers to Variations2 to avoid duplication of effort. We are teasing apart the descriptive elements devised for physical artifacts and are associating the data instead with digitized works and instantiations. Although we have been criticized for remaining too dependent on the USMARC format, we find this level of detail useful, particularly in authoritative headings and controlled vocabularies, in providing successful navigation among the entities. However, if our project is to become internationally cooperative, we may need to look at other standards as well, and at the very least develop a crosswalk from our descriptive metadata to the Dublin Core standard and/or the emerging Metadata Object Description Schema (MODS).[10]

We established our metadata entities based on earlier conceptualization about music in descriptive catalogs by Richard Smiraglia and Sherry Vellucci, who in turn derived theirs in part from that of their mentor Barbara Tillett.[11] Tillett was a consultant to the International Federation of Library Associations and Institutions' Functional Requirements for Bibliographic Standards (FRBR), a final draft of which was issued in 1998 (IFLA, 1998).[12] Future work will examine how we might better exploit FRBR, since our metadata construct is so similar, with a view toward exploring how metadata entry could be encouraged and facilitated in a distributed fashion. We will also investigate other appropriate standards such as the Metadata Encoding and Transmission Standard (METS) (Library of Congress, 2002b)[13] and the Moving Picture Experts Group's MPEG-7 and MPEG-21 designed expressly for digital objects (Fraunhofer, 2001a, 2001b). It has also been suggested that we devise administrative metadata that would track the kinds of uses being made of these objects (assignment preparation by classroom or studio faculty or student, recital-program design, background listening) to facilitate our research with respect to intellectual property.

Usability

Usability is a primary research focus of Variations2, with the aim not simply to create a digital library system that is easy to use, but one that actually proves useful to its target user population. By integrating a user focus into the system design and development process, we can help to ensure that we meet this goal.

The project's Usability Specialist is an integrated part of the software development team, helping the team to define system requirements based on user needs. Usability work on the project has included three primary activities: (1) study of current user practices in order to establish a usability baseline for future comparison and help guide design decisions; (2) investigation of emergent interaction technologies which may be of benefit; and (3) usability evaluation of the Variations2 system through contextual interviews, lab-based testing of prototypes and finished releases, and pilot studies of actual use.

A study of current practice has been accomplished via a usability test of the existing Variations system, a satisfaction survey of current Variations users, and by contextual inquiry into music classroom pedagogical practices, Variations use in the Music Library, and the information habits of voice students. These studies revealed a generally high level of satisfaction among users with the current Variations system; however, some complaints were noted, including latency in requests for recordings and in moving around within recordings and the fact that access is restricted to within the Music Library. User interviews using paper prototypes help to validate user interface and information architecture design concepts before the expense of implementation, while lab-based testing allows us to make adjustments to the user interface before the system is widely deployed to users. Finally, pilot studies in which the project Usability Specialist works with faculty and students in the context of a specific class unit or assignment allow us to examine the system in use rather than in the more contrived setting of a lab-based usability test. To date, automated logging of user actions and a web-based satisfaction survey have been used to gather data during pilot studies.

Of all these activities, the most fruitful in terms of identifying system design issues have been usability testing and observational studies. Both methods yield rich data about users' experiences with the system, and both methods provide enough context to render the data meaningful and actionable. Surveys and session logging have been less valuable because it is difficult to know what thought is behind a particular mouse click or Likert scale rating.

Future usability work will include broadening the scope of our studies to include the satellite sites, so that we can be more certain that the Variations2 system will be applicable generally and not just to IU. We will continue to engage in prototype testing and lab-based usability testing of current and future versions of the system and will also conduct field studies of Variations2 use and of the ways instructors prepare lessons and use technology in the classroom.

Intellectual Property

Variations2 embraces research in intellectual property, given that the issues are complex in a digital music library that will be shared with public and private institutions in three different countries. Although the US Copyright Law is generally more liberal than its Canadian or European counterparts, particularly in its concept of Fair Use, the digital issues are complex and confusing. Music libraries have depended on the Fair Use provision more heavily than have other libraries because of the generally more restrictive rubrics for music in Section 108 of the US Copyright Law (exceptions for libraries). Exceptions for performance and displays (in Section 110) are generally limited to face-to-face teaching, although the recently enacted so-called 'TEACH Act' has broadened these some-what (Technology, 2002). At issue, however, is whether or not libraries may make digital copies of documents they have lawfully acquired for the purpose of digital display, as they did for photocopying or microfilming, in the context of teaching and learning in non-profit educational institutions.

Kenneth Crews has written a number of working papers for Variations2 research examining the constraints of Sections 107 and 108, and the difficulties of establishing whether or not something is in the public domain (Crews, 2001). Naturally, we will exercise our right of Fair Use to the extent possible, but we are also watching as the music industry attempts to establish new business models in a period of rapidly declining sales and confusion of new media standards. It appears that given the failure of the marketplace to establish convenient and cost-effective methods of licensing musical content, reliance upon Fair Use is our only option at the moment. Based on observations gleaned from our usability studies, we are creating a set of scenarios that we will test to see how broadly we might interpret this doctrine. Because the project is underway in geographical areas with three different sets of intellectual property laws, we will need to develop a complex grid of rights management with corollary rules for users' access and authentication.

Conclusions

The Variations2 project is a true work in progress. It serves as a platform for research in six different but closely related domains – metadata, usability, pedagogy, intellectual property, networking, and system architecture – and provides a basis for a useful experiment that will address issues identified in our grant proposal. We will also continue to investigate emerging technologies, such as content-based music information retrieval, which could prove useful to music digital library users.

As Variations2 develops, we continue to ask questions that touch on many aspects of the system and its users. Are we creating a digital library system that can be used in production at one or more of the music libraries involved in this work? If so, how do we integrate it within other existing local systems, or should we? In a project involving more than one library, what are the political issues involved? Will the music industry develop convenient and cost-effective licensing plans relevant to the use of music teaching and research in a non-profit educational environment? How far can, or should, we extend the concept of fair use in a multinational project in order not to limit our library to music in the public domain? Are any of the existing metadata schemas more appropriate, or should we continue to develop our own? How can we lessen the intensity of the labor now necessary to populate Variations2 and thus reduce the costs? How may cataloging and digitization efforts be shared? What kinds of networking designs are necessary to provide interactive access to the system to all campuses of the same university, and to other universities in the US, the UK, and elsewhere? Is the system architecture we are developing sufficient to support all these activities?

In designing the current system, we have made choices with future expansion in mind, but work will need to be done to add support for sharing metadata records and content between Variations2 repositories at different institutions. In addition, depending on outcomes in the intellectual property area, increased authentication, access control, and digital rights management functionality will need to be provided.

Another question to address for the future is that of how to continue development of the Variations2 software. A number of models are possible. At first glance, given the economics of music libraries, it seems unlikely that a commercial spin-off could be a success, but that option may merit further investigation. Another more promising option might be to form a collaborative development project among the set of institutions using the software. This could be carried out as a 'pay to play' model in which institutions contribute development efforts in order to have access to the software; alternatively, an open source model would allow free distribution of the software and source code to any interested user.

In order for Variations2 to be successfully deployed in production at multiple institutions, more work is needed to make it adaptable to a wider variety of technical environments. In addition, many institutions are starting to look at implementing institution-wide digital library repository systems or digital asset management systems. These systems include those born in the academic world, such as Fedora (Fedora Project, 2001) as well as commercial systems such as IBM Content Manager and Artesia TEAMS. Variations2 will need to be able to make use of such systems for content and metadata storage if it is to be integrated into university structures for supporting digital content.

Finally, to be successfully integrated into classroom and distance education, Variations2 must be able to interoperate with course management systems beyond IU's own Oncourse system. Several efforts to standardize course management system interoperability are starting to emerge, including the Open Knowledge

Initiative (OKI) effort (Massachusetts Institute of Technology, 2002), in which IU is a participant.

'... Thus from the very beginning we see foreshadowed the twofold musical meanings of variation as technique and as form' (Sisman, 2003). The Variations2 project creates and relies on a vast array of techniques to construct a form with many dimensions. The idea of a searchable digital library, even for music, is certainly not new. What is new, and of significance, is the creation of a working, extensible model that accommodates searching, display, and navigation among music in all its formats, for a variety of uses in personal and classroom learning and teaching, in many academic institutions.

Acknowledgements

The authors would like to thank Mark Notess and Doug Pearson for their assistance with this chapter. We would also like to acknowledge the work of present and past members of the Variations and Variations2 project teams in the development of these systems. This material is based upon work supported by the National Science Foundation under Grant No. 9909068. Any opinions, findings, and conclusions or recommendations expressed in this material are those of the authors and do not necessarily reflect the views of the National Science Foundation.

Notes

1 For detailed technical descriptions of Variations hardware, software, networking, and methods of sound capture see especially Dunn and Mayer (1999).
2 For a recent brief survey of these projects, see Davidson (2001, pp. 400–402); Griscom (2003) surveys digital audio reserve and preservation projects in music libraries.
3 The institutions were Northwestern University, University of Illinois at Urbana-Champaign, University of Massachusetts at Amherst (United States); King's College London, University of Loughborough, and University of Oxford (United Kingdom); and Waseda University (Japan). City University London has recently become an additional site in the UK.
4 For further information on music information retrieval research, see Downie, (2002), and the online proceedings of the ISMIR conference series at http://www.ismir.net/.
5 Bamberger (2003) has shown that a curriculum for elementary music fundamentals classes at the college level should recognize, build on, and help students develop their musical intuitions in part by giving easy access to 'a *variety of representations* that include: multiple sensory modalities, multiple graphics and multiple levels of musical structure' (italics in original).
6 For more detailed description of the various interfaces, see IU (2002a).
7 This software was developed at Indiana University. For a description, see IU (1997–2003). For an overview of the specific application, see Fern *et al.* (2002).
8 For commentary on the music appreciation and music theory applications, see Isaacson (2002).
9 For a detailed chart showing the details of the entities with their associated types of metadata, see Davidson *et al.* (2002). See also Minibayeva and Dunn (2002).
10 Dublin Core Metadata Initiative (1995–2003). MODS (Library of Congress, 2003) is based closely on a simplified MARC format, using textual instead of numeric labels.

11 Smiraglia (2002), Vellucci (1997) and Tillett (1987). These sources provide insight into
    Smiraglia's and Vellucci's most recent writing about the nature of musical works, and
    Tillett's seminal thought upon which they are based.
12 See also Tillett (2001).
13 METS grew out of the Digital Library Federation's 'Making of America II' project
    (Digital Library Federation, 2001) and is maintained in the Network Development and
    MARC Standards Office at the Library of Congress.

References

Bamberger, J. (2003), 'The Development of Intuitive Musical Understanding: A Natural
    Experiment', *Psychology of Music*, 31(1), 43.
Burroughs, M. and Fenske, D. (1990), 'Variations: A Hypermedia Project Providing
    Integrated Access to Music Information', in S. Arnold and G. Hair, (eds), *ICMC Glasgow
    1990. Proceedings of the International Computer Music Conference, 1990*, Glasgow:
    ICMC for the Computer Music Association, pp. 221–224.
Byrd, D. and Isaacson, E. (2002), *Music Representation Requirement Specification for
    Variations2, Version 1.1*, http://variations2.indiana.edu/pdf/v2-music-rep-req-11.pdf.
Crews, K. (2001a), *Copyright Law for the Digital Library: Framework of Rights and
    Exceptions*, http://variations2.indiana.edu/pdf/CopyrightLawforDLibFramework.pdf.
Crews, K. (2001b), *The Expiration of Copyright Protection: Survey and Analysis of U.S.
    Copyright Law for Identifying the Public Domain*, http://variations2.indiana.edu/pdf/dml-
    copyright-duration-report.pdf.
Crews, K. (2001c), *Digital Libraries and the Application of Section 108 of the U.S.
    Copyright Act*, http://variations2.indiana.edu/html/crews-sec108/.
Crews, K. (2001)d, '*A&M Records, Inc., v. Napster, Inc.*': Implications for the Digital
    Music Library*, http://variations2.indiana.edu/pdf/AnalysisOfNapsterDecision.pdf.
Davidson, M. (2001), 'Trends and Issues in Digital Technology,' *Fontes artis musicae*,
    48(4), October–December, 398–410.
Davidson, M., Hemmasi, H., and Minibayeva, N. (2002) *Data Dictionary: Metadata
    Elements for Version 1*, http://variations2.indiana.edu/pdf/DML-metadata-elements-v1.
    pdf.
Digital Library Federation (2001), *Making of America II* (website), http://sunsite.berkeley.
    edu/MOA2/.
Downie, S.J. (2002), *Music Information Retrieval Research Bibliography* (website), http://
    music-ir.org/, last updated 20 September.
Dublin Core Metadata Initiative (1995–2003), *Dublin Core Metadata Initiative* (website)
    http://dublincore.org/.
Dunn, J.W. and Mayer, C.A. (1999), 'VARIATIONS: A Digital Music Library System at
    Indiana University', in: E.A. Fox and N.C. Rowe (eds) *Digital Libraries 99 The Fourth
    ACM Conference on Digital Libraries*, 11–14 August 1999, Berkeley, CA (New York:
    Association for Computing Machinery), pp. 12–19.
Fedora [Flexible Extensible Digital Object and Repository Architecture] *Project* (2001)
    (website), http://www.fedora.info/.
Fern, J., Lindsey, R. and Scull, E. (2002), 'The distributed music appreciation class and the
    Indiana University Digital Library Project: Phase One', paper presented at the College
    Music Society – Great Lakes Chapter meeting, Northfield, MN, 16 March.
Fraunhofer Institut Intigrierte Publikations- und Informationssystem (2001a). *MPEG-7*
    (website), http://ipsi.fraunhofer.de/delite/Projects/MPEG7/.

Fraunhofer Institut Intigrierte Publikations- und Informationssystem (2001b). *MPEG-21* (website), http://ipsi.fraunhofer.de/delite/Projects/MPEG7/Mpeg21.html.

Griscom, R. (2003), 'Distant Music: Delivering Audio over the Internet', *Notes: Quarterly Journal of the Music Library Association*, 59(3), 521–541.

IFLA Study Group on the Functional Requirements for Bibliographic Records (1998), *Functional Requirements of Bibliographic Records: Final Report*, UBCIM publications, new series, vol. 19 (Munich: K.G. Saur). Also available at http://www.ifla.org/VII/s13/frbr/frbr.htm, last updated 10 April 2000.

Indiana University (1997–2002), *Digital Library Program* (website), http://www.dlib.indiana.edu/index.htm, last updated 24 February 2003.

Indiana University (1997–2003), 'What is Oncourse', *Indiana University Knowledge Base* (website), http://kb.indiana.edu/data/agku.html.

Indiana University (1999), 'Creating the digital music library', proposal to the National Science Foundation, Program Announcement NSF 98–63: Digital Libraries Initiative, Phase 2 (DLI2), 17 May; available at http://variations2.indiana.edu/overview/, last updated 9 May.

Indiana University (2001), 'General Description', *School of Music* (website), http://www.music.indiana.edu/about/general.html, last updated 2 November.

Indiana University (2002a), *IUDML Version 1 Interface Specification*, http://variations2.indiana.edu/pdf/DML-UI-V1.pdf, last updated 19 February.

Indiana University (2002b), *Variations Project* (website), http://www.dlib.indiana.edu/variations/, last updated 13 May.

Indiana University (2002c), *William and Gayle Cook Music Library* (website), http://www.music.indiana.edu/muslib.html, last updated 20 November.

Indiana University (2003), *Variations2 Project* (website), http://variations2.indiana.edu/, last updated 24 February.

Internet2 (2003), *Shibboleth Project* (website), http://shibboleth.internet2.edu/.

Isaacson, E.J. (2002), 'Music Learning Online: Evaluating the Promise', National Association of Schools of Music, *Proceedings, the 77th Annual Meeting, 2001*, 90, July, pp. 120–126.

Library of Congress (2002a), *Digital Audio-Visual Preservation Prototyping Project* (website), http://lcweb.loc.gov/rr/mopic/avprot/, last updated 25 March.

Library of Congress (2002b), *Metadata Encoding & Transmission Standard* (website) http://www.loc.gov/standards/mets/, last updated 19 February.

Library of Congress (2002c), *NISO Metadata for Images in XML Schema* (website) http://www.loc.gov/standards/mix/, last updated 16 April.

Library of Congress (2003), *Metadata Object Description Schema* (website) http://www.loc.gov/standards/mods/, last updated 7 February.

MARC21 (1999) *MARC 21 Format for Bibliographic Data, including Guidelines for Content Designation* (Washington, DC: Library of Congress, Cataloging Distribution Service).

Massachusetts Institute of Technology (2002), *Open Knowledge Initiative* (website), http://web.mit.edu/oki/.

Minibayeva, N. and Dunn, J.W. (2002), 'A Digital Library Data Model for Music', in *Proceedings of the Second ACM/IEE-CS Joint Conference on Digital Libraries*, Portland, Oregon, (New York: ACM Press), pp. 154–155.

Papakhian, A.R. (1985), 'The Frequency of Personal Name Headings in the Indiana University Music Library Card Catalogs', *Library Resources & Technical Services* 29, 273–285.

Payette, S. and Staples, T. (2002), 'The Mellon Fedora Project: Digital Library Architecture Meets XML and Web Services', in M. Agosti, and C. Thanos, (eds), *Research and*

Advanced Technology for Digital Libraries: 6th European Conference, ECDL 2002, Rome Italy, 16–18 September, Proceedings (Berlin: Springer), pp. 406–421.

Sisman, E. (2003) 'Variations', *The New Grove Dictionary of Music Online*, L. Macy (ed) (Accessed 24 January 2003), http://www.grovemusic.com/.

Smiraglia, R.P. (2002), 'Musical Works and Information Retrieval', *Notes: The Scholarly Journal of the Music Library Association* 58(2), 747–767.

Staples, T. and Wayland, R. (2000), 'Virginia Dons FEDORA: A Prototype for a Digital Object Repository', *D-Lib Magazine*, 6(7/8), July/August, http://www.dlib.org/.

'Technology, Education, and Copyright Harmonization Act of 2002', in *21st Century Department of Justice Appropriations Act*, US PL 107–273, stat. 1910, §13301. Available online at http://www.copyright.gov/legislation/pl107–273.html.

Tillett, B.B. (1987), 'Bibliographic relationships: toward a conceptual structure of bibliographical information used in cataloging', unpublished PhD thesis, University of California at Los Angeles.

Tillett, B. B. (2001), 'Bibliographic Relationships', in C.A. Bean, and R. Green (eds), *Relationships in the Organization of Knowledge* (Dordrecht; Boston: Kluwer Academic Publishers), pp. 19–35.

Vellucci, S.L. (1997), *Bibliographic Relationships in Music Catalogs* (Lanham, MD., Scarecrow Press).

Chapter 13

Beyond Bricks and Mortar: Building a Digital Library Program at the Library of Congress

Diane Nester Kresh

Introduction

History and technology provided the Library of Congress with a unique opportunity at the close of the 20th century and the beginning of the 21st to realize fully the potential of a digital library – a virtual library without walls, not bound by time or place. History's greatest innovations have been about mass communication. The printing press linked communities and created a literary culture, the automobile linked urban and rural America, and the internet has spawned a virtual community where, with a PC and a modem, a person can connect, any time, anywhere, with another human being to share information, seek advice, buy or sell a product – the opportunities are limitless.

The Library of Congress has enjoyed tremendous success in creating the National Digital Library Program (NDLP), an initiative that has been applauded and recognized as much for its technical innovations as its freely available content. Technology, and the experience gained through the NDL, now make it possible for the Library of Congress to provide an even higher level of connectivity to anyone in the world and to provide such services to a scholar in the Main Reading Room of the Library of Congress, to a teacher creating lesson plans in Topeka, Kansas, or to a student able to talk to a library curator during a live video conference.

A digital library program, however, is not just a 21st century equivalent of the 19th century storehouse. Its potential is limited primarily by the imagination of its creators. The proliferation of websites (at last count over 50 million) and the explosion of e-commerce and other e-activities all argue for a robust Library program that integrates content and access services (Billington, 2001).

Windows on the Past: The Launch of the National Digital Library Program

For the general public, the Congress has endorsed the creation of a National Digital Library through a private–public partnership that will create high-quality content in electronic form and thereby provide remote access to the most interesting and education-ally valuable core of the Library's Americana collections. Schools, libraries, and homes will have access to new and important material in their own localities along with the same freedom readers have always had within public reading rooms to interpret, rearrange, and use the material for their own individual needs. (Billington, 1995)

It was with these words that Librarian of Congress James Billington launched one of the most visionary and successful programs in the Library's then almost 200 year history. For the program not only made available millions of unique materials from its collection, it also established technical standards and digitizing benchmarks that have informed the library and archival communities.

In 1990, the Library of Congress began its *American Memory Project*[1] with the goal of disseminating, in electronic form, the Library's unique special collections of photographs, maps, manuscripts, and other special format materials. In 1995, coupled with the rise in importance of the World Wide Web, *American Memory* became part of the newly established National Digital Library (NDL) Program and so began an ambitious program to present online 5 million items from the Library's collections – 5 million items in 5 years. With money provided by the Congress, private donors and corporate sponsors, the Library reached its goal of digitizing 5 million items in its bicentennial year of 2000 (Library of Congress, 1998).

Since its inception, *American Memory* has been a popular and award-winning site. In 2001 alone, more than 1,025,276,805 visitors came to the site, among them teachers, students, genealogists, researchers, and just plain dabblers. The Library receives countless letters from patrons who applaud what it has done and who urge it to do more. *American Memory* is a gateway to rich primary source materials relating to the history and culture of the United States.[2] A quick review of the site reveals a large collection – close to eight million digital items from more than 110 historical collections – in a variety of media formats and subject areas.

The online collections cover a broad range of American history, from the exploration of the Americas to the travels of Lewis and Clark and the settlement that followed; the development of trade and commercialism in America, immigration, and the social change and activism of the late 19th and early 20th centuries. These archival or theme-based collections include maps and atlases from the 16th century to the 21st; daguerreotypes from the Civil War and tens of thousands of documentary photographs from the Farm Security Administration–Office of War Information in the mid 20th century; the papers and diaries of several US presidents (including George Washington, Thomas Jefferson and Abraham Lincoln); late 19th and early 20th century silent films from the Thomas Edison Company; audio collections from the American Folklife Center, focusing on personal histories and songs of regions across the country; the papers of Samuel F. B. Morse and Alexander Graham Bell; and printed broadsides and bulletins from the earliest colonial times to the early 20th century. A treasure trove of Americana.

More recently, the Library has begun to collect data on the use of *American Memory*, data that will be used to help identify additional collections for digitization. Feedback from patrons tells us that, among the collections, the presidential papers (Washington, Jefferson and Lincoln) prompt lots of reference inquiries, followed closely by a Century of Lawmaking, the Historic American Buildings Survey and the Historic American Engineering Record (HAEBS-HAER) and the sheet music collections. Teachers and students who may not know our collections query the Library about specific subjects for history day projects or other educational activities. For curriculum support, sites on immigration, the women's right to vote, the Civil War and the American Depression have proven the most heavily used. The release of collections that appeal to a specific community also generates many questions and requests to link to the site. Similar responses were witnessed with the release of the *Slave Narratives*, *Florida Folklife* and the Aaron Copeland Collection.

The Library is also digitizing materials representing world cultures and histories, from both its own collections and in cooperation with other national libraries. *Global Gateways*[3] provides access to a variety of cooperative international digitization projects, creating virtual digital libraries on various historical themes. Other international resources from the Library's own collections are also being digitized, including materials from Europe, the Middle East, Asia, and other parts of the Americas. Of special significance, 'Meeting of Frontiers' was the Library's first major digital project involving international material and extensive cooperation with foreign institutions to obtain materials for the Library's collections in digital form.

In addition to making the unique materials from the Library of Congress available, the National Digital Library established many of the digitizing benchmarks and technical standards and practices that persist today.[4] In order to reproduce collections of books, pamphlets, motion pictures, manuscripts and sound recordings, the Library created a wide array of digital entities: bitonal document images, gray-scale and color pictorial images, digital video and audio, and searchable texts (Arms, 1999). To provide access to the reproductions, the project developed a range of descriptive elements: bibliographic records, finding aids, and introductory texts and programs, as well as indexing of the full texts for certain types of content.

A Library Without Walls

One of the goals of *American Memory* was to serve as a bridge to other libraries. The Library used part of the private money that largely funded the NDL to subsidize adding unique American historical materials from other institutions, libraries, and repositories from all over America to this *American Memory* website. With a gift from Ameritech, the Library of Congress sponsored a competition from 1996 through 1999 to enable public, research, and academic libraries, museums, historical societies, and archival institutions (except federal institutions) to create digital collections of primary resources (Arms, 1996).

Highlights of the competitions included: African-American sheet music; history of the American west, 1860–1920; emergence of advertising (here you can find that Jello was America's most famous dessert), American landscape design 1850–1920; Sunday school books from 19th century America; prairie settlement (photographs and letters from Nebraska); small-town America, 1850–1920; stereoscopic views, and Edward Curtis's photos of American Indians. All of these digitized collections were presented through the *American Memory* website and the home institution's site.

Nuts and Bolts: Staffing, Selection for Digitization and Attracting New Audiences

Staff with a range of skills were required to create the *American Memory* online collection. The Library's Conservation staff assisted with addressing the care and handling needs of the collections and determined whether a collection item could indeed withstand the scanning process. Digital conversion specialists – a newly established library position – were hired to provide project coordination and technical oversight. The more experienced specialists oversaw teams and directed the activities of item selection, rights clearance and production. They also served as brokers among the divisions, automation staff and contractors. In addition, curatorial staff were assigned from subject/format divisions to assist in the preparation and processing of the materials to be digitized. To support the needs of the emerging audience of teachers and educators, a newly formed educational services staff focused on outreach for the use of the historical collections by the K-12 (Kindergarten to 12th Grade) community.

In many respects, the technical issues attending the creation of digital libraries were the easy ones to solve. What has been harder to determine and codify is what to digitize and why (Hazen, 1998). To date, the definition of selection criteria has come from a variety of sources: library curators and specialists interested in promoting their collections to a broader audience; staff interested in the preservation uses of the technology; and educators interested in having the Library's digitized collections supplement K-12 school curriculum.

With the integration of the *American Memory* conversion project into the Library's core operations, the Library has instituted an annual call for proposals for digital conversion. Each proposal describes the content, quantities, physical description, preservation needs, copyright status, anticipated funding, and calendar-related requirements. The projects are then evaluated against technical criteria to determine their feasibility within the allotted time frame. This scoring system attempts to evaluate and balance priorities by the division or sponsor, audience interest, copyright status, technical implementation requirements, physical state of the collection materials, and amount of descriptive (bibliographic) information available for the collection. In addition, each project is assessed against selection criteria to ensure that through digitization the Library can fill content gaps in current online collections; take advantage of synergies with other Library initiatives or events; and gauge potential scholarly use to ensure that it is continuing to digitize the most important Library materials.

With the creation of the National Digital Library, the Library of Congress assumed a broad and nationwide educational function. This was new territory for an institution that was previously focused on serving the Congress, the government, the scholarly community, and the general public. To prepare for its role in providing educational content, the Library brought together leading history and social studies K-12 teachers and librarians to consider how archival online resources could best be used in the nation's schools. The participants at this Educator's Forum, held in 1995, validated earlier findings: that while the primary sources were in great demand, for teachers to be able to make effective use of them they needed additional materials to frame the collections and the topics represented in the collections.

The Learning Page was an initial response to this need and it debuted in 1996. The Learning Page is described as a gateway to the online collections and provides contextual material, search help, sample lesson plans and activities, special presentations, and descriptions of the digital collections for K-12 school teachers and media specialists. New material is continuously added to this site.

In 1997, the Library initiated the American Memory Fellows Program, which brought together 25 two-person teams of K-12 educators to explore the collections and to develop sample lesson plans, teaching activities, and websites that could be used in their local communities. The American Memory Fellows Program continued through 2001, graduating more than 250 teachers and educators. The Library continues to offer a range of programs to teachers and students, primarily in the areas of history and language arts. Participants learn online search skills, background and context for using archival collections in the classroom, and strategies for integrating web-based material into teaching.

Special Initiatives

I Hear America Singing

In the fall of 2003, the Music Division of the Library of Congress released an ambitious, interactive website on roots of American Music. *I Hear America Singing* will allow a library patron to select dates from a time line and experience, through sheet music, photographs, sound recordings and other media, the collections of the Library and the development of American music. From folk to gospel, choral to musical theater, chamber to jazz . . . it will all be here.

The International Children's Digital Library (ICDL)

The Library of Congress is a participant and contributor to an exciting new program developed by the Internet Archive and the University of Maryland. The International Children's Digital Library, with funding provided by the National Science Foundation (NSF), will make available to children around the world, a prestigious collection of international literature. This online digital library will provide free access to stories that can enable children to become familiar with literature from around the world and, through that familiarity, increase their understanding of global society. The materials included in the collection reflect similarities and differences in cultures, societies, interests, lifestyles, aspirations, and priorities of peoples around the world. The ICDL's primary audiences are children aged 3–13, librarians, teachers, parents, caregivers, and others concerned with the interests and welfare of children. Titles included from the Library's Rare Book and Special Collections Division are the usual suspects, such as *Alice in Wonderland*, *Aesop's Fables*, *A Child's Garden of Verses*, several varieties of fairy tales and folk tales, and some titles perhaps less familiar, such as *More Goops and How Not to be Them: a Manual of Manners for Polite Infants*.

Cataloging Enrichment

In 1992, a team of catalogers and reference staff was formed to develop and implement tools to aid catalogers, reference specialists, and searchers in creating and locating information. The result was BEAT, which stands for the Bibliographic Enrichment Advisory Team, and which is a cross-departmental team at the Library of Congress, comprising representatives from cataloging, reference, acquisitions, operations, the Cataloging Distribution Service, and the Network Development and MARC Standards Office. Its mission is to explore ways in which the content of Library of Congress bibliographic records can be enriched in order to improve access to the data the records represent. A major focus of the group is to carry out pilot research and development projects that support this goal. Among BEAT's recent catalog enrichment projects are the addition of links in selected catalog records to tables of contents, back-of-book indexes, annotations, book reviews, and publisher-supplied descriptions and sample pages of text. Several recent initiatives focus on providing links in our bibliographic records to the full digitized text of the items described: these include freely available 'born-digital' internet resources, monographic series of working papers, and digitized publications in the public domain.

Virtual Reference Services

When new collections are created and brought to new audiences, new questions naturally arise (Kresh, 2002a). The Library of Congress is now in the position of being able to serve the public's need for information more effectively through its development and implementation of a virtual reference service, *QuestionPoint*.[5] Co-developed by the Library of Congress and the Online Computer Library Center (OCLC), *QuestionPoint* allows for seamless exchange of reference questions within the Library of Congress (LC), as well as with colleagues around the United States and worldwide. The Library's version of *QuestionPoint*, called *Ask A Librarian*, is featured on the homepage. This service has resulted in outreach that helps patrons discover new resources and provides a link between more traditional reference services and those that are online. This is part of an ongoing process to bring libraries throughout the country into strong local, online networks – redirecting patrons to their local libraries and local resources, as well as to specialized materials that would not ordinarily be available to them. OCLC and LC and other library partners share a vision of producing and improving *QuestionPoint* so that it will allow librarians to manage their online reference more effectively and provide access to unique collections. *QuestionPoint* enables libraries throughout the world to share their riches with a broad audience, and the role of the Library of Congress in the development of *QuestionPoint* ensures that LC has a central role in the future direction of reference practice in the United States and beyond.

Lessons Learned

Many challenges accompany digital reformatting and developing a digital library. A few of the lessons learned by the Library through its five-year effort are worth noting here.

Establish Protocols and Standards to Facilitate the Assembly of Distributed Digital Libraries

Interoperability and the development of technical standards for a sustainable resource between digital libraries are of significant importance. To that end, the Library of Congress has been a participant in a number of distributed digital library programs, including the RLG Cultural Alliance and the Open Archival Information System (OAIS) protocol. Numerous *American Memory* collections have been made available for harvesting via the OAIS Reference Model and incorporated into distributed digital libraries.

Integrate Access to Both Digital and Physical Materials

As we created the Library's digital collections, we discovered variant bibliographic description policies among types of material and formats. This is an ongoing challenge when dealing with an integrated multi-format digital library. All *American Memory* collections now have standard MARC records and appear in the Library's Integrated Library System (ILS) as electronic sources. With the addition of the ILS, it became possible to provide item-level cataloging where it was unavailable before – a key element to providing access to digitized resources. As a result, all digitized maps have links between MARC records and their digitized *American Memory* or *Global Gateway* presentation, as do newly catalogued prints and photographs. Linking of digitized items to bibliographic records is now a standard operating procedure.

Ensure that the National Digital Library is Useful to Different Communities of Users

The historical collections digitized by the National Digital Library are used by different communities (educational, research, library, lifelong learner, commercial). However, the material is generally not presented with any specific community in mind. The Library of Congress, through the Fellows program and other initiatives, is collecting data to demonstrate that the online collections have lasting value.

Provide More Efficient and More Flexible Tools for Transforming Digital Content to Meet the Needs of End-users

The original conception of use of a digital library environment mimicked the use of a physical library. Books are stacked on shelves, readers are guided in the proper direction and allowed to do their own discovery. While this is also true in the digital library environment, there is such a range of directions for users, we often try to guide them through the historical material, providing context and explanation of the importance of these materials, relationships to other materials, and supplemental digital items or information. In the early days of the National Digital Library program, the technical architecture designed to support the digital library centered on the presentation of materials in a 'collection' structure, as many of the materials selected for digitization were held as archival collections. As the library expanded, however, structuring the presentation of materials as 'collections' has sometimes proved problematic. The expectations of dealing with a defined group of materials are often more custom-tailored to that particular group of materials than is wise for the needs of overall sustainability. In addition, the temptation is to tailor the presentation of the collection to the individual elements of the historic collection and tie it together with its identity as a collection – we have found, however, that doing so creates a very complicated process for growing and sustaining the digital resource. In current efforts, metadata standards are being developed that allow for individual digital objects to be associated with all information relevant to their presentation, structure, preservation and description, external to their archival provenance. We are working towards utilizing a similar approach for future growth.

Develop Economic Models for the Support of the National Digital Library

In fund-raising and development for digital programs, it is often easiest to point a potential donor to the tangible digitized material – the presentation of a book online, an archival collection of manuscripts, a gallery display of many photographs. However, what is intangible but necessary to the coherence and sustainability of that digital resource is often the most expensive part of the process. These expenses include the conservation and stabilization of materials for handling and scanning, the development of descriptive metadata to provide adequate access in a digital environment, the technical architecture and network development necessary to sustain any digital library effort. At the Library of Congress, we are attempting to institutionalize these costs, integrating the program with other initiatives that share common needs.

Where Do we Go From Here?

A library's digital future depends upon creating and sustaining a balanced program that has all of the critical components; digital *content* (what we choose to capture in digital form; both the historic and born digital), digital-based *services* (information, cataloging, cybercasting), and a robust *delivery* mechanism. Many digital library projects have, to date, focused on the creation of digital resources, but we must also further understand the power of the internet to inform and educate. As librarians, our challenge will be to develop and sustain accompanying service and delivery aspects of the digital library so that the collections will not be 'warehoused' but will be accessible to anyone who wants to use them.

In an essay on 'Aids to Readers', Ainsworth Rand Spofford, the Librarian of Congress from 1864–97, wrote: 'Remember always, that readers are entitled to the best and most careful service, for a librarian is not only a keeper, but the interpreter of the intellectual stores of a library. It is a good and safe rule to let no opportunity of aiding a reader escape' (Spofford, 1900). Librarians are knowledge navigators, trusted advisors, the keepers, interpreters, and mediators of information and knowledge. Librarians perform this role because all citizens are entitled to equal access to information and knowledge. These statements form fundamental principles on which to base the digital information services libraries we can provide. Through the provision of online reference services, such as the Library's groundbreaking collaborative reference service *QuestionPoint*, any member of the public can become informed about any topic 24 hours a day, 7 days a week; online discussions with curators can bring artifactual material to life; online chats can enable communities and affinity groups to draw on each other's knowledge and can promote resource sharing previously only dreamed of; the collections of the Library can come alive for viewers through the cyber-casting of cultural events; and our own in-house 'treasures', the Library's specialists and curators, can offer online interpretations of the Library's rarities.

Each of the service initiatives described here depends on addressing the challenges that accompany maintaining a digital library of any size and scope. To bring the collections and curatorial expertise of this or any other library to the world, libraries must build strong repositories, and address and begin to resolve some of the copyright challenges. We also need to refresh and maintain digital data, and to support a library's core activities so that libraries continue to acquire the most important digital research materials, to catalog and link these materials to the most important resources in all subject fields, and to preserve for all time those digital items and collections once they are created. Thus, providing a sense of where we need to direct our energy is necessary.

Material that is only in digital form, and especially that which is only on the web, is an enormous challenge to collect, store and preserve and the Library of Congress has only begun to experiment in this area. Libraries, including the Library of Congress, need to put a large amount of extra effort in this direction, or risk putting scholars of the future at a disadvantage. With the average life of a website lasting less than 75 days, capturing 'at risk' born-digital material must be a priority. Libraries also need to develop 'potential loss' lists that will stir the concern of funders, and so help attract congressional funding for collection of this born-digital material.

Archiving the Web[6]

The MINERVA (Mapping the INternet Electronic Resources Virtual Archive) Web Preservation Project was established in 2000 to initiate a broad program to collect and preserve primary source materials. A multi-disciplinary team of Library staff, representing cataloging, legal, public, and technology services, studied methods to evaluate, select, collect, catalog, provide access to, and preserve these materials for future generations of researchers.

Collection activities have focused on individual historic events, selecting sites for capture using subject specialist recommendations and the information resources available to the Library. We at the Library of Congress have partnered with outside organizations on a variety of programs.

The Library's first large-scale collection of data-searchable websites to be archived and made available online was Election 2000.[7] As a first step, site owners were notified by e-mail of the Library's intent to collect. The completed collection comprises more than two terabytes, or about 200 million pages, of election-related information gathered between August 1, 2000 and January 21, 2001. Sites were archived many times a day – and often hourly – in order to record candidate responses to each other and simultaneously to demonstrate the dynamic nature of internet content.

Following the events of September 11, the Library of Congress, again in collaboration with outside partners, began work on a *September 11 Web Archive*.[8] The Library's subject and language specialists recommended sites for inclusion in the Archive, just as they recommend items for the permanent collections of the Library. Essentially, we wanted everything – American and international responses, responses from the US government and the military, the terrorists' response, and the responses of religious, ethnic, mental health and educational communities. We also sought personal accounts and public discussion from listservs and online newsgroups.

The research potential of the *September 11 Web Archive* has been noted both in print media and, not surprisingly, on the web itself. The internet portal Yahoo selected the *Archive* as its top site of the year 2001. The site was also included in the *Librarians' Index to the Internet*, was featured in *The Scout Report* and selected as both a Yahoo Pick of the Week and a *USA Today* Hot Site. Articles have also appeared in both the US and international press. The collection team made a concerted effort to include as many sites from languages other than English and from all points of view as possible, deciding not to censor any of the content (Kresh, 2002a).

Projects recently initiated include a small collection on the 2002 Winter Olympics, Election 2002 (pursued once again in collaboration with the Internet Archive and WebArchivists.org), and a capture of the websites of the 107th Congress, which ceased to exist on December 31, 2002. Each pilot project initiated under MINERVA enables the Library to explore further the issues surrounding the archiving of internet-distributed information. While we continue to develop both our thinking and our processes, we capture this ephemeral data reflecting our cultural heritage that may otherwise disappear.

Preservation of Digital Information

In December 2000, the Library of Congress was tasked by the US Congress (Public Law 106–554) to develop a national program to preserve the burgeoning amounts of digital information, especially materials that are created only in digital formats, to ensure their accessibility for current and future generations. The National Digital Information Infrastructure and Preservation Program (NDIIPP)[9] will provide a national focus on important policy, standards and the technical components necessary to preserve digital content. Investments in modeling and testing various options and technical solutions will take place over several years, resulting in recommendations to the US Congress about the most viable and sustainable options for long-term preservation.

To meet its mandate, the Library is working closely with federal partners to assess considerations for shared responsibilities in the preservation of digital information. Federal legislation calls for the Library to work jointly with the Secretary of Commerce, the director of the White House Office of Science and Technology Policy, and the National Archives and Records Administration (NARA). The legislation also directs the Library to seek the participation of 'other federal, research and private libraries and institutions with expertise in the collection and maintenance of archives of digital materials', including the National Library of Medicine (NLM), the National Agricultural Library (NAL), the Research Libraries Group (RLG), the Online Computer Library Center (OCLC) and the Council on Library and Information Resources (CLIR).

The Library is also seeking participation from the non-federal sector. The overall strategy (LC21, 2000) will be executed in cooperation with the library, creative, publishing, technology and copyright communities. In early 2001, the Library established a National Digital Strategy Advisory Board to help guide it through the planning process. This board is made up of experts from the technology, publishing, internet, library and intellectual-property communities as well as government.

Conclusion

The advent of the World Wide Web and the internet has provided a watershed moment for all libraries. We now have technology that enables us to reach more people than ever before and enables us to ensure that the American people not only have the means to record and share their unique stories but continue to enjoy free access to information, a freedom that is at the heart of their ability to participate in the democratic process. Creating the digitized items is only part of the story. Integrating the digitized content with services that help interpret, organize and make accessible is also important. And providing an infrastructure that ensures that the digital bits and bytes persist in perpetuity is the final leg of the three-legged stool.

Digital libraries have the potential to increase learning and knowledge. The challenge for libraries is to take that same content and make it usable and searchable in ways that can engender discovery, creativity and invention (Larson, 2002).

Notes

1   American Memory home page for Historical collections from the National Digital Library Program. URL: http://lcweb2.loc.gov/ammem/ammemhome.html.
2   Accessible at http://memory.loc.gov.
3   Accessible at http://international.loc.gov. These collections include the exploration of Alaska, a partnership project with the national libraries of Russia and several Alaskan institutions; the Spanish exploration of the Americas with the National Library of

Spain; a cooperation with the National Library of Brazil regarding 19th-century Brazil and its relationships with, and similarities to, the United States as a multicultural democracy rich in natural resources; and a project with the Royal Dutch Library on the influence of Dutch exploration and immigration in the US.

4 The site itself has many text documents which provide concrete advice http//memory.loc.gov/ammem/ftpfiles.html.
5 Accessible at http://www.questionpoint.org/.
6 The Internet Archive (www.sarchive.org) provides actual webcrawling technology and a group of social scientists, www.webarchivist.org, contribute resources for selection and description tool development.
7 The collection may be viewed at www.loc.gov/minerva.
8 The Internet Archive, captured and stored the web pages and WebArchivist.org, (http://www.webarchivist.org) is in the process of creating archival metadata. The Library also worked closely with The Pew Internet & American Life Project (www.pewinternet.org) which creates and funds original, academic-quality research that explores the impact of the internet on children, families, communities, the workplace, and schools.
9 Accessible at National Digital Information Infrastructure and Preservation Program. *Digital Preservation* URL: http://www.digitalpreservation.gov/ndiipp/.

References

Arms, C.R. (1996), 'Historical Collections for the National Digital Library', *D-Lib Magazine*, April and May. URL: Part I http://www.dlib.org/dlib/april96/loc/04c-arms.html [Viewed February 8, 2003]. URL: Part II http://www.dlib.org/dlib/may96/loc/05c-arms.html [Viewed February 8, 2003].

Arms, C.R. (1999), 'Getting the Picture: Observations from the Library of Congress on Providing Online Access to Pictorial Images,' *Library Trends*, 48(2), Fall, 379–409. URL: http://memory.loc.gov/ammem/techdocs/libt1999/libt1999.html [Viewed February 8, 2003].

Billington, J.H. (1995), Mission and Strategic Priorities of the Library of Congress. FY1997–2004. Fall. URL: http://lcweb.loc.gov/ndl/mission.html.

Billington, J.H. (2001), 'Humanizing the information revolution', in *67th International Federation of Libraries and Institutions Conference*, Boston, MA, August 21, *IFLA Journal*, 27(5–6), 301–307.

Hazen, D., Horrell, J. and Merrill-Oldham, J. (1998) 'Selecting Research Collections for Digitization. Council on Library and Information Resources. August 1998. URL: http://www.clir.org/pubs/reports/hazen/pub74.html.

Kresh, D. (2002a), 'Courting Disaster: Building a Collection to Chronicle 9/11 and Its Aftermath. Witness and Response: Remembering September 11', *The Library of Congress Information Bulletin*, 61(9).

Kresh, D. (2002b), 'High Touch or High Tech: the Collaborative Digital Reference Services as a Model for the Future of Reference', *Advances in Librarianship*, 26, 149–173.

Larson, C. (2002), *The Internet and the Changing Face of Scholarship: Challenges and Opportunities for Libraries*, Bibliography (Washington, DC: Library of Congress).

LC21 (2000) A digital strategy for the Library of Congress. Committee on an information technology strategy for the Library of Congress, Computer Science and Telecommunications Board, Commission on Physical Sciences, Mathematics, and Applications, National Research Council (Washington, DC: National Academy Press), 265p. URL: http://www.nap.edu/books/0309071445/html/index.html.

Library of Congress (various years) *National Digital Library Annual Review* 1998, 1999, 2000 and 2001. (Washington DC: Library of Congress).

Spofford, A.R. (1900) *A Book for all Readers, Designed as a Aid to the Collection, Use and Preservation of Books and the Formation of Public and Private Libraries* (New York: G.P. Putnam & Sons).

PART 3
THE WAY AHEAD

Chapter 14

After the Digital Library Decade: Where are the Next Frontiers for Library Innovation?[1]

Mel Collier

Introduction

In the late 1980s and early 1990s the new library at Tilburg University was planned and built. Perhaps more than any library building in Europe, it became a model and a 'must see' for those planning libraries in preparation for the digital age. It is difficult to find a library or learning centre in Europe and beyond which was built in the last ten years, where the librarians and architects did not visit Tilburg. For their vision and strategy we pay tribute to the then librarian, Hans Geleijnse, his predecessor Leo Wieërs, Solke Veling and the University Computer Centre, the board of Tilburg University and the architect Martien Janssen and all the others whom is it not possible to mention here (Geleijnse and Grootaers, 1994).

The Decade of the Digital Library

The design of the new Tilburg University library was based on the vision that the digital library would soon arrive. As part of that design it was decided to provide a large number of computer workplaces for students, each with integrated desktop software. To create a library in the early 1990s with over 400 computer study places was an important innovation, preceding similar developments elsewhere by a few years. The vision of the Tilburg planners turned out to be well founded. Indeed, within a few years the digital library moved from concept to reality and many other universities rushed to emulate the Tilburg example.

The first ten years of the new Tilburg library have actually coincided with the first decade of the so-called 'digital library'. As far as the library world is concerned, the last decade has been the digital library decade. This is not to say that the digital library has only been a product or achievement of librarians. Far from it, because many other groups have been involved: computer scientists, publishers, educationalists, to name but a few. During this decade, the digital library, which had been foreseen for quite some time, suddenly became practicable. On the other hand, those of us who were active in the field in the late 1980s and early 1990s can well remember how the notion of the digital library was regarded by many at that time with a great deal of scepticism. A momentous change has taken place in the library world. As with many other major innovations, the sudden practicality of the digital library was more to do with the felicitous convergence of several factors than with one brilliant discovery. The following critical success factors for the emergence of the digital library can be identified.

- The World Wide Web (in itself, of course, a brilliant development).
- The (relatively) quick development of electronic publishing (particularly scholarly journals).
- The availability of affordable technology (communications, storage, processing).

Tilburg University Library played a leading role in the realization of the digital library, not only by creating a landmark building as an exemplar, but also through active participation in projects, including:

- The integrated desktop.
- The first licence agreement for presentation of electronic journals (with Elsevier).
- The Elise project: early work on digital images (as part of a European Third Framework project led by De Montfort University).
- The Decomate project: a European project led by Tilburg and precursor of the now ubiquitous portal concept and foundation of the I:port product, marketed by OCLC Pica.

One can say then, that the Tilburg University Library decade has, in fact, also been the digital library decade.

The Digital Library: Revolution or Evolution?

In assessing innovations there is often a debate about whether they should be seen as the product of many years of arduous preparatory build-up or whether they are a defining occurrence. The authors of the book *Delivering Digitally* (Inglis *et al.*, 1999) are first inclined to think of the appearance of the web as a revolutionary event, but then seem to have second thoughts, wondering if it should not more correctly be seen as the culmination of many years of earlier ICT developments. Their first thought was the right one. To deny it would be like asserting that the French Revolution was not a revolution because the conditions that caused it had been building up for years. The realization of the digital library is indeed a revolution for culture and scholarship, to be compared with the invention of printing. There is now, to all intents and purposes, no limit to the storage capacity and speed of the digital library. With a few exceptions (to which we return below) libraries as storehouses and preservers of *new* scientific knowledge are obsolete. There are, of course, a number of underlying professional principles that endure, as pointed out by Brophy in his excellent book on the library in the 21st century (Brophy, 2001), but the library has changed for ever. A revolution did indeed take place in the last decade. A frontier has been crossed. Now, we have to ask, where is the next frontier for library innovation?

Previous Landmarks

The library world has witnessed many landmark developments over the last 30 or 40 years. From the early computerization projects, such as automated indexing and abstracting in the 1960s, development moved to the first online library management systems in the 1970s, the first microcomputer based library systems in the 1980s, and also the first local area networks and microcomputer networks applied to libraries. Within the field of library innovation these were all new frontiers: they changed the way we operated libraries. However, they did not change the nature of the library itself, which was, of course, still built around the printed word.

Visions and Transitions

With the early digital library projects, the people involved had a vision. Via those projects we started heading towards the last frontier within the library domain, the frontier which, when crossed, meant that – theoretically at least – the digital library made the traditional library obsolescent.

At this point, however, it is appropriate to say a word about the transitional phases. Those writing about the management of change always emphasize that the important factors are to do with people, not technology, or that the underlying principles of the profession, or user needs, or service quality are what really matter. Others may observe that despite the introduction of new technology, not much has changed. All these things may be true. To take an example, it became fashionable towards the end of the e-Lib programme in Britain, to talk of 'hybrid libraries'. This terminology reflects the fact that, in most cases, the digital and the analogue will coexist for the foreseeable future. The author's criticism of this is that it is only a statement of the obvious (Collier, 1997), and that if one is trying to develop a theory or philosophy of the digital library, it does not help very much. This may be very much a minority opinion (Oppenheim and Smithson, 1999), but it can be observed, in agreement with Chowdhury and Chowdhury (2003), that now, six years on, there is still no generally accepted theory of the digital library. The point is that there is no problem with the formulation of strategies for the transitional phases, but not if it provides a comfort zone for inaction or hinders the recognition that a fundamental change has taken place.

Returning to the crossing of the frontier, if we were to pinpoint a defining moment when the traditional library became obsolete, it would be when a critical mass of scientific research output became available in electronic form, around the period 2000–2002. This is a generalization, of course. The defining moment will differ for various libraries according to their mission and goals. That does not matter: the fact that a theoretical frontier has been passed is enough. The totally digital library is now feasible. Some have already done it. Whether particular libraries do in fact go fully digital is a matter of local policy.

Now that we have crossed that frontier there is much work to do in the library world. There are almost innumerable challenges to do with content development, further development of standards and metadata, discussions about rights and access, technologies for authentication, consolidating the theory and managing the change. These, and others, are tremendously important activities. They are about clearing the land beyond the frontier, cultivating it and populating it, but they are not new frontiers.

Some Enabling Developments

There are many activities that can enable the population of the digital library landscape. Brophy (2001) provides a useful inventory of many of these. The following may be highlighted, but there are probably others.

- Interoperability
- Middleware
- User interface
- Identifiers
- Document formats
- E-business

These are topics that are already well known in the library world. In addition, the work of IMS, the Global Learning Consortium, should also be mentioned here. This body develops open technical specifications to support distributed learning. It announced, on 13 March 2003, an alliance with the Coalition for Networked Information (CNI) to explore the development of common architectural and functional models, leading to specifications in the areas of digital libraries and learning object repositories. This is an important link between the world of scholarly communication, which tends to be research orientated, and the world of e-learning.

Key Research Areas

It is likely that work in the fields just mentioned is primarily in the form of developing and implementing new tools, standards, and policies: highly important, detailed and intensive work but not ground-breaking. If we look at research areas identified by those focusing on the digital future, a few key research areas seem to be emerging. Deegan and Tanner (2002), in their excellent book, single out digital preservation as one of the most important issues facing librarians and information in the digital world. The problem is already immense, growing exponentially, with no certainty of being solved in the near future, either in terms of method, or of scale. The main responsibility for solving this must lie with national libraries. Uncoordinated efforts will almost certainly be less productive. Brophy, on the one hand, and Garrison and Anderson (2003) on the other identify the distribution of digital objects as a major development. Depending on one's perspective, these can be called information objects, or educational objects or learning objects. Garrison and Anderson, in their framework for research and practice in e-learning, expect a fifth generation in which more intelligence is added to the web to promote much more fruitful searching, navigation and exploitation of web resources – the so-called 'semantic web'. Tim Berners-Lee and his colleagues indeed believe that the semantic web is itself the new 'killer application' (Berners-Lee *et al.*, 2001). Personalization is also seen by many authors as an increasingly important trend in information services, encouraged perhaps by the general trend in the marketing of other goods to cater for individual preference. Personalization can offer user profiling for e-commerce, tools for personal workspace, alerting and push services, and portability of personal workspace.

Probably wisely, most authors avoid making predictions. Mention may be made of a new storage device, or mobile telephony or digital TV, but it is not so easy nowadays to identify a single technology that will make an important difference. The technological patchwork is so much more complicated now than it was ten years ago. As Brophy (2001) points out, the unexpected ground-breaking development is, by definition, unpredictable, but perhaps the new killer application will be found in one of these research areas.

The Next Frontier?

We have said that, the in the last decade, the library community crossed a frontier into the digital library world. It is true that for some time the stakeholding in library development, which was once primarily in the hands of librarians, has been passing into the hands of many others. Librarians are now just one group among many with a stake. Now that the digital library frontier has been crossed, and effort in that domain is mostly to do with populating it, a further proposition may be made, that the next frontier will not lie in the library domain at all. It will lie in other domains where the digital library can have a fundamental impact.

In the university world it is tempting to look at the activities that are closest: namely research and learning. Arguably, the new frontier will not lie in research. Already researchers for whom digital information is the staple commodity have fundamentally changed their behaviour in the direction of working at the desktop, using pre-print servers and collaborative working via conferencing and other communications. True, they still rely in the main for their research reputation on publication in established journals, which may or may not be electronic, but this is surely transitional. The world of research communication has already changed fundamentally. This has happened remarkably quickly and researchers now have a range of tools that will further consolidate this change.

In the digital library applied to learning, however, there are changes underway, which will have an effect of an altogether different dimension. We know already that ICT can support and enable learning that is collaborative, adaptive and asynchronous. The digital library has the potential to support those qualities and characteristics even further by promoting learning that is investigative, responsive to learning styles and by giving access to an unprecedented richness of learning resources.

Why in E-learning?

Librarians have been in a prime position for some time to observe at first hand spontaneous changes taking place on the part of students. We at Tilburg University Library, having been early leaders in the provision of digital resources and facilities, can now see students working in ways for which the building was not designed. We refer particularly to a clear trend towards working in groups around a PC, to a more informal approach, to a preference even to work in a noisy and bustling environment. The learning centre developments in the UK, such as Sheffield Hallam and Hertfordshire Universities, are wonderful exemplars of response to these changes. The subject of learning centres has been admirably and recently covered by Edward Oyston of Sheffield Hallam (Oyston, 2003).

In learning however, the long heralded fundamental changes have generally been slower to arrive than predicted. There have been numerous experiments, developments and projects over the last decade. Much has been learned and it is clear that ICT has become thoroughly embedded into the infrastructure of universities. ICT as a tool of communication and of information management has become indispensable. It is strikingly clear that ICT as a tool in the educational process is an important quality factor, and the quality of ICT facilities and resources is a critical factor in student choice and institutional competitiveness. Latterly the role of ICT in the educational process itself has progressed from a mosaic of individual experiments and projects to something more integrated and structural through the introduction of digital learning environments. The digital library is now meeting the digital learning environment.

At Tilburg, we can see that students are choosing *en masse* for study that is supported by access to ICT, but we readily admit to not knowing precisely what is going on, how they are using the digital resources and the impact this is having on their learning. It is clear that e-learning can already be effective in certain markets: training, professional development and distance education. The promise is as yet unfulfilled in mainstream education. It has yet to have a significant effect on the structure of programmes.

The Barriers Before the Frontier

Compared to the introduction of the digital library itself, and to its application to research, the integration of the digital library into the learning process is a far greater challenge. Learning itself is a highly complex human process and we are, moreover, at the early stages of understanding how it will adapt to e-learning. The structures and procedures surrounding education, particularly in universities can be very conservative. This is often for good reason because change brings risks and risks can threaten quality. The two most important things in university business are quality of research and quality of learning and therefore universities and academics are naturally cautious. This is, perhaps, paradoxical given that universities are essentially about independence and creativity of thought. It is also possible to avoid innovation by hiding behind protestations of quality.

A barrier of an entirely different kind is the high cost of, and protectiveness accorded to, learning content. It is notoriously difficult to persuade academics to use learning content in their programmes that has been developed elsewhere. This is another paradox, as they generally have no resistance to using textbooks written by others. The digital revolution now offers the potential of content development in a different paradigm from the book: smaller chunks of learning content that can be individually packaged and identified with metadata through the facilitation of the semantic web and standards such as those promoted by IMS. These kinds of learning object repositories have been predicted for some time but have not yet taken hold. There is an embryonic market is these products but it is not yet clear when market conditions will be right both from the supply and the consumer side.

Over the Frontier

In the past, one could see the frontiers looming within the library domain, which offered enticing opportunities for research, development and structural change. Now that we have crossed the digital library frontier, the next frontier is not to be seen within the library domain at all, but beyond in the learning domain where the digital library should combine with e-learning activities to effect structural change and quality improvement. Over that frontier would lie learning, which has the characteristics of being interactive, collaborative, independent and investigative. These characteristics are not necessarily to do with distance learning, although they could be. They are not an alternative to good quality interaction with tutors, but an enrichment of it. At Tilburg University we are committed to a learning approach that is based on face to face interaction with tutors, taking place in an excellent campus-based environment. The approach in the land over the frontier would be a balance of e-learning and the interpersonal. The digital library's role over that frontier will be to populate a new landscape with content that can be shared between tutors, supported by a thriving industry in learning objects and enabled by infrastructures such as the semantic Web and open standards.

The Tilburg Learning Centre Initiative

At Tilburg, these ideas are finding expression in our planning for a new learning centre in 2005. Based on the conversion and renovation of an existing high-quality building, the facility will provide an excellent physical environment for learning supported by e-learning and groupwork. The digital library facilities will naturally be a fundamental asset in the centre, although we have yet to discuss seriously how the digital library will need to be configured to integrate with, and support, an e-learning environment. Most importantly, the development will be grounded in the Tilburg approach to learning and on an agreed vision for e-learning. We are busy with defining those two key elements at this time. As there is still so much that is unknown about how learning can, and should be, supported by ICT, it will provide us with a testbed for research and continuous improvement. As an e-learning centre it will complement the library, which will continue as an integrated learning environment. Together, these two facilities will provide our students with a huge range of choice of learning environment to suit their preference of study style.

The Library of the Future

The motto of the new Tilburg Library in 1992 was 'the library of the future today'. It was a memorable and effective motto that captured the imagination of library planners for a decade. However, visitors to the Tilburg library today will see that there is new work in progress. Although the library is only ten years old, we are in the later stages of some major changes. We have moved 7000 linear metres of journals into a store to provide more and improved space for our growing numbers of students. We are increasing the number of individual computer work places and have converted a third of the entrance level into an e-learning facility. The e-learning facility is giving us valuable experience and ideas for the design of our new learning centre in 2005. The library of the future, good though the motto was, is by definition something that is never attained, but the spirit of it, the commitment to innovation, lives on in Tilburg University Library.

Note

1   This is a revised version of a paper presented at 'Ten years of the library of the future', a symposium at Tilburg University on 21 March 2003, to mark the tenth anniversary of the opening of the Tilburg University Library building.

References

Berners-Lee, T. Hendler, J. and Lassila, O. (2001), 'The semantic web', *Scientific American*, May, 35–43.

Brophy, P. (2001), *The Library in the Twenty-first Century: New Services for the Information Age* (London: Library Association Publishing).

Chowdhury, G.G. and Chowdhury, S. (2003), *Introduction to Digital Libraries* (London: Facet).

Collier, M. (1997), 'Towards a general theory of the digital library', *International Symposium on the Research, Development and Practice in Digital Libraries*, Tsukuba, Japan, pp. 80–84.

Deegan, M. and Tanner, S. (2002), *Digital Futures: Strategies for the Information Age* (London: Library Association Publishing).

Garrison, D.R. and Anderson, T. (2003), *E-learning in the 21st Century: A Framework for Research and Practice* (London: Routledge Falmer).

Geleijnse, H. and Grootaers, C. (1994), *Developing the Library of the Future: the Tilburg Experience* (Tilburg University Press).

Inglis, A., Ling, P. and Joosten, V. (1999), *Delivering Digitally: Managing the Transition to the Knowledge Media* (London: Kogan Page).

Oppenheim, C. and Smithson, D. (1999), 'What is the hybrid library?', *Journal of information Science*, 25(2), 97–112.

Oyston, E. (2003) *Centred on Learning: Academic Case Studies on Learning Centre Development* (Aldershot: Ashgate).

Bibliography

Arms, C.R. (1996), 'Historical Collections for the National Digital Library', *D-Lib Magazine*, April and May. URL: Part I http://www.dlib.org/dlib/april96/loc/04c-arms.html [Viewed February 8, 2003]. URL: Part II http://www.dlib.org/dlib/may96/loc/05c-arms.html [Viewed February 8, 2003].

Arms, C.R. (1999), 'Getting the Picture: Observations from the Library of Congress on Providing Online Access to Pictorial Images', *Library Trends*, 48(2) Fall, 379–409. URL: http://memory.loc.gov/ammem/techdocs/libt1999/libt1999.html [Viewed February 8, 2003].

Ashcroft, L. (2000), 'Win-win-win: can the evaluation and promotion of electronic journals bring benefits to library suppliers, information professionals and users?', *Library Management*, 21(9), 466–471.

Association of College and Research Libraries (1998), *Task Force on Academic Library Outcomes Assessment Report*. (Available at: http://www.ala.org/acrl/outcome.html.

Atkins, A. (2002), *Resources for Developers of ETD databases*. Website http://scholar.lib.vt.edu/ETD-db/developer/.

Atkins, A., Fox, E.A., France, K.R., and Suleman, H. (2001), *ETD-ms: an Interoperability Metadata Standard for Electronic Theses and Dissertations version 1.00*, NDLTD. Available http://www.ndltd.org/standards/metadata/.

Bamberger, J. (2003), 'The Development of Intuitive Musical Understanding: A Natural Experiment', *Psychology of Music*, 31(1), 43.

Banwell, L. and Gannon-Leary, P. (1999), 'A review of the literature for the JUBILEE Project (JISC User Behaviour Information Seeking: Longitudinal Evaluation of Electronic information services)', *The New Review of Academic Librarianship*, 5, 81–114.

Barton, J. and Blagden, J. (1998) *Academic Library Effectiveness: A Comparative Approach*, British Library Research and Innovation Centre, British Library Research and Innovation Report 120.

Beagrie, N. and Jones, M. (2000), 'Preservation Management of Digital Materials Workbook: A Pre-publication Draft', October 2000. Available: http://www.jisc.ac.uk/dner/preservation/workbook.

Beck, M., and Moore, T. (1998), 'The I-2 DSI Project: An Architecture for Internet Content Channels', *Computer Networking and ISDN Systems*, 30(22–23), 2141–2148.

Berners-Lee, T. Hendler, J. and Lassila, O. (2001), 'The semantic web', *Scientific American*, May, 35–43.

Berthon, H. (2000), 'The Moving Frontier: Archiving, Preservation and Tomorrow's Digital Heritage', In *VALA 2000–10th VALA Biennial Conference and Exhibition*,

Melbourne, Victoria, 16–18 February 2000 [Online], available: http://www.nla. gov.au/nla/staffpaper/hberthon2.html.

Bertot, J.C. and McClure, C.R. (1998), *The 1998 National Survey of US Public Library Outlet Internet Connectivity: Final Report* (Washington, DC: National Commission on Libraries and Information Science).

Billington, J.H. (1995), 'Mission and Strategic Priorities of the Library of Congress', FY1997–2004. Fall. URL: http://lcweb.loc.gov/ndl/mission.html.

Billington, J.H. (2001), 'Humanizing the information revolution', in *67th International Federation of Libraries and Institutions Conference*, Boston, MA, August 21, *IFLA Journal*, 27(5–6), 301–307.

Blixrud, J.C. (2002), 'Measures for electronic use: The ARL e-metrics project', paper presented at the *Statistics in Practice: Measuring and Managing IFLA Satellite Conference*, 13–25 August 2002, Loughborough, UK (available at: http://www.arl.org/stats/newmeas/emetrics/Blixrud_IFLA.pdf).

Boezerooy, P. (2003), 'Keeping up with our neighbours: ICT developments in Australian Higher Education LTSN Generic Centre', [n.p.].

Borgman, C.L. (1999), 'What are digital libraries? Competing visions', *Information Processing and Management*, 35(3), 227–243.

Bowen, W.G. (2001), The Academic Library In a Digitized, Commercialized Age: Lessons from JSTOR, January 2001, http://www.jstor.org/about/bowen.html.

Brindley, L. (2000), 'Preservation 2000: Keynote Speech', in *Preservation 2000: An International Conference on the Preservation and Long Term Accessibility of Digital Materials*. 7–8 December 2000, York, UK. Conference Papers [Online], available: http://www.rlg.org/events/pres-2000/brindley.html.

Brodie, N. (2000), 'Authenticity, Preservation and Access in Digital Collections', in *Preservation 2000: An International Conference on the Preservation and Long Term Accessibility of Digital Materials*. 7–8 December 2000, York, UK. Conference Papers [Online], available: http://www.rlg.org/events/pres-2000/ brodie.html.

Brophy, P. (2001), *The Library in the Twenty-first Century: New Services for the Information Age* (London: Library Association Publishing).

Brophy, P. (2001),'The historical context of eLib: practice based library research in the UK', *Library Management*, 22(1/2), 15–18.

Brophy, P. and Wynne, P.M. (1997), *Management Information Systems and Performance Measurement for the Electronic Library: eLib Supporting Study* (MIEL2). Final report, JISC (available at: http://www.ukoln.ac.uk/dlis/models/ studies/mis/mis.rtf).

Burroughs, M. and Fenske, D. (1990), 'Variations: A Hypermedia Project Providing Integrated Access to Music Information', in S. Arnold, and G. Hair, (eds), *ICMC Glasgow 1990. Proceedings of the International Computer Music Conference, 1990*, Glasgow: ICMC for the Computer Music Association, pp. 221–224.

Byrd, D. and Isaacson, E. (2002), *Music Representation Requirement Specification for Variations2, Version 1.1*, http://variations2.indiana.edu/pdf/v2-music-rep-req-11.pdf.

Calado, P., da Silva, A.S., Ribeiro-Neto, B., Laender, A.H.F., Lage, J.P., Reis, D.C., Roberto, P.A., Vieira, M.V., Gonçalves, M.A., and Fox E.A. (2003), 'From the Web to a Digital Library: The Web-DL Architecture', *ACM/IEEE*

2003 Joint Conference on Digital Libraries (JCDL 2003), 27–31 May, Houston, Texas, USA, Proceedings. IEEE Computer Society 2003.

Carr, L., Hitchcock, S., Hall, W. and Harnad, S. (2000), 'A usage based analysis of CoRR [A commentary on "CoRR: a Computing Research Repository" by Joseph Y. Halpern]', *ACM SIGDOC Journal of Computer Documentation*. May 2000. http://www.cogsci.soton.ac.uk/'harnad/Papers/Harnad/harnad00.halpern. htm. http://www.garfield.library.upenn.edu/papers/cseimpactfactor05092000. html.

Carr, R. (1998), 'Integrate, co-operate, innovate: an introduction', *The New Review of Information and Library Research*, 4, 17–26.

Carr, R. (2002), 'Towards the academic digital library in the UK: a national perspective', in: S.K. Hannesdottir, (ed.), *Global Issues in 21st Century Research Librarianship* pp. 221–233 (Helsinki: NORDINFO).

Chapman, S., Conway, P. and Kenney, A.R. (1999), 'Digital Imaging and Preservation of Microfilm: The Future of the Hybrid Approach for the Preservation of Brittle Books', *RLG DigiNews* 3(1) 15, [Online], available: http://www.rlg.org/preserv/diginews/diginews3–1.html.

Chowdhury, G.G. and Chowdhury, S. (1999), 'Digital Library Research: Major Issues and Trends', *Journal of Documentation*, 55(4), 409–448.

Chowdhury, G.G. and Chowdhury, S. (2003), *Introduction to Digital Libraries* (London: Facet).

Chun Wei Choo (1997), 'IT2000: Singapore's Vision of an Intelligent Island', in P. Droege (ed.), *Intelligent Environments* (Amsterdam: North-Holland).

Collier, M. (1997), 'Towards a general theory of the digital library', *International Symposium on the Research, Development and Practice in Digital Libraries*, Tsukuba, Japan, pp. 80–84.

Covey, D.T. (2002) *Usage and Usability Assessment: Library Practices and Concerns* (Washington, DC: Digital Library Federation; Council on Library and Information Resources) (available at: http://www.clir.org/pubs/reports/pub105/pub105.pdf).

Crawford, J. (2000), *Evaluation of Library and Information Services*, 2nd edn (London: Aslib).

Crews, K. (2001), *The Expiration of Copyright Protection: Survey and Analysis of U.S. Copyright Law for Identifying the Public Domain*, http://variations2.indiana.edu/pdf/dml-copyright-duration-report.pdf.

Crews, K. (2001), *'A&M Records, Inc., v. Napster, Inc.': Implications for the Digital Music Library*, http://variations2.indiana.edu/pdf/AnalysisOfNapster Decision.pdf.

Crews, K. (2001), *Copyright Law for the Digital Library: Framework of Rights and Exceptions*, http://variations2.indiana.edu/pdf/CopyrightLawforDLib Framework.pdf.

Crews, K. (2001) *Digital Libraries and the Application of Section 108 of the U.S. Copyright Act'*, http://variations2.indiana.edu/html/crews-sec108/.

Currier, S., Brown, S. and Ekmekioglu, F.C. (2001), *INSPIRAL: Investigating Portals for Information Resources and Learning: Final report*, available at: http://inspiral.cdlr.strath.ac.uk/documents/INSPfinrep.doc).

Dalton, J. and Seamans, N.H. (2004), 'Electronic Theses & Dissertations: Two

Surveys of Editors & Publishers', in: E.A. Fox, S. Feizbadi, J. M. Moxley, and C.R. Weisser, (eds), *The ETD Sourcebook: Theses and Dissertations in the Electronic Age* (New York: Marcel Dekker), in press.

Davidson, M. (2001), 'Trends and Issues in Digital Technology', *Fontes artis musicae*, 48(4), 398–410.

Davidson, M., Hemmasi, H. and Minibayeva, N. (2002) *Data Dictionary: Metadata Elements for Version 1*, http://variations2.indiana.edu/pdf/DML-metadata-elements-v1.pdf.

Dawson, A. (1999), 'Inferring User Behaviour from Journal Access Figures', *Serials Librarian*, 35(3), http://bubl.ac.uk/archive/journals/serlib/v35n0399/dawson.htm.

Deegan, M. and Tanner, S. (2002), *Digital Futures: Strategies for the Information Age* (London: Library Association Publishing).

Dempsey, L. (2000), 'The subject gateways: experiences and issues based on the emergence of the Resource Discovery Network', *Online Information Review*, 24(1), 8–23. Also available at http://www.rdn.ac.uk/publications/ior-2000–02-dempsey/.

Dempsey, L., Russell, R., Murray, R. and Heseltine, R. (1998), 'Managing access to a distributed library resource: report from the fifth MODELS workshop', *Program*, 32(3), 265–282.

Digital Library Federation (2001), *Making of America II* (website), http://sunsite.berkeley.edu/MOA2/.

Downie, S.J. (2002), *Music Information Retrieval Research Bibliography* (website), http://music-ir.org/, last updated 20 September.

Dublin Core Metadata Initiative (1995–2003), *Dublin Core Metadata Initiative* (website) http://dublincore.org/.

Duff, A.S. (2003), 'Four "e"pochs: the story of informatization', *Library Review*, 5(2), 58–64.

Dunn, J.W. and Mayer, C.A. (1999), 'VARIATIONS: A Digital Music Library System at Indiana University', in: E.A. Fox and N.C. Rowe (eds), *Digital Libraries 99 The Fourth ACM Conference on Digital Libraries*, 11–14 August, Berkeley, CA, (New York: Association for Computing Machinery) pp. 12–19.

Duranceau, E. and Harnad, S. (1999), 'Electronic Journal Forum: Resetting Our Intuition Pumps for the Online-Only Era: A Conversation With Stevan Harnad', *Serials Review*, 25(1), 109–115. http://www.cogsci.soton.ac.uk/'harnad/Papers/Harnad/harnad99.ejforum.html.

Eaton, J. (2002), 'Measuring user statistics', *Cilip Update*, 1(6), 44–45.

Effective Academic Library (1995), *The Effective Academic Library: A Framework for Evaluating the Performance of UK Academic Libraries*. A consultative report to the HEFCE, SHEFC, HEFCW and DENI by the Joint Funding Councils' Ad-Hoc Group on Performance Indicators for Libraries.

ETD (2002), *The ETD Guide*, www.etdguide.org.

eVALUEd Paper 1 (2002), *Questionnaire to Higher Education Institutions in the UK: Analysis of Responses*, (available at: http://www.cie.uce.ac.uk/evalued/Library/Paper1_QuAnalysis.pdf.

Fedora [Flexible Extensible Digital Object and Repository Architecture] *Project*, [2001] (Web site), http://www.fedora.info/.

Fern, J., Lindsey, R. and Scull, E. (2002), 'The distributed music appreciation class and the Indiana University Digital Library Project: Phase One', paper presented at the College Music Society – Great Lakes Chapter meeting, Northfield, MN, 16 March.

Follett, B. (chair) (1993), *Joint Funding Council's Libraries Review Group: Report*, Bristol: Higher Education Funding Council for England. Available at: http://www.niss.ac.uk/education/hefc/follett/.

Ford, G. (1996), 'Performance assessment: the way forward,' in: S. Morgan, (ed.), *Performance Assessment in Academic Libraries* (London: Mansell), pp. 156–173.

Ford, G. (2001), 'Theory and practice in the networked environment: a European perspective', in: C.R. McClure, and J.C. Bertot, (eds), *Evaluating Networked Information Services: Techniques, Policy and Issues*, (Melford, NJ: Information Today), pp. 1–22.

Fox, E.A. and Marchionini, G. (1998), 'Toward a Worldwide Digital Library', Guest Editors' Introduction to special section (pp. 28–98) on *Digital Libraries: Global Scope, Unlimited Access. Communications of the ACM*, 41(4), 28–32. http://purl.lib.vt.edu/dlib/pubs/CACM199804.

Fox, E.A. (1999), 'Digital Libraries Initiative: Update and Discussion', *Bulletin of the American Society for Information Science*, 26(1), 7–11.

Fraunhofer Institut Intigrierte Publikations- und Informationssystem (2001) *MPEG-7* (website), http://ipsi.fraunhofer.de/delite/Projects/MPEG7/.

Fraunhofer Institut Intigrierte Publikations- und Informationssystem (2001) *MPEG-21* (website), http://ipsi.fraunhofer.de/delite/Projects/MPEG7/Mpeg21.html.

Fuhr, N., Hansen, P., Mabe, M., Micsik, A. and Sølvberg, I. (2001a), 'Digital Libraries: A Generic Classification and Evaluation Scheme', in: *Proceedings of the European Conference on Digital Libraries*, (Berlin: Springer).

Fuhr, N., Hansen, P., Mabe, M., Micsik, A. and Sølvberg, I. (2001b), 'Digital libraries: a generic classification and evaluation scheme', in: P. Constantopoulos, and I.T. Sølvberg (eds), *Research and Advanced Technology for Digital Libraries*. Proceedings 5th European Conference, ECDL 2001, Darmstadt, Germany, 4–9 September 2001. (Springer), pp. 187–199.

Garfield, E. (1955), 'Citation Indexes for Science: A New Dimension in Documentation through Association of Ideas', *Science*, 122, 108–111, http://www.garfield.library.upenn.edu/papers/science_v122(3159)p108y1955.html.

Garrison, D.R. and Anderson, T. (2003), *E-learning in the 21st Century: A Framework for Research and Practice* (London: Routledge Falmer).

Geleijnse, H. and Grootaers, C. (1994), *Developing the Library of the Future: The Tilburg Experience* (Tilburg University Press).

Giles, C.L., Bollacker, K.D., and Lawrence, S. (1998), 'CiteSeer: An Automatic Citation Indexing System', in: *Proceedings of Third ACM Conference on Digital Libraries*, Pittsburgh, USA, 23–26 June, pp. 89–98.

Gonçalves, M.A., Fox, E.A., Watson, L.T. and Kipp, N.A. (2003), 'Streams, Structures, Spaces, Scenarios, Societies (5S): A Formal Model for Digital Libraries', Technical Report TR-03–04, Computer Science, Virginia Tech. http://eprints.cs.vt.edu:8000/archive/00000646/.

Gorman, G.E. (ed) (2002), *The Digital Factor in Library and Information Services*,

International Yearbook of Library and Information Management, 2002–2003 (London: Facet).

Gratch-Lindauer, B. (2002), 'Comparing the regional accreditation standards: outcomes assessment and other trends', *Journal of Academic Librarianship*, 28(1–2), 14–25.

Green, A. (1997),'Towards the digital library: how relevant is eLib to practitioners?', *The New Review of Academic Librarianship*, 3, 39–48.

Greenstein, D. (2000), 'Strategies for developing sustainable and scalable digital library collections', http://www.diglib.org/collections/collstrat.htm.

Griffin, S.M. (1998), 'NSF/DARPA/NASA Digital Libraries Initiative: A Program Manager's Perspective', *D-Lib Magazine*, July/August. http://www.dlib.org/dlib/july98/07griffin.html. Accessed April 15, 2003.

Griscom, R. (2003), 'Distant Music: Delivering Audio over the Internet', *Notes: Quarterly Journal of the Music Library Association*, 59(3), 521–541.

Guardian (2002), *The Education Guardian*, Thursday 9 May 2002 [news item] http://education.guardian.co.uk/higher/humanities/story/0,9850,712877,00.html.

Harnad, S. (1990), 'Scholarly Skywriting and the Prepublication Continuum of Scientific Inquiry', *Psychological Science*, 1, 342–343 (reprinted in *Current Contents*, 45, 9–13, 11 November 1991). http://cogsci.soton.ac.uk/'harnad/Papers/Harnad/harnad90.skywriting.html.

Harnad, S. (1991), 'Post-Gutenberg Galaxy: The Fourth Revolution in the Means of Production of Knowledge', *Public-Access Computer Systems Review*, 2(1), 39–53 (also reprinted in *PACS Annual Review*, **2**, 1992; and in R.D. Mason (ed.) *Computer Conferencing: The Last Word* (Beach Holme Publishers), 1992; and in: M. Strangelove and D. Kovacs (1992) *Directory of Electronic Journals, Newsletters, and Academic Discussion Lists* 2nd edn, (A. Okerson, ed.), (Washington, DC: Association of Research Libraries, Office of Scientific & Academic Publishing); and in Hungarian translation in REPLIKA 1994; and in Japanese in *Research and Development of Scholarly Information Dissemination Systems* 1994–1995. http://cogsci.soton.ac.uk/harnad/Papers/Harnad/harnad91.postgutenberg.html.

Harnad, S. (1992), 'Interactive Publication: Extending American Physical Society's Discipline-Specific Model for Electronic Publishing', *Serials Review*, Special Issue on Economics Models for Electronic Publishing, pp. 58–61. http://cogsci.soton.ac.uk/harnad/Papers/Harnad/harnad92.interactivpub.html.

Harnad, S. (1995a), 'The PostGutenberg Galaxy: How to Get There From Here', *Information Society*, 11(4), 285–292. Also appeared in: *Times Higher Education Supplement*. Multimedia. p. vi, 12 May 1995. http://cogsci.soton.ac.uk/'harnad/THES/thes.html.

Harnad, S. (1995b), 'Sorting the Esoterica from the Exoterica: There's Plenty of Room in Cyberspace: Response to Fuller', *Information Society*, 11(4), 305–324. Also appeared in: *Times Higher Education Supplement*. Multimedia. p. vi, 9 June 1995, http://cogsci.soton.ac.uk/'harnad/THES/harful1.html.

Harnad, S. (1995c), 'Interactive Cognition: Exploring the Potential of Electronic Quote/Commenting', in: B. Gorayska and J.L. Mey (eds) *Cognitive Technology: In Search of a Humane Interface* (Elsevier) pp. 397–414. http://cogsci.soton.ac.uk/harnad/Papers/Harnad/harnad95.interactive.cognition.html.

Harnad, S. (1995d), 'Electronic Scholarly Publication: Quo Vadis?', *Serials Review*, 21(1), 70–72. (Reprinted in *Managing Information*, 2(3) 1995). http://cogsci.soton.ac.uk/harnad/Papers/Harnad/harnad95.quo.vadis.htm.

Harnad, S. (1995e), 'A Subversive Proposal', in: A. Okerson and J. O'Donnell (eds), *Scholarly Journals at the Crossroads: A Subversive Proposal for Electronic Publishing* (Washington, DC: Association of Research Libraries, June 1995). http://www.arl.org/scomm/subversive/toc.html.

Harnad, S. (1996), 'Implementing Peer Review on the Net: Scientific Quality Control in Scholarly Electronic Journals', in: R. Peek, and G. Newby, (eds) *Scholarly Publishing: The Electronic Frontier* (Cambridge, MA: MIT Press) pp. 103–108. http://cogsci.soton.ac.uk/'harnad/Papers/Harnad/harnad96.peer.review.html.

Harnad, S. (1997a), 'How to Fast-Forward Serials to the Inevitable and the Optimal for Scholars and Scientists', *Serials Librarian*, 30, 73–81. http://www.cogsci.soton.ac.uk/'harnad/Papers/Harnad/harnad97.learned.serials.html. Reprinted in C. Christiansen and C. Leatham (eds) *Pioneering New Serials Frontiers: From Petroglyphs to CyberSerials* (New York: Haworth Press), and in French translation as *Comment Accelerer l'Ineluctable Evolution des Revues Erudites* vers la Solution Optimale pour les Chercheurs et la Recherche, http://www.enssib.fr/eco-doc/harnadinteg.html.

Harnad, S. (1997b), 'The Paper House of Cards (And Why It is Taking So Long to Collapse)', *Ariadne*, 8, 6–7. Longer version http://cogsci.soton.ac.uk/harnad/Papers/Harnad/harnad97.paper.house.ariadne.html.

Harnad, S. (1997c), 'Learned Inquiry and the Net: The Role of Peer Review, Peer Commentary and Copyright', *Learned Publishing*, 11(4), 283–292. Short version appeared in 1997 in *Antiquity*, 71, 1042–1048. Excerpts also appeared in the *University of Toronto Bulletin*, 51(6), p. 12. http://citd.scar.utoronto.ca/EPub/talks/Harnad_Snider.html. http://www.cogsci.soton.ac.uk/'harnad/Papers/Harnad/harnad98.toronto.learnedpub.html.

Harnad, S. (1998/2000), 'The invisible hand of peer review', *Nature* [online] (5 Nov. 1998) http://helix.nature.com/webmatters/invisible/invisible.html. Longer version in *Exploit Interactive*, 5 (2000), http://www.exploit-lib.org/issue5/peer-review/. http://www.cogsci.soton.ac.uk/'harnad/nature2.html.

Harnad, S. (1998a), For Whom the Gate Tolls? Free the Online-Only Refereed Literature. American Scientist Forum. http://amsci-forum.amsci.org/archives/september98-forum.html. http://www.cogsci.soton.ac.uk/'harnad/amlet.html.

Harnad, S. (1998b), 'On-Line Journals and Financial Fire-Walls', *Nature*, 395(6698), 127–128. http://www.cogsci.soton.ac.uk/'harnad/nature.html.

Harnad, S. (1999a), 'The Future of Scholarly Skywriting', in: A. Scammell (ed.) *I in the Sky: Visions of the Information Future* (Aslib), http://www.cogsci.soton.ac.uk/'harnad/Papers/Harnad/harnad99.aslib.html.

Harnad, S. (1999b), 'Free at Last: The Future of Peer-Reviewed Journals', *D-Lib Magazine*, 5(12) December. http://www.dlib.org/dlib/december99/12harnad.html.

Harnad, S. (1999c), 'Advancing Science By Self-Archiving Refereed Research', *Science dEbates* [online] 31 July 1999. http://www.sciencemag.org/cgi/eletters/285/5425/197#EL12.

Harnad, S. (2000a), 'E-Knowledge: Freeing the Refereed Journal Corpus Online', *Computer Law & Security Report*, 16(2), 78–87. [Rebuttal to Bloom Editorial in Science and Relman Editorial in *New England Journal of Medicine*]. http://www.cogsci.soton.ac.uk/'harnad/Papers/Harnad/harnad00.scinejm.htm.

Harnad, S. (2000b), 'Ingelfinger Over-Ruled: The Role of the Web in the Future of Refereed Medical Journal Publishing', *The Lancet Perspectives*, 256 (December Supplement): s16. http://www.cogsci.soton.ac.uk/'harnad/Papers/Harnad/harnad00.lancet.htm.

Harnad, S. (2001a), 'AAAS's Response: Too Little, Too Late', *Science dEbates* [online], 2 April 2001. http://www.sciencemag.org/cgi/eletters/291/5512/2318b. Fuller version: http://www.cogsci.soton.ac.uk/'harnad/Tp/science2.htm.

Harnad, S. (2001b), 'The Self-Archiving Initiative', *Nature*, 410, 1024–1025. http://www.cogsci.soton.ac.uk/'harnad/Tp/nature4.htm. *Nature WebDebates* version: http://www.nature.com/nature/debates/e-access/Articles/harnad.html. Fuller version: http://www.cogsci.soton.ac.uk/'harnad/Tp/selfarch.htm.

Harnad, S. (2001c), 'The Self-Archiving Alternative', *Nature WebDebates* http://www.nature.com/nature/debates/e-access/index.html. http://www.cogsci.soton.ac.uk/'harnad/Tp/nature3.htm.

Harnad, S. (2001d), 'The (Refereed) Literature-Liberation Movement', *New Scientist*. http://www.cogsci.soton.ac.uk/'harnad/Temp/newsci1.htm. Fuller version: http://www.cogsci.soton.ac.uk/'harnad/Temp/newscientist.htm.

Harnad, S. (2001e), 'Research Access, Impact and Assessment', *Times Higher Education Supplement*. http://www.cogsci.soton.ac.uk/'harnad/Tp/thes1.html.

Harnad, S. and Carr, L. (2000), 'Integrating, Navigating and Analyzing Eprint Archives Through Open Citation Linking (the OpCit Project)', *Current Science* 79(5), 629–638. http://www.cogsci.soton.ac.uk/'harnad/Papers/Harnad/harnad00. citation.htm. http://www.iisc.ernet.in/'currsci/sep102000/629.pdf.

Harnad, S. and Hemus, M. (1997), 'All or None: There Are No Stable Hybrid or Half-Way Solutions for Launching the Learned Periodical Literature in the PostGutenberg Galaxy', in: I. Butterworth, (ed.) *The Impact of Electronic Publishing on the Academic Community* (London: Portland Press). http://cogsci.soton.ac.uk/'harnad/Papers/Harnad/harnad97.hybrid.pub.html.

Harnad, S., Carr, L. and Brody, T. (2001), 'How and Why To Free All Refereed Research' from Access- and impact-barriers online, now. http://www.cogsci.soton.ac.uk/'harnad/Tp/science.htm.

Harnad, S., Varian, H. and Parks, R. (2000), 'Academic publishing in the online era: What Will Be For-Fee And What Will Be For-Free?', *Culture Machine*, 2 (Online Journal) http://www.cogsci.soton.ac.uk/'harnad/Temp/Varian/new1.htm. http://culturemachine.tees.ac.uk/frm_f1.htm.

Hayes, P., Harnad, S., Perlis, D. and Block, N. (1992), 'Virtual Symposium on Virtual Mind', *Minds and Machines*, 2(3), 217–238. http://cogsci.soton.ac.uk/harnad/Papers/Harnad/harnad92.virtualmind.html.

Hazen, D., Horrell, J. and Merrill-Oldham, J. (1998) 'Selecting Research Collections for Digitization. Council on Library and Information Resources', August 1998.http://www.clir.org/pubs/reports/hazen/pub74.html.

Hitchcock, S., Carr, L., Jiao, Z., Bergmark, D., Hall, W., Lagoze, C. and Harnad, S. (2000), 'Developing services for open eprint archives: globalisation, integration and the impact of links', *Proceedings of the 5th ACM Conference on Digital Libraries*. San Antonio, Texas, June 2000. http://www.cogsci.soton.ac.uk/'harnad/Papers/Harnad/harnad00.acm.htm.

Hodge, G.M. (2000), 'Best Practices for Digital Archiving: An Information Life Cycle Approach', *D-Lib Magazine*, 6(1), January, [Online], available: http://www.dlib.org/dlib/january00/01hodge.html.

IFLA Study Group on the Functional Requirements for Bibliographic Records (1998), *Functional Requirements of Bibliographic Records: Final Report*, UBCIM publications, new series, vol. 19 (Munich: K.G. Saur). Also available at http://www.ifla.org/VII/s13/frbr/frbr.htm, last updated 10 April 2000.

Indiana University (1997–2002), *Digital Library Program* (website), http://www.dlib.indiana.edu/index.htm, last updated 24 February 2003.

Indiana University (1997–2003), 'What is Oncourse', *Indiana University Knowledge Base* (website), http://kb.indiana.edu/data/agku.html.

Indiana University (1999), 'Creating the digital music library', proposal to the National Science Foundation, Program Announcement NSF 98–63: Digital Libraries Initiative, Phase 2 (DLI2), 17 May; available at http://variations2.indiana.edu/overview/, last updated 9 May.

Indiana University (2001), 'General Description', *School of Music* (website), http://www.music.indiana.edu/about/general.html, last updated 2 November.

Indiana University (2002), *IUDML Version 1 Interface Specification*, http://variations2.indiana.edu/pdf/DML-UI–V1.pdf, last updated 19 February.

Indiana University (2002), *Variations Project* (website), http://www.dlib.indiana.edu/variations/, last updated 13 May.

Indiana University (2002), *William and Gayle Cook Music Library* (website), http://www.music.indiana.edu/muslib.html, last updated 20 November.

Indiana University (2003), *Variations2 Project* (website), http://variations2.indiana.edu/, last updated 24 February.

Inglis, A., Ling, P. and Joosten, V. (1999), *Delivering Digitally: Managing the Transition to the Knowledge Media* (London: Kogan Page).

Internet2 (2003), *Shibboleth Project* (website), http://shibboleth.internet2.edu/.

Isaacson, E. J. (2002), 'Music Learning Online: Evaluating the Promise', National Association of Schools of Music, *Proceedings, the 77th Annual Meeting, 2001*, 90, July, pp. 120–126.

Joint Information Systems Committee (2003), 'E-collections: exploiting the opportunities' [JISC collections folder] (Bristol: JISC) www.jisc.ac.uk/collections/.

Joint Information Systems Committee (1994), *Circular 4/94 – FIGIT Framework*, (Bristol: JISC). Available at http://www.jisc.ac.uk/pub/c4_94.html.

Joint Information Systems Committee (1995), *Circular 11/95 – Electronic Libraries Programme (eLib):Targeted Call for New Proposals* (Bristol: JISC). Available at http://www.jisc.ac.uk/pub/c11_95.html.

Joint Information Systems Committee (1997), *Circular 3/97 Electronic Information Development Programme: eLib Phase 3* (Bristol: JISC). Available at http://www.jisc.ac.uk/pub97/c3_97.html.

Jones, M. (2000), 'A Workbook for the Preservation Management of Digital Materials', in: *Preservation 2000: An International Conference on the Preservation and Long Term Accessibility of Digital Materials*. 7–8 December 2000,

York, UK. Conference Papers [Online], available: http://www.rlg.org/events/pres-2000/jones.html.

Jones, M.L.W., Gay, G.K. and Rieger, R.H. (1999), 'Project soup: comparing evaluations of digital collection efforts', *D-Lib magazine*, 5(11). (Available at: http://www.dlib.org/dlib/november99/11jones.html).

Kaushik, R. (2003), 'Spreading The Digital Word', *ExtremeTech*, 29, April. http://www.extremetech.com/article2/0,3973,1047454,00.asp.

Kelleher, J., Sommerlad, E. and Stern, E. (1996), *Evaluation of the Electronic Libraries Programme: Guidelines for Elib Project Evaluation* (London: Tavistock Institute) Available at: http://www.ukoln.ac.uk/services/elib/papers/tavistock/evaluation-guide/intro.html).

Kenney, A.R. and Rieger, O.Y. (2000), *Moving Theory into Practice: Digital Imaging for Libraries and Archives* (Mountain View, CA: Research Libraries Group).

Kresh, D. (2002), 'High Touch or High Tech: The Collaborative Digital Reference Services as a Model for the Future of Reference', *Advances in Librarianship*, 26, 149–173.

Kresh, D. (2002), 'Courting Disaster: Building a Collection to Chronicle 9/11 and Its Aftermath. Witness and Response: Remembering September 11', *The Library of Congress Information Bulletin*, 61(9).

Lagoze, C., Van de Sompel, H., Nelson, M. and Simeon W. (2002), *The Open Archives Initiative Protocol for Metadata Harvesting – Version 2.0*, Open Archives Initiative, June 2002. Available at http://www.openarchives.org/OAI/2.0/openarchivesprotocol.htm.

Larson, C. (2002), *The Internet and the Changing Face of Scholarship: Challenges and Opportunities for Libraries*, Bibliography (Washington, DC: Library of Congress).

Law, D. (1994), 'The development of a national policy for dataset provision in the UK: a historical perspective', *Journal of Information Networking* 1(2), 103–116.

Law, D. (2002), 'The Library in the Market: information arbitrage as the new face of an old service', *IATUL Proceedings*, 11 (New Series) (Delft: Delft University of Technology), 2002.

Law, D. and Dempsey, L. (2000), 'A Policy Context – e-Lib and the emergence of subject gateways', *Ariadne*, 25, 5. http://www.ariadne.ac.uk/issue25/subject-gateways.

Lawrence, S. (2001a), 'Online or Invisible?', *Nature*, 411 (6837), 521. http://www.neci.nec.com/~lawrence/papers/online-nature01/.

Lawrence, S. (2001b), 'Free online availability substantially increases a paper's impact', *Nature Web Debates*, http://www.nature.com/nature/debates/e-access/Articles/lawrence.html.

Lazinger, S.S. (2001), *Digital Preservation and Metadata: History, Theory, Practice* (Englewood, CO: Libraries Unlimited).

Lazinger, S.S. and Adler, E. (1998), *Cataloging Hebrew Materials in the Online Environment: A Comparison of American and Israeli Approaches* (Englewood, CO: Libraries Unlimited).

LC21 (2000), 'A Digital Strategy for the Library of Congress. Committee on an Information Technology Strategy for the Library of Congress, Computer Science and Telecommunications Board, Commission on Physical Sciences, Mathematics, and Applications, National Research Council' (Washington, DC: National Academy Press) c2000, 265p. URL: http://www.nap.edu/books/0309071445/html/index.html.

Lesk, M. (1999), 'Perspectives on DLI-2 – Growing the Field', *Bulletin of the American Society for Information Science*, 26(1), 12–13.

Library and Information Commission (1999) 2020 Vision. http://www.lic.gov.uk/publications/policyreports/2020.pdf.

Library of Congress (2002), *Digital Audio-Visual Preservation Prototyping Project* (website), http://lcweb.loc.gov/rr/mopic/avprot/, last updated 25 March.

Library of Congress (2002), *Metadata Encoding & Transmission Standard* (website), http://www.loc.gov/standards/mets/, last updated 19 February.

Library of Congress (2002), *NISO Metadata for Images in XML Schema* (website), http://www.loc.gov/standards/mix/, last updated 16 April.

Library of Congress (2003), *Metadata Object Description Schema* (website), http://www.loc.gov/standards/mods/, last updated 7 February.

Library of Congress National Digital Library Annual Review 1998, 1999, 2000 and 2001 (Washington DC: Library of Congress).

Light, P., Light, V., Nesbitt, E. and Harnad, S. (2000), 'Up for Debate: CMC as a support for course related discussion in a campus university setting', in: R. Joiner, K. Littleton, D. Faulkner and D. Miell (eds) *Rethinking Collaborative Learning* (London: Free Association Books). http://www.cogsci.soton.ac.uk/'harnad/Papers/Harnad/harnad00.skyteaching.html.

Lindauer, B.G. (2000), *Measuring What Matters: a Library/LRC Outcomes Assessment Manual* (Fairfield, CA: Learning Resources Association of California Community Colleges).

MARC 21 (1999), *Format for Bibliographic Data, including Guidelines for Content Designation* (Washington, DC: Library of Congress, Cataloging Distribution Service).

Marchionini, G., Plaisant, C. and Komlodi, A. (2001), 'The people in digital libraries: multifaceted approaches to assessing needs and impact', *Digital Library Use: Social Practice in Design and Evaluation*. Available at: http://ils.unc.edu/'march/revision.pdf.

Marchionini, G. (2000), 'Evaluating Digital Libraries: A Longitudinal and Multifaceted View', *Library Trends*, 49(2), 304–333.

Massachusetts Institute of Technology (2002), *Open Knowledge Initiative* (website), http://web.mit.edu/oki/.

McClure, C.R. (2003), 'Developing evaluation strategies in academic libraries' (unpublished paper) (Tallahassee, Florida: Florida State University, Information Institute).

McClure, C.R. and Bertot, J.C. (2001), *Evaluating Networked Information Services: Techniques, Policy and Issues* (Medford, New Jersey: Information Today).

McMillan, G. (2001a). 'Do ETDs Deter Publishers? Coverage from the 4th Inernational Symposium on ETDs', *College and Research Libraries News*, 62(6), 620–621.

McMillan, G. (2001b), 'What to Expect from ETDs: Library Issues and Responsibilities' *Fourth International Conference on ETDs*, 24 March, Cal Tech.

Milunovich, S. (2002), 'Micropayment's big potential', *Red Herring*, 5, November.

Minibayeva, N. and Dunn, J.W. (2002), 'A Digital Library Data Model for Music', in *Proceedings of the Second ACM/IEE-CS Joint Conference on Digital Libraries* Portland, Oregon (New York: ACM Press), pp. 154–155.

Mischo, W.H. and Cole, T.W. (1998), 'Processing and Access Issues for Full-Text Journals', in: S. Harum and M. Twidale (eds) *Successes and Failures of Digital Libraries: Papers Presented at the 35th Annual Clinic on Library Applications of Data Processing.*

Morais, R. (2002), 'Double Dutch No Longer', *Forbes*, 11 November.

Nelson, W.N. and Fernekes, R.W. (2002), *Standards and Assessment for Academic Libraries: a Workbook* (Chicago: American Library Association).

Nicholson, D. and Macgregor, G. (2002), 'Learning lessons holistically in the Glasgow Digital Library', *D-Lib Magazine*, July/August. http://dlib.org/dlib/july02/nicholson/07nicholson.html.

Nicholson, D., Dawson, A. and Macgregor, G. (2003), 'GDL: Model infrastructure for a regional digital library?', *Widwisawn*, 1, January. http://widwisawn.cdlr.strath.ac.uk/Issues/issue1.htm.

Oakland, J.S. (2000), *Total Quality Management: Text with Cases*, 2nd edn, (Oxford: Butterworth-Heinemann).

OCLC (2003) Five year information format trends. OCLC, March. www.oclc.org/info/trends/.

Odlyzko, A.M. (1998), 'The economics of electronic journals', in: R. Ekman and R. Quandt, (eds), *Technology and Scholarly Communication* (University of California Press). http://www.dtc.umn.edu/'odlyzko/doc/eworld.html.

Odlyzko, A.M. (1999a), 'Competition and cooperation: Libraries and publishers in the transition to electronic scholarly journals', *Journal of Electronic Publishing* 4(4) (June 1999)

Odlyzko, A.M. (1999b) *Journal of Scholarly Publishing*, 30(4) (July 1999), 163–185. The definitive version appears in *The Transition from Paper: A Vision of Scientific Communication in 2020*, S. Berry and A. Moffat (eds) (Springer, 2000). http://www.press.umich.edu/jep/04–04/odlyzko0404.html. http://www.research.att.com/'amo/doc/competition.cooperation.pdf.

Odlyzko, A.M. (2002), 'The rapid evolution of scholarly communication', *Learned Publishing*, 15, 7–19. http://rosina.catchword.com/vl=11319436/cl=24/fm=docpdf/nw=1/rpsv /catchword/alpsp/09531513/v15n1/s2/p7. http://www.si.umich.edu/PEAK-2000/odlyzko.pdf.

Oppenheim, C. (1998), 'Beyond e-lib: how does e-lib fit into the wider context of electronic information research?', *Library and Information Research News*, 21(69), 17–23.

Oppenheim, C. and Smithson, D. (1999), 'What is the hybrid library?', *Journal of Information Science*, 25(2), 97–112.

Oppenheim, C. (2001), *The Legal and Regulatory Environment for Electronic Information*, 4th edn (Tetbury: Infonortics). http://www.infonortics.com/publications/legal4.html.

Oyston, E. (2003), *Centred on Learning: Academic Case Studies on Learning Centre Development* (Aldershot: Ashgate).

Paepcke, A., Baldonado, M., Chang, C.-C.K., Cousins, S., Garcia-Molina, H.

h(2000), 'Building the InfoBus: A Review of Technical Choices in the Stanford Digital Library Project', Stanford Database Group Publication Server. http://dbpubs.stanford.edu/pub/2000–50. Accessed 15 April 2003.

Pantry, S. and Griffiths, P. (2003), *Creating a Successful e-information Service* (London: Facet).

Papakhian, A.R. (1985), 'The Frequency of Personal Name Headings in the Indiana University Music Library Card Catalogs', *Library Resources & Technical Services* 29, 273–285.

Payette, S. and Staples, T. (2002), 'The Mellon Fedora Project: Digital Library Architecture Meets XML and Web Services', in: M. Agosti, and C. Thanos, (eds), *Research and Advanced Technology for Digital Libraries: 6th European Conference, ECDL 2002*, Rome Italy, 16–18 September 2002, (Berlin: Springer), pp. 406–421.

Pinfield, S. (2000), 'The relationship between national and institutional electronic library developments in the UK: an overview'. *The New Review of Academic Librarianship*, 6, 2000, 3–20. Revised version published in Ershova, T.V. and Hohlov, Y.E. (eds) *Libraries in the Information Society* (Munich: K.G. Saur) 2002, IFLA Publications 102, pp. 134–148.

Pinfield, S. (2001), 'Beyond eLib: lessons from Phase 3 of the Electronic Libraries Programme', report to JISC. Available at http://www.ukoln.ac.uk/services/elib/papers/other/pinfield-elib/elibreport.html.

Pinfield, S. (2003), 'Open Archives and UK Institutions', *D-Lib Magazine*, 9(3).

Pinfield, S. and Dempsey, L. (2001) The Distributed National Electronic Resource (DNER) and the hybrid library, *Ariadne*, 26, January. Available at http://www.ariadne.ac.uk/issue26/dner/.

President's Information Technology Advisory Committee. (2001), 'Report to the President. Digital Libraries: Universal Access to Human Knowledge.' http://www.itrd.gov/pubs/pitac/pitac-dl-9feb01.pdf. February. Accessed 15 April 2003.

Reich, V., and Rosenthal D.S.H. (2001), 'LOCKSS: A Permanent Web Publishing and Access System', in *D-lib magazine*, 7(6), June. Available http://www.dlib.org/dlib/june01/reich/06reich.html.

Revill, D. and Ford, G. (1996) *User Satisfaction: Standard Survey Forms for Academic Libraries*, SCONUL Advisory Committee on Performance Indicators.

Richtel, M.A. (2002), 'Shift Registers in Willingness to Pay for Internet Content', *The New York Times*, 1 August.

Rose, M.R. (2002) '2001 was a hard read for e-books', *Wired News*. http://www.wired.com/news/culture/0,1284,49297,00.html.

Rothenburg, J. (2000), 'An Experiment in Using Emulation to Preserve Digital Publications'. Revision 2000–05–11. Published by the Koninklijke Bibliotheek, Den Haag [Online], available: http://www.kb.nl/coop/nedlib/results/emulationpreservationreport.pdf.

Rusbridge, C. (1995a), 'The Electronic Libraries Programme', *Serials*, 8(3), 231–240.

Rusbridge, C. (1995b), 'The UK Electronic Libraries Programme', *D-Lib Magazine*, 1 (6). Available at http://www.dlib.org/dlib/december95/briefings/12uk.html.

Rusbridge, C. (1998), 'Towards the hybrid library', *D-Lib Magazine*, 4(7). Available at http://www.dlib.org/dlib/july98/rusbridge/07rusbridge.html.

Rusbridge, C. (2001), 'After eLib', *Ariadne*, 26, January. Available at http://www.ariadne.ac.uk/issue26/chris/.

Saracevic, T. (2000), 'Digital Library Evaluation: Toward Evolution of Concepts', *Library Trends*, 49(2), 350–369.

Saracevic, T. (1997), 'Studying the value of library and information services: I establishing a theoretical framework; II methodology and taxonomy', *Journal of the American Society for Information Science*, 48(6), 527–563.

Saracevic, T. (2000), 'Digital library evaluation: toward an evolution of concepts', *Library Trends*, 49(2), 350–369.

Seville, C. and Weinberger, E. (2000), 'Intellectual Property Rights Lessons from the CEDARS Project for Digital Preservation', in: *Preservation 2000: An International Conference on the Preservation and Long Term Accessibility of Digital Materials. 7–8 December 2000*, York, UK. Conference Papers [Online], available: http://www.rlg.org/events/pres-2000/weinberger.html.

Shim, W., McClure, C.R., Fraser, B. and Bertot, J.C. (2001a) *Measures and Statistics for Research Library Networked Services: Procedures and Issues*, ARL e-metrics phase II report (Washington, DC: Association of Research Libraries). [The authors refer to a former online version of this report. Pagination may have changed in the published report].

Shim, W., McClure, C.R., Fraser, B.T. and Bertot, J.C. (2001b), *Data Collection Manual for Academic and Research Library Network Statistics and Performance Measures* (Washington, DC: Association of Research Libraries). Available at: www.arl.org/stats/newmeas/emetrics/phase3/ARL_Emetrics_Data_Collection_manual.pdf.

Shim, W. and McClure, C.R. (2002), 'Improving database vendors' usage statistics reporting through collaboration between libraries and vendors', *College and Research Libraries*, 63(6), 499–514.

Sisman, E. (2002), 'Variations', in: Macy, L. (ed.), *The New Grove Dictionary of Music Online*, http://www.grovemusic.com/ (Accessed 24 January 2003).

Smiraglia, R.P. (2002), 'Musical Works and Information Retrieval', *Notes: The Scholarly Journal of the Music Library Association*, 58(2), 747–767.

Soergel, D. (2002), 'A Framework for Digital Library Research: Broadening the Vision', *D-Lib Magazine*, December. http://dlib.org/dlib/december02/soergel/12soergel.html.

Sparks, M., Neisser, G. and Hanby, R. (1999) 'An Initial Statistical Analysis of the Performance of the UK National JANET Cache. http://wwwcache.ja.net/papers/initial_analysis/.

Spofford, A.R. (1900), *A Book for all Readers, Designed as a Aid to the Collection, Use and Preservation of Books and the Formation of Public and Private Libraries* (New York: G.P. Putnam's Sons).

Staples, T. and Wayland, R. (2000), 'Virginia Dons FEDORA: A Prototype for a Digital Object Repository', *D-Lib Magazine*, 6 (7/8), http://www.dlib.org/.

Suleman, H. (2002), *ODL-based ETD Union Catalog*, Website http://purl.org/net/etdunion.

Sun (2003) Sun Microsystems Educational Consultation Forum. Creating the Distributed National Research Library, paper ECF04 February, 2003.

Technology, Education, and Copyright Harmonization Act of 2002, in: *21st Century Department of Justice Appropriations Act*, US PL 107–273, stat. 1910, §13301. Available online at http://www.copyright.gov/legislation/pl107–273.html.

Tillett, B.B. (1987), 'Bibliographic relationships: toward a conceptual structure of bibliographical information used in cataloging', unpublished PhD thesis, University of California at Los Angeles.

Tillett, B.B. (2001), 'Bibliographic Relationships', in: C.A. Bean, and R. Green (eds), *Relationships in the Organization of Knowledge* (Dordrecht; Boston: Kluwer Academic Publishers), pp. 19–35.

University of Oxford (1999), Scoping the Future of Oxford's Digital Collections. A Study funded by the Andrew W. Mellon Foundation [Online], available: http://www.bodley.ox.ac.uk/scoping/.

Urs, S.R. and K.S. Raghavan, (2001), 'Vidyanidhi: Indian digital library of electronic theses', *Communications of the ACM*, 44(5), 88–89.

Vellucci, S.L. (1997), *Bibliographic Relationships in Music Catalogs* (Lanham, MD: Scarecrow Press).

VTLS (2002) *VTLS*. Website http://www.vtls.com.

West, C. (2001), *Measuring User Satisfaction: a Practical Guide for Academic Libraries*. SCONUL briefing paper.

Whitelaw, A. and Joy, G. (2000) *Summative Evaluation of Phases 1 and 2 of the eLib Initiative: Final Report* (Guildford: ESYS). Available at http://www.ukoln.ac.uk/services/elib/papers/other/intro.html#elib-evaluation.

Whitelaw, A. and Joy, G. (2001), *Summative Evaluation of Phase 3 of the eLib Initiative: Final Report* (Guildford: ESYS). Available at http://www.ukoln.ac.uk/services/elib/papers/other/intro.html#elib-evaluation.

Winiata, W. (2002), 'Ka purea e ngā a hau a Tāwhirimātea: Ngā Wharepukapuka o Ngā Tau Ruamano', Keynote address, LIANZA Conference, Wellington, 2002. http://www.confer.co.nz/lianza2002/PDFS/Whatarangi%20Winiata.pdf.

Winkworth, I. (2001), 'Innovative United Kingdom approaches to measuring service quality', *Library Trends*, 49(4), 718–731.

Wolf, M. (2001), 'Electronic journals: use, evaluation and policy', *Information Services and Use*, 21(3–4), 249–261.

Xie, H and Wolfram, D. (2002), 'State Digital Library Usability: Contributing Organizational Factors', *Journal of the American Society for Information Science and Technology*, 53(13). http://www.asis.org/Publications/JASIS/vol53n13.html.

Index

Page numbers in *italics* refer to figures and tables, *n* indicates chapter note.